Library of Arabic Linguistics

The reasons behind the establishment of this Series on Arabic linguistics are manifold.

First: Arabic linguistics is developing into an increasingly interesting and important subject within the broad field of modern linguistic studies. The subject is now fully recognised in the universities of the Arabic-speaking world and in international linguistic circles as a subject of great theoretical and descriptive interest and importance.

Second: Arabic linguistics is reaching a mature stage in its development, benefiting both from early Arabic linguistic scholarship and modern techniques of general linguistics and related disciplines.

Third: The scope of this discipline is wide and varied, covering diverse areas such as Arabic phonetics, phonology and grammar, Arabic psycho-linguistics, Arabic dialectology, Arabic lexicography and lexicology, Arabic sociolinguistics, the teaching and learning of Arabic as a first, second or foreign language, communications, semiotics, terminology, translation, machine translation, Arabic computational linguistics, history of Arabic linguistics, etc.

Viewed against this background, Arabic linguistics may be defined as the scientific investigation and study of the Arabic language in all its aspects. This embraces the descriptive, comparative and historical aspects of the language; it concerns itself with the classical form as well as the modern and contemporary standard forms and their dialects. Moreover, it attempts to study the language in the appropriate regional, social and cultural settings.

The Series will devote itself to all issues of Arabic linguistics in all its manifestations on both the theoretical and applied levels, through Monographs written in either English or Arabic, or both, for the benefit of wider circles of readership. The results of these studies will be of use in the field of linguistics in general, as well as related subjects.

The Series Editors

The Sociolinguistic Market of Cairo:
Gender, Class, and Education

Library of Arabic Linguistics

Series Editors
Muhammad Hasan Bakalla
King Saud University, Riyadh, Kingdom of Saudi Arabia
Bruce Ingham
School of Oriental and African Studies, University of London
Clive Holes
Oriental Institute, University of Oxford

Advisory Editorial Board
Peter F. Abboud, *University of Texas at Austin*; M.H. Abdulaziz, *University of Nairobi*; Yousif El-Khalifa Abu Bakr, *University of Khartoum*; Salih J. Altoma, *Indiana University*; Arne Ambros, *University of Vienna*; El Said M. Badawi, *American University in Cairo*; Michael G. Carter, *New York University*; Ahmad al-Dhubaib, *King Saud Univerity (formerly University of Riyadh)*; Martin Forstner, *Gutenberg University at Mainz*; Otto Jastrow, *University of Heidelberg*; Raja T. Nasr, *University College of Beirut*; C.H.M. Versteegh, *Catholic University at Nijmegen*; Bougslaw R. Zagorski, *University of Warsaw*.

Library of Arabic Linguistics
North East Arabian Dialects: Bruce Ingham
Transivity, Causation and Passivization: George Nemeh Saad
Language and Linguistic Origins in Bahrain: Mehdi Abdalla al-Tajir
A Linguistic Study of the Development of Scientific Vocabulary in Standard Arabic: Abdul Sahib Mehdi Ali
Language Variation and Change in a Modernising Arab State: Clive Holes
Saudi Arabian Dialects: Theodore Prochazka, Jr.
From Code Switching to Borrowing: Jeffrey Heath
Sibawayh the Phonologist: A. A. al-Nassir
Modality, Mood and Aspect in Spoken Arabic: T.F. Mitchell and Shahir al-Hassan
Siculo Arabic: Dionisius A. Agius

Niloofar Haeri

Monograph No. 13

The Sociolinguistic Market of Cairo: Gender, Class, and Education

LONDON AND NEW YORK

First published in 1997 by
Kegan Paul International

This edition first published in 2010 by
Routledge
2 Park Square, Milton Park, Abingdon, Oxfordshire OX14 4RN

Simultaneously published in the USA and Canada
by Routledge
711 Third Avenue, New York, NY 10017

First issued in paperback 2016

Routledge is an imprint of the Taylor and Francis Group, an informa business

© Niloofar Haeri, 1997

All rights reserved. No part of this book may be reprinted or reproduced or utilised in any form or by any electronic, mechanical, or other means, now known or hereafter invented, including photocopying and recording, or in any information storage or retrieval system, without permission in writing from the publishers.

British Library Cataloguing in Publication Data
A catalogue record for this book is available from the British Library

ISBN 13: 978-1-138-98243-7 (pbk)
ISBN 13: 978-0-7103-0503-9 (hbk)

Publisher's Note
The publisher has gone to great lengths to ensure the quality of this reprint but points out that some imperfections in the original copies may be apparent. The publisher has made every effort to contact original copyright holders and would welcome correspondence from those they have been unable to trace.

Editor's Note

The field of Arabic sociolinguistics has made rapid strides since the appearance of the first correlational studies in the early 1980s. Up to that point, studies of non-standard Arabic had largely been confined to the field of dialectology, in which the researcher's frame of reference tended to be historical (e.g. the relationship of the dialects to Classical Arabic) or, if synchronic, cultural (e.g. the study of dialect poetry, or oral culture in general). With the development of the Labovian sociolinguistic paradigm, the importance of socially conditioned variation in language, as an engine of language change, began to be recognized by Arabic linguists, as it already had been by their non-Arabist colleagues two decades earlier. In fact, variation has always been there, but was often relegated to the margins of Arabic dialectological enquiry, the object of which was seen as getting at the 'real' dialect which had been unaffected by outside influence (i.e. the dialect of the old and uneducated). Twenty-five years on, there have been many data-based enquiries into linguistic variation in contemporary Arab societies, inevitably, perhaps, focusing on the centres of population in the eastern Mediterranean. The field is now an established one, and although Niloofar Naeri's work fits squarely into the Labovian paradigm, it is far from being a blind application of his approach. Dr Haeri is acutely aware of the local social backdrop to her linguistic investigations and how this needs to be integrated into any correlational work, just as she is of the general Arab sociolinguistic frame of reference of which the situation in Cairo forms a part. The work which is in the reader's hands represents another solid contribution to the growing body of data-based studies of language variation and change in the Arab world, as well as to the field of language and gender.

Clive Holes
Series Co-editor

To my mother,
Behjat Altoma
& my father,
Jamaleddin Haeri

Table of Contents

Preface and Acknowledgments	xiii
Notes on Transcription	xviii

Chapter 1 Introduction — 1

Overview of the Sociolinguistic Setting: Ways of Co-Existence	7
The Problem: Gender and "Standard" Varieties	10
A Monolithic "Colloquial"?	12
Footnotes	18

Chapter 2 Methodology — 19

Description of the Speech Community	19
Details of Fieldwork: Contacting and Sampling Speakers	23
Details of Fieldwork: General Pattern of the Interviews	28
Experiments	31
Children's Speech and the Use of the Qaf	33
Social Class Distribution in Cairo and in the Sample	34
Sample of Speakers Analyzed for Each Sociolinguistic Variable	37
Footnotes	40

Chapter 3 Palatalization: A Non-classical Stylistic Resource of Cairene Arabic — 43

Part I Linguistic Characterization — 43

Articulatory Features of Palatalization from a Cross-Linguistic Perspective	45
Spectrographic Analysis	48
Coding Procedure	50
Following environments	51
Results of Statistical Analyses	53
Palatalization of Pharyngeal Segments: Contradictory Processes?	55
Effects of Following Environment	57
Other Linguistic Factors	61
Weak and Strong Palatalization: One Process or Two?	63

Table of Contents

Part II An Innovation of Women: Sociolinguistic Characterizations — 68
Coding the Social Factors — 69
Is Palatalization a Sound Change in Progress? — 70
Locating the Innovators: Gender and Social Class — 73
Education and Type of School — 83
Speakers' Reactions to Palatalization — 86
Differential Effects of Interviewers — 88
The "Paradox" in Women's Linguistic Behavior: A Critique of Sociolinguistic Theory — 91
Varieties of Social Meaning: Individual Portraits of Speakers — 96
Summary and Conclusion — 100
Footnotes — 101

Chapter 4 The Re-appearance of a Classical Sound: The Qaf — 103

Part I Diachronic and Synchronic Analyses — 103
History of the Glottal Stop and the Qaf — 106
Disappearance of the Qaf: A Case of Languages in Contact? — 112
Review of the Literature: The Lexical Borrowing Model — 115
Review of the Literature: Variationist Studies — 117
The Qaf in Cairene Arabic: Linguistic Analysis — 126
Borrowing from the Classical Language — 129
Types, Tokens, and Morphological Characteristics — 131
Quoted Names — 133
Phonological Variation in the Ten Most Frequent Nouns — 135
Phonological Integration or Segment Substitution? — 137
Use of Qaf Lexical Items Among Children: An Experiment — 139

Part II In Whose Speech Has the Qaf Re-appeared? Sociolinguistic Considerations — 144
The Qaf Index: A Problem of Measurement — 144
Differences between Women and Men — 145
Education and Social Class — 147
Emerging Questions — 154
The Re-appearance of a Sound and the Formation of a Sociolinguistic Variable: What Happens to Old Variables in a Diglossic Setting — 154
Footnotes — 157

Table of Contents

Chapter 5 Searching for Explanations: Gender, Class, and Education ... 159

The Sociolinguistic Market of Cairo: "Standard" Arabic ... 160
Urban Cairene: A Non-classical "Standard" ... 168
Explaining Gender Differences: A Matter of Access? ... 174
Language Change, Linguistic Behavior, and Ideology ... 183
Footnotes ... 191

Chapter 6 Language Attitudes and Ideologies ... 193

Review of the Literature ... 194
Signs of Ambivalence: Fear, Habit, and Identity ... 200
Perceptions of Differences in the Speech of Men and Women ... 220
Footnotes ... 223

Chapter 7 Conclusion ... 226

Evaluations and Categorizations of Linguistic Varieties ... 235
Diglossia Without Contact? ... 237
Sociolinguistic Variables for Future Research ... 239

Appendix 1 ... 243

Appendix 2 ... 248

Bibliography ... 252

Index ... 267

Glossary of Technical Terms

Preface and Acknowledgments

There is an unstated consensus in North American linguistics that foreign students should write on their own native languages. The supreme authority of "native speaker intuitions" too often defines the task of the linguist as emptying out what is already in one's head. I decided instead to do my research on Arabic, rather than on my native language—Persian—believing that I had much to learn from what I could not readily intuit, and because of a strong interest in understanding other parts of the Middle East.

Upon my arrival in Egypt, I discovered that while Egyptians are accustomed to researchers from Europe and the United States, those from other parts of the Middle East are considered something of a novelty. I began to wonder at the histories, colonial and otherwise, that have produced this state of affairs. But this has not been nor is it now a fixed reality, and in so far as my personal experiences were concerned, the exotic status of being a researcher from Iran did not in any way hamper my research. At times, it even seemed to produce a special sympathy, which, along with my Muslim identity, made fieldwork quite rewarding.

The present book is a substantially revised version of my doctoral dissertation. Its central concern is an understanding of the effects of the co-existence of Classical and Egyptian Arabic on stylistic variation. Within the context of the sociolinguistic setting in Cairo, I examine stylistic variation as the meaningful use of heterogeneous linguistic resources—resources that have different histories, users, and meanings.

Preface and Acknowledgments

Before, during, and after my fieldwork in Cairo, numerous Egyptians rewarded my interest in their country. Dr. Fattouh Abul-Azm of the Sadat Academy in Alexandria worked untiringly for seven months to help me obtain a visa to enter Egypt. Without his assistance, I might have never been able to carry out my research. In Cairo, Professor Abbas El-Tonsi of the American University taught me Egyptian Arabic in private tutorials, offered hours of insightful discussions regarding my research, and helped with translations and experimental recordings. I am deeply grateful to both for their major contributions to the possibility of this study.

I would like to thank William Labov and Gillian Sankoff for having encouraged me to pursue my research on Arabic and saving me from the general constraints on foreign students' research interests. I thank them also for their many contributions to the work that has culminated in this book. With detailed comments on my written works, e-mail exchanges, and his own continuing research, my ongoing dialogue with Bill helps ground my work in sociolinguistics and inspires me to explore fruitful bridges to anthropology. I am also grateful to Charles Ferguson for his interest in my research and for having accepted to share his encyclopedic knowledge of Arabic with me. I have benefited greatly from conversations with Penny Eckert, who read parts of this manuscript and offered insightful comments. Clive Holes read the entire manuscript, saved me from careless mistakes, and provided valuable suggestions. I thank Clive for his patience and interest in bringing this book to fruition.

Professors El-Said Badawi, Zeinab Ibrahim, and Qassem Wahba guided and assisted me in a variety of ways—Dr. Badawi with discussions and his then recently published Dictionary of Egyptian Arabic, which proved invaluable; Zeinab Ibrahim with friendship, contacts, trips, and more; and Qassem Wahba with experimental recordings and discussions

Preface and Acknowledgments

on the vowel systems of Cairo and Alexandria. My deep interest in learning Arabic was nurtured and encouraged by the unrivaled group of professors with whom I had the good fortune to study in the Arabic Language Program at Middlebury College, among them Mahmoud Al-Batal and Muhammad Sawaie. Together with Abbas El-Tonsi, they are all my "first teacher." I am indebted to Yahya Abdel-Latif, who conducted a number of outstanding interviews on my behalf; to Amr Sherif for his brotherly protection during my stay in Cairo, and for having introduced me to Yahya. I thank three other friends, Ragui Assaad, Iman Ghazala, and Hanan Sabea, who have helped me generously with access to census data, its interpretation, statistical methods, and long discussions on everything Egyptian.

Other friends, professors, and family members whose names deserve more than a brief mention, but who nevertheless appreciate brevity are: Mark Liberman and Tom Veatch for their assistance with the spectrographic analysis; Kathryn Woolard, Bambi Schieffelin, Fernando Tarallo, Ruth Herold, John Myhill, Otto Santa Anna, Mae Thamer, Neill Matheson, and Carlos Schwartzman. Fernando Tarallo's untimely death in 1992 ended one of those rare friendships I have been fortunate to experience. I cherish all the memories of our years together. Richard Cameron gave me valuable comments at lightning speed on two chapters. Brian Spooner generously provided me with a research assistant to help with data entry upon my arrival from the field. Devin Stuart helped me with that process and with the general organization of what seemed like an overwhelming amount of data. I thank Shahla Haeri for guiding me through many an academic rite of passage; and my other siblings Shirin, Muhammad-Reza, and Shokoofeh Haeri for taking care of the rest. I have benefited from lively discussions with Kirk Belnap, Dilworth Parkinson, Keith Walters, and Kamran Ali. Kirk has also helped me generously with

Preface and Acknowledgments

hard to find references. I am grateful to Felicity Northcott and Jean Kang for their editorial comments on various chapters.

I thank my husband Lanfranco Blanchetti-Revelli for having been by my side throughout the interminable process of re-writings and revisions. His gift for seeing and articulating connections between subjects and across disciplines has clarified my thinking on many difficult topics.

I would like to express my gratitude to my colleagues at the Department of Anthropology at Johns Hopkins University: Eytan Bercovitch, Ashraf Ghani, Gillian Feeley-Harnik, Sidney W. Mintz, Michel-Rolph Trouillot, and Katherine Verdery. Katherine and Gillian in their respective capacities as Chair eased my job requirements when possible. Discussions with Ashraf, starting at the time of my job interview, made me increasingly aware of the importance of historical specificity. Rolph's comments on Chapters 1 and 5 sparked some much needed lucidity in thinking and presentation. Brackette Williams's presence in 1995 provided many occasions for lively debates. I am grateful for her support of my research. I owe thanks to Bernadette Butler and Daphne Klautky for always being ready to untangle the many tangles that often define our work days.

The fieldwork for this study (November 1987-August 1988) was supported by a grant from the Wenner-Gren Foundation for Anthropological Research, a grant-in-aid from the Institute for Intercultural Studies, and an Andrew Mellon Fellowship from the University of Pennsylvania. My second intensive training in Classical Arabic was funded by a Foreign Language and Area Studies fellowship again provided through the University. The support of all these institutions is gratefully acknowledged here. I would also like to thank Penelope Parker for much computer assistance, and Kaori O'Connor and Sarah Harries at Kegan Paul International.

Preface and Acknowledgments

It is difficult to simply give thanks to the many Egyptians who gave of their time, heart, and friendship. They taught me much in the realm of linguistics, and far beyond it. I owe them more than I would be able to express in a few lines. I hope their ideas and thoughts are reflected in this study.

Notes on Transcription

Transcription symbols used in this study appear in the following chart. In addition, it should be noted that where speakers are quoted at some length, as for example in Chapter 6, assimilation of the definite article to the following sound is not shown. Glottal stops which do not historically derive from the /q/ are transcribed as / '/. Most transcriptions in this study are attempts at phonemic representation, and exceptions are provided within the usual phonetic brackets. The chart is adapted from Broselow (1976) *The Phonology of Egyptian Arabic*.

	Labial	Dental	Palatal	Velar	Uvular	Phar	Glottal
Stop	b	t, T		k	q		ʔ, '
		d, D		g			
Spirant	f	s, S	š		x	H	h
		z, Z			ɣ	ʕ	
Nasal	m	n					
Lateral		l, L					
Flap		r, R					
Glide	w		y				

Chapter One
Introduction

In a walk around the city of Cairo, through markets, cafés, offices, universities, and mosques, one hears many languages. The powerful recitation of the *azaan* in Classical Arabic offers respite for a few brief moments from the racket of street noises that Cairo is so famous for. Upper Egyptian dialects can be heard in the exchanges of *buwwaabs* sipping tea and chatting in front of the buildings they manage. Cairene Arabic, with or without resonances of the classical language, of English, Greek, or French, is the variegated media of countless others in their daily interactions. The sociolinguistics of the city of Cairo presents students of language use with an array of dazzling challenges.

The present investigation aims to bring together contributions from sociolinguistics, sociology of language, and studies of Arabic (socio)linguistics, including diglossia (Altoma 1969; Schmidt 1974; Abdel-Jawad 1981), in an attempt to meet some of these challenges. The extraordinary success of empirical sociolinguistics since the mid-1960s is partly due to the applicability of its methods in diverse speech communities. By 1982, variationist studies had already been carried out in New York, Norwich, Belfast, Montreal, Paris, Panama City, Bahia

Introduction

Blanca, Tehran, Cairo, Amman, Bahrain, Sidney, and other urban centers around the globe (Labov 1982). Through detailed and careful analyses, such studies document aspects of the interaction of language and social structure. Although their approach to social analysis is largely within a quantitative sociological framework (with important exceptions such as Milroy 1980; Milroy and Milroy 1992; Eckert 1989a,b), they have contributed greatly to the deciphering of one of the most difficult and enduring puzzles in linguistics—how and why do languages change? This question which has been at the center of sociolinguistic theory leads to, among other things, a search for social groups that initiate and advance change, and those that resist it. Hence when a new form enters a given language, it is crucial to locate both those groups that "choose" it over its competing older variant and propagate it, as well as those who continue to employ the older form. Often, what is older is also part of the sociolinguistic variety that the speech community recognizes as the "standard" and "correct" variety. Thus, the principal way in which sociolinguists characterize the linguistic behavior of social groups is on the basis of the relative frequency of older, newer, "standard" or "non-standard" forms in their speech.

I began the fieldwork for this study by exploring the role of gender in the use of classical and non-classical Arabic in Cairo. This angle proved to be a highly productive beginning for a number of reasons. A look at the role of gender in the variationist framework necessarily forces us to employ the construct of "standard" sociolinguistic varieties in order to determine and compare men's and women's relations to the standard variety. The generalization that is sought is whether it is men or women who are "innovators" of linguistic changes; or keepers of the standard forms. But since the construct of a standard variety is inseparable from power, *some* analysis of social class becomes critical. In turn, the question of class brings into focus the issue of social mobility, which puts education, or more specifically the role that knowledge of the "standard" language plays, in the spotlight. An investigation of the roles of gender, social class, and education in the sociolinguistic setting of Cairo thus constitutes a central aim of this study.

But there are inherent tensions in applying theories and methods developed for speech communities like New York, to those such as Cairo. The study of the *vernacular* occupies a privileged position in sociolinguistics. Labov has repeatedly spoken of the vernacular as the "most systematic data for linguistic analysis" (Labov 1984: 29), defining it not as "illiterate or lower class speech," but as that most spontaneous style of each social group "relative to their careful and literary forms of speech" (Labov 1971: 112). Arabic linguistics, on the other hand, following a tradition that has historically privileged *Classical* Arabic as its legitimate focus, expresses ambivalence or strong disapproval towards the study of non-classical varieties.[1] Even *socio*linguistic studies of Arabic, unperturbed by the "activism" inherent in the elevated status of the vernacular, have in practice defined for all "social groups" identical means of style shifting that are provided by "Standard Arabic"—that is, Classical Arabic.[2] Such a direct application of the variationist paradigm fails to illuminate specificities of Arabic speech communities that can serve to enhance it.

The clash of two approaches—one exalting the "vernacular" and the other the "classical"—is fertile ground for asking a number of important questions: Are "standard" varieties socio-historical formations closely associated with the native speech of a group of powerful speakers within the speech community, or desired norms that are privileged largely through *textual authority* without reflecting the habitual and daily speech of any particular group? Is there only one "standard" per speech

Introduction

community? Is the use of "standard" varieties always interpretable as constitutive of "conservative" linguistic behavior; and how do we evaluate the use of institutionally sanctioned "standards" in contrast to those that are covertly sanctioned? Are both "conservative"? Are "standard" varieties of diverse speech communities directly comparable to each other as sociohistorical entities? Do they play similar roles in the attainment of social mobility everywhere and for all segments of the society? These and similar questions are pursued in the present study through a framework that treats means of style-shifting and social dialect differentiation in broader terms, taking into account not only resources that originate from Classical Arabic, but also those that are created as a result of the dynamics of Cairene Arabic.

If some of the weaknesses of sociolinguistic theory are due to the specificities of speech communities different from those for which it was developed, others are of a more fundamental nature. The treatment of the social meaning of linguistic forms and hence that of their transition and evaluation is a general problem. Since the 1980s one of the major controversies in sociolinguistics has been the "paradoxical" linguistic behavior of women—their simultaneous "conservativeness" in situations of stable variability, and their "innovativeness" in cases where there is a change in progress. But a "paradox" can exist only if we assume that the social meanings of all variable forms are directly comparable to each other theoretically, and from the point of view of the speakers who use them. While the social meanings of older and well-established forms may be crucially captured in labels such as "standard" and "conservative," those of *new* forms often escape the theory's minimalist paradigm of "non-standard" and "innovative"—exhibiting a range of uses and users in a larger social field. Hence, methodologically as well, empirical sociolinguistics is ill-equipped to explore such meanings. In addition, sociolinguistic theory does not adequately address the problem of speakers' characterizations of their own linguistic behavior, in particular where self-description and actual practice do not match. In order to understand more fully the causes of linguistic change, some attention must be paid to the relation between behavior and ideology. A fuller discussion of this problem is undertaken in Chapter 5.

Moving on from an appraisal of the variationist paradigm to that of "diglossia" as a model for the classification and description of Arabic speech communities, a few points need to be discussed. Diglossia as introduced and applied to Arabic speech communities by Marçais (1930) and Ferguson (1959, 1991) focused attention on the co-existence of Classical and non-classical Arabic. This was and continues to be necessary for the understanding and analysis of numerous sociolinguistic phenomena. However, a glance at the vast literature on Arabic diglossia that has appeared to date (Hudson 1992; Fernández 1993) shows three fundamental shortcomings. One is that "diglossia" has come to be used for the most part as a convenient short-hand in lieu of empirically grounded sociolinguistic and ethnographic research. Secondly, it has been extended to cover any "functionally differentiated language varieties of whatever kind" (Fishman 1972: 92). Thus, for some, it came to mean in essence any setting in which there is functional differentiation of language use. On the one hand, it is difficult to conceive of any sociolinguistic setting in which such a situation would not obtain. On the other, the concept of functional differentiation encourages ahistorical accounts in which the domains of appropriate varieties never seem to change, merge, or disappear. Finally, contrary to the interpretation of some scholars, Ferguson's original model is not one of "actual language use" but rather of overarching societal norms (Caton 1991: 145). Indeed, the merit of the model resides in calling attention to such norms and to the ways in which

Introduction

the superposed variety is acquired. Caton argues that Ferguson's description is a more adequate model of the "metapragmatic" norms or "cultural generalizations" that speakers share, rather than one of constraints on actual language use. In part, this may explain why some scholars found the dichotomous nature of the model inadequate. Since my central focus in this study is on stylistic variation, the model is relevant to the degree that it helps a historical understanding of the use of linguistic forms that originate from the classical language. I will use the term where it is more convenient than other lengthy labels. However, I have found the theories and methods of the variationist paradigm, with the reservations that were already articulated, better developed for an understanding of stylistic variation in Cairo.

I will analyze some aspects of the roles of education and social class by way of developments in the sociology of language and social reproduction theory using the construct of a "linguistic market" (Bourdieu 1977, 1982, 1991; Bourdieu and Passeron 1977). The concept of the linguistic market is meant to explain the source, maintenance, values, and reproduction of a "standard" linguistic variety. It goes some way in helping us understand the language situation in Egypt. However, where such a construct assumes the existence of a unified or "integrated" linguistic market in which all institutions produce and reproduce the same values for one "standard" variety, it seems to ignore the impact of the global economy on countries like Egypt. The linguistic market in Egypt is not so fully integrated due in part to the fact that the public educational system alone does not create linguistic value.

The analytic challenges of Egypt's sociolinguistic setting would require us to combine the methods of sociolinguistics with those of anthropology and history to look at the impact of political and economic systems and ideologies, religion, education, and the roles of colonialism and imperialism during any given historical period. The theoretical and methodological demands of such an investigation would go beyond what the variationist model, adopted and adapted in this study, has to offer. The present book is intended as a beginning, a first installment in a holistic line of inquiry into the dynamics of Egypt's linguistic repertoire.

Overview of the Sociolinguistic Setting: Ways of Co-Existence

It is useful to consider briefly how Classical Arabic continued its presence in the daily lives of different kinds of speakers during the centuries following the Islamic conquest of Egypt. To my knowledge, there are no detailed and comprehensive studies of the language habits of Egyptians (or other Arabs) for any given historical period. That is, there are no published social histories of Classical and non-classical Arabic varieties.[3] Considering the contact of those that can be considered members of a reading-writing elite with the classical language, in particular after the establishment of such important centers of learning as the Al-Azhar in Cairo, we know that the language of texts they read, wrote, and analyzed was Classical Arabic. Classical Arabic, throughout the centuries following the emergence and spread of Islam, served as a lingua franca connecting Muslim scholars around the globe. For the majority outside of the reading-writing elite, it is more difficult to ascertain the ways in which the classical language continued its presence in their lives. But we may infer that before the spread of mass education, their contact with Classical Arabic was through recitations of daily prayers, reading, hearing or memorizing parts of the Quran, and listening to sermons or political speeches.[4]

The gradual development of mass education beginning with Muhammad Ali's military schools, brought Classical Arabic more forcefully to the domain of public education (Heyworth-Dunn 1939;

Hourani 1991a; Vatikiotis 1991). The process through which Classical Arabic was finally declared as the official language of Egypt and the many debates surrounding the "language question" that various individuals and groups engaged in during different periods would require a separate study (see Chejne 1969; Gershoni and Jankowski 1986). But this brief historical discussion helps to contextualize the linguistic influences of Classical Arabic on present-day non-classical varieties. One example of this influence, which has attracted much attention, is dealt with in Chapter 4 where the "re-appearance" of the Classical Arabic sound "qaf" is considered in detail.

At present, Classical Arabic as the official language of the country, is the medium of education at all levels in the public state schools where the majority of Egyptians acquire their education. Basic literacy skills such as reading and writing are taught in Classical Arabic. The classical language dominates all official domains including most published material such as newspapers, magazines, journals, books of non-fiction, as well as fiction. The use of Classical Arabic in most written domains, includes instructions of use on commercial products such as fire extinguishers, nose sprays, insect repellents and so on.

Egyptian Arabic, on the other hand, is the mother tongue of elite and non-elite Egyptians. It is the language of daily life and interactions, not only within the home and among intimates, but also in institutions and between strangers. As long as interactions are oral and face to face, Egyptian Arabic dominates. Egyptian Arabic has been the vehicle of epic poems, folklore, plays, proverbs, and songs. In the print media, there are publications in Egyptian Arabic. These include satirical newspapers and weeklies, poetry, and plays (Booth 1992). Comic strips are published both in Classical and Egyptian Arabic (Douglas and Malti-Douglas 1994); translation of comic strips such as Tintin (Belgian French in the original) are in Classical Arabic. The dialect of the capital, Cairo, has much national and regional prestige. At the moment, almost all films are produced using Egyptian Arabic. The Egyptian film industry is quite prolific and since the 1930s has exported hundreds of films to other parts of the Arab world. Most television productions are also in Egyptian Arabic. These include soap operas, films made for television, children's programs, the announcement of programs by mostly female announcers, farmers' programs, documentaries, and so on. The one program that is entirely in Classical Arabic is the news, usually with two announcers, a woman and a man, or less frequently, two men. There are at times, issue-centered programs in which several experts debate a particular issue or topic. Here, participants sometimes attempt to speak in the classical language. But even in this context where the topic of discussion is "formal," the matrix language remains Egyptian Arabic, at times with lexical borrowings, and less frequently with brief switches to what the speaker believes is Classical Arabic. A brief observation regarding television commercials should be mentioned here. I did not undertake their detailed study in terms of language use, but in general, commercials for high technology, expensive products such as personal computers, involved the booming voice of a man who praised the product in some version of Classical Arabic, and who never appeared on the screen. On the other hand, for more common and less expensive products such as cookies, soft drinks, baby diapers and so on, either a man or woman was shown describing the product or singing a jingle in Egyptian Arabic. Thus, on television as well, it is the latter that is employed in the majority of programs.

With this brief sketch of the co-existence of Classical and Egyptian Arabic, we are now in a position to pose questions regarding conceptualizations of stylistic variation in Arabic-speaking speech

Introduction

communities. Again, the role of gender in the differentiation of stylistic resources exposes the weaknesses of assumptions and practices both in sociolinguistics and in Arabic linguistics.

The Problem: Gender and "Standard" Varieties

In attempting to account for linguistic change, variationist theory attaches the labels of "standard" and "conservative" to forms that in comparison to their variant realizations, are older and well-established. Thus "conservative" forms are both those that are older and also those that belong to the "standard" language.[5] Newer forms that emerge as variants or "competitors" are characterized as "non-standard" and "innovative" (Labov 1972, 1990; Trudgill 1974). In this way, the linguistic behavior of different social classes and ethnic groups, as well as men and women, are related to each other and compared. Labov (1982, 1990) summarizes the findings of numerous investigations around the world, and formulates the fundamental and recurrent patterns in the linguistic behavior of women and men. Where competing forms have been in use for a long time and neither is replacing the other—contexts that are defined as "stable variation"—women use the more "standard" forms more frequently than men in all social classes and educational backgrounds. Thus in cases of stable variation, women's linguistic behavior is characterized as "conservative." However, where newer and more recent forms emerge as variants of older forms—"change in progress"—women use these "non-standard" forms more than men. In such cases their behavior is therefore "innovative." This has appeared as "paradoxical," and remains as one of the major sources of debate and controversy in sociolinguistics.

Yet the literature reporting on the linguistic behavior of men and women in several Arabic-speaking speech communities suggests patterns that differ from this model. Men were found to use Classical Arabic forms, that is, "standard" forms, more than women. Thus, it was the linguistic behavior of *men* that turned out to be "conservative." Such results prompted the conclusion that this pattern of gender differences was the reverse of that found in Western, non-diglossic settings where it is women who use "standard" variants more frequently than men. We will address this "reversal" fully in Chapters 4 and 5. For now, we might note that, once more, questions of explanation centered on the linguistic behavior of *women*. Thus an older explanation was reiterated that women in Arabic-speaking speech communities are seemingly less "conservative" in their linguistic behavior because they do not have access to the norms of Classical Arabic. With access, their "conservativeness" would follow (Labov 1990: 213). Earlier, in a study of Amman, Abdel-Jawad had suggested that women have a more limited access to education; and their less intensive participation in "public" life where Classical Arabic is used, accounts for their lower usage of "standard" forms, and for their more frequent employment of urban non-classical forms (Abdel-Jawad 1981).

Many of the issues discussed above center around a particular conceptualization of stylistic variation in Arabic speech communities as consisting exclusively of competing forms between Classical and non-classical Arabic. We know far too little about variation that does not involve Classical Arabic.[6] In Egyptian Arabic, for example, there is clearly much variation that does not travel along the "classical-colloquial" hierarchy. If so, forms have both "standard" and "non-standard" variants also outside of this hierarchy. That is, "different ways of saying the 'same' thing" in Egyptian Arabic are not all "non-standard" ways of speaking just because they are non-classical. In this study, we will examine two kinds of variables, one that originates from the classical language, and another that does not. These are respectively the use of the *qaf* and palatalization. Palatalization is a phonological process whose

Introduction

sociolinguistic dynamics do not involve the classical language. Where speakers use different degrees of palatalization, or do not use it at all, we cannot consider all these forms as "non-standard" because none belong to Classical Arabic. Methodologically, contrasting these two kinds of variables both in their linguistic and sociolinguistic features provides us with a powerful analytic tool. The contrast also enables us to give a more complete picture of variation in Cairo; and we are better able to locate similarities and differences with other sociolinguistic settings.

A Monolithic "Colloquial"?

The conceptualization of variation as essentially the product of competing forms between Classical and non-classical Arabic may be addressed by a re-examination of assumptions underlying one of the most basic terms in Arabic linguistics: the "colloquial." This term implies that when people speak Egyptian Arabic, for example, they cannot style shift, particularly in the direction of an elevated style, and still remain within the resources provided by Egyptian Arabic. It implies the existence of a monolithic linguistic variety that however much may vary in forms and features remains "colloquial." Thus, the language of those playwrights and poets who write in Egyptian Arabic is "colloquial" and the language of those who cannot read or write is also "colloquial." It further implies that as Egyptian society has changed and transformed, as it has become increasingly more complex in occupational, educational, economic, and cultural terms, its language has remained "colloquial" incapable of nuances, elevations, and rhetorical devices *unless* the speaker resorts to Classical Arabic. Moreover, even when scholars may agree that one can move down within the "colloquial" and speak "deep colloquial," one cannot move up without using elements belonging to the classical language, that is, without moving in part at least, *out* of the "colloquial."

Such problems are not alleviated by resorting to labels such as "educated colloquial Arabic," "Educated Spoken Arabic" and the like. In fact, many scholars who write on "intermediate" varieties speak of the emergence of "Educated Spoken Arabic" (Sallam 1980; Mitchell 1982; Mahmoud 1986; Al-Muhannadi 1991 among others). Using the resources of Classical Arabic as a sociolinguistic phenomenon is not "new" among those who acquire education and master to various degrees its lexical, phonological, syntactic, and rhetorical features. Because of the spread of education, there are now more people capable of using such resources. Abdel-Jawad (1981: 21) rightly criticizes approaches that "concentrate on one group of speakers, namely educated speakers, claiming that they are the carriers of linguistic variation in the speech community. Sociolinguistic studies so far have shown that variation exists in the speech community along the whole spectrum."

There is much insistence on the part of some scholars to define a *distinct* variety that is said to belong to the speech of educated speakers. It is not clear why the speech of such speakers should be set apart and treated as a "third language." Some have asserted the putative distinctness of this language to result from a "mixture of written and vernacular" (Mitchell 1990: 254-256).[7] Others argue that the language of educated speakers is neither Classical Arabic, nor "colloquial" Arabic (El-Hassan 1977: 113). El-Hassan states that on "formal" grounds and "analytically," ESA can be distinguished from both varieties. However, his specific examples show the use of Classical Arabic features in the speech of educated speakers while speaking a non-classical variety. Simultaneously, he objects to analyses that search for "well-defined" and "homogeneous" varieties:

Introduction

> In short, one searches in vain for a miraculously homogeneous and well-defined Cairene that is spoken in an INVARIABLE way by old and young, educated and uneducated, Muslim and Christian, male and female, Azhar and AUC graduates, of urban and rural origin, in a multiplicity of situations ranging from an informal chit-chat to a formal talk at the Arab Socialist Union, say (El-Hassan 1977: 117).

But again he seems to assume that sociolinguistic variation for the educated, uneducated, Azhar or AUC graduates, is only possible through the resources of Classical Arabic. The speech of educated speakers everywhere shows influences from learned varieties. Thus, just as in the United States where we would not treat the speech of educated speakers as something distinct, such as "Educated Spoken English," so we cannot treat Arabic influenced by the classical variety as a *separate* entity. For Morocco, Heath (1989: 10) argues against the existence of a distinct intermediate variety. The speech of educated Egyptians, (where such education has been in Classical Arabic) is part and parcel of what is often called "Colloquial Egyptian Arabic." That is, it is one of the styles in which Egyptian Arabic under certain conditions is spoken. In his "Analysis of Linguistic Borrowing," Haugen (1950) rightly cautions us against treating the use of features from one language while speaking another as a special linguistic phenomenon and states:

> A further inaccuracy is introduced if the resulting language is called 'mixed' or 'hybrid'. Mixture implies the creation of an entirely new entity and the disappearance of both constituents [...] *It implies that there are other languages which are 'pure', but these are scarcely any more observable than a 'pure race' in ethnology"* (Ibid: 211, emphasis added).

Chapter One

Thus the point is not to deny that "mixing" takes place—it certainly does—but to stress that it is not unique to Arabic, and that its existence does not justify a theoretical machinery that renders the language situation opaque. In his revisiting of diglossia, Ferguson argues against a distinct, third variety without denying that depending on myriad factors, most unpredictably the extreme variation in knowledge of Classical Arabic among individuals, some use its words, phrases, sounds, and syntax, in their speech: ". . .in the diglossia case the analyst finds two poles in terms of which intermediate varieties can be described; there is no third pole" (Ferguson 1991: 226).

A consequence of the narrow view of variation in Arabic is also a proliferation of terms meant to divide the Arabic stylistic continuum into anywhere from three to seven (or more) levels (Badawi 1973; Blanc 1960). Although the criteria for such divisions are never stated explicitly, what all such attempts have in common is their conceptualization of variation as the degree to which elements from the classical are used in the "colloquial." Meiseles, for example, proposes a "quadriglottic approach to the hierarchization of language varieties in contemporary Arabic" (Meiseles 1980:118). Such an approach assumes that some speakers of Arabic codeswitch between four or more varieties. Attempts to simply label styles as "Low," "a level below L[ow]," "plain colloquial," "colloquial of the illiterate," "Educated Colloquial," "Educated Spoken Arabic," "the third language" and so on fail to provide a theoretically and empirically coherent picture of the sociolinguistic setting.

I believe the key to consistent and realistic analyses of variation in Arabic is to bury the notion that the non-classical varieties are "colloquial" languages. Languages that have been serving such complex societies as Egypt, Syria, or Lebanon cannot be *monolithic* entities unless we are ready to argue that Classical Arabic *alone* (which saw a decline for

Introduction

at least 5 centuries) has served the needs of their speakers. And if we agree that the non-classical varieties of Arabic are not monolithic, then why persist in calling them "colloquial"? Furthermore, elements from Classical Arabic can and do in time become integrated into Egyptian Arabic (and other varieties) so that as Holes (1987: 7) has argued, variation in non-classical Arabic "should not be discussed, for example, as 'interference' from the standard, but incorporated into dialectological description, since from the speaker's point of view it is every bit as much part of his speech behavior as the 'dialect'." Thus for every feature of Classical Arabic that is borrowed, we must examine its history and the degree of its integration. In this way, many classical features that from the point of view of linguists continue to be considered as classical, become part of the resources for speakers of *Egyptian* Arabic. In short, Egyptian Arabic is a language, not a "colloquial" language, whose stylistic resources depend on its contact with Classical Arabic, on its own sociolinguistic dynamics, and on its contact with other languages. It is a language like other languages in which sociolinguistic variation cannot be understood outside of the social differentiation that is its context of use. If it were to be accepted that non-classical varieties of Arabic are full fledged languages, then the confused and mystifying machinery of so many labels and "levels" could be dispensed with.

The foregoing bring us to the last discussion of this chapter and that is the issue of terms. Based on the usage of the Egyptians that I interviewed, I use the terms Classical Arabic, Egyptian Arabic, and Cairene Arabic. Speakers used the terms *il luɣa il ʕarabiyya* (the Arabic language); *il fuSHa* (lit: 'the eloquent'); and somewhat less frequently *(il) naHawi* ('the grammatical language') to refer to the classical language. Following their usage and that of most scholars (e.g. Altoma 1969, Heath 1989), I translate these terms into "Classical Arabic" without wishing to

Chapter One

imply that there is only one classical which has remained unchanged since its appearance in the Quran. The speakers used the terms (*il luɣa il) ſammiyya*, and *maSri*, which I translate into, as have others, Egyptian and Cairene Arabic. These were sometimes employed interchangeably by the speakers. Where the discussion is equally applicable to Egyptian Arabic as to Cairene Arabic, I will use the more inclusive term. Dialects of the capital city are often treated as representing the "national" language, e.g. French for *Parisian* French; or *maSri* for Egyptian Arabic or Cairene Arabic. The usage is vague to the degree that "Egyptian Arabic" is also used to cover all non-classical varieties of Arabic spoken in Egypt—regional and social. But it seems to be accepted. In the case of the variable of palatalization, however, reference to Egyptian Arabic would be inaccurate, and therefore I will only use Cairene Arabic. In so far as I am aware, palatalization is an urban feature and does not exist in rural dialects in Egypt. At times, some speakers made a distinction between *ſammiyya* and *baladi*. The former is the more inclusive term, while the latter refers to the social dialect of lower class, less educated speakers.

Some scholars prefer to use the term "Modern Standard Arabic" for the version(s) of Classical Arabic that are employed today. Since at the level of the lexicon in particular the classical language has changed, such scholars find Modern Standard Arabic to be more appropriate. No speaker that I interviewed, however, used terms that could be translated into "Modern Standard Arabic" or "Educated Spoken Arabic"—terms that are mostly used by linguists writing in English. Finally, the term "colloquial Arabic" will not be employed in the present investigation to refer to Cairene or Egyptian Arabic; where there is a need, it will always appear in quotation marks.

Introduction

. Authors who have critiqued this ambivalence in various ways are: Altoma 1969; Beeston 1970; Ibrahim 1983, among others. Taha Hussein, one of the most famous public intellectuals of Egypt and a minister of education in the 1950s has written, for example "The colloquial lacks the qualities to make it worthy of the name of a language" (Hussein 1954: 86). See Chapter 6 for a fuller discussion.

2. I am borrowing the term "activism" from Fasold (1986: 361) who characterized "research on language variation" as having always had an "activist flavor."

3. Brief but very useful comments can be found in the works of Gabriel Baer who has written much on the social history of Egypt, see for example Baer 1961.

4. This is not at all an obvious historical outcome. Although it may be somewhat difficult to imagine, if the Quran had been translated into, published, and disseminated in the non-classical varieties of Arabic; if the daily prayers had been passed on from generation to generation in non-Classical Arabic; and if scholarly production had been carried out in the latter, the sociolinguistic situation today would have been different.

5. There is a potential for confusion here with regard to the different ways in which sociolinguists on the one hand, and Arabic dialectologists on the other, use terms such as "conservative," "innovative" and so on. I will address this problem more fully in Chapter 5. It should be emphasized that throughout this study, I use such terms in the senses used by sociolinguists.

6. Lack of research in this area may be attributed to lack of attention to and interest in non-classical Arabic, which in turn is difficult to dissociate from an ideology that considers non-classical varieties of Arabic as less than "real languages."

7. See Abdel-Jawad (1981:18-22) for a valuable critique of the methodology of the Leeds Group.

Chapter Two
Methodology

The present study is an empirical investigation of the Cairene speech community in the tradition of variationist studies embedded in their social contexts (Labov 1966, 1972). The fieldwork for this study was carried out between November 1987 and August 1988. The data analyzed are mainly drawn from sociolinguistic interviews. In addition, four linguistic experiments were carried out which will be described below. Radio and television programs for children and adults were also recorded. I will provide a description of Cairo, as well as the sample of speakers chosen for this study. Next, the structure of the interviews and the details of the experiments will be presented.

Description of the Speech Community
The main reason for choosing Cairo as the site of this investigation was that the Cairene dialect is a well-established, urban dialect. My intention was to focus on *social* variation within a dialect whose historical depth as an urban variety is not in dispute. This is in contrast to Amman, for example, which is an "emergent" urban dialect where the factor of place of origin plays an important role (see Abdel-Jawad 1987). Furthermore,

Methodology

thanks to the existence of Egyptian movies dating as far back as the late 1920s, it is possible to carry out some diachronic "fieldwork." Although this opportunity is not exploited in the present study, it was an important factor in my original decision. A map of Cairo with its neighborhoods is provided below.[1]

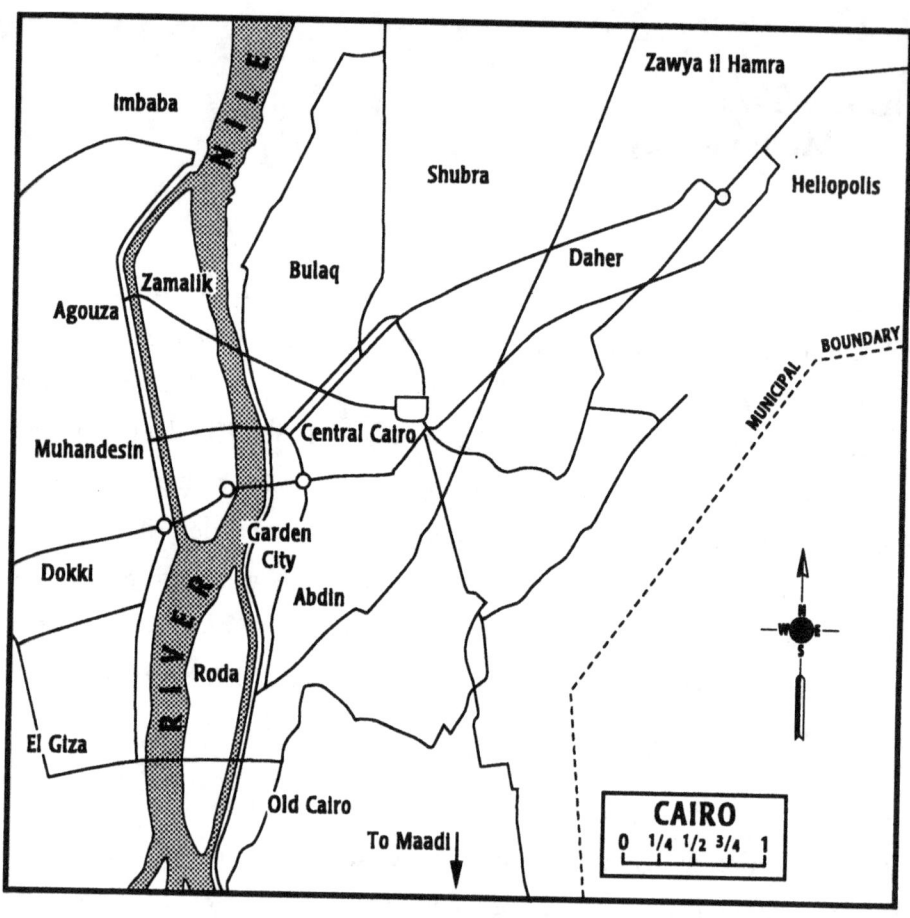

It is difficult to convey a picture of Cairo through numbers and words. The reason can perhaps be gleaned from the following passage written by Janet Abu-Lughod in her remarkably comprehensive study of Cairo:

Chapter Two

The colossus of Cairo today dominates the two continents Egypt bridges. Even as Africa and Asia Minor find their cultural and geographic nexus in the heartland of Egypt, so also do both continents turn inevitably toward its core, Cairo. One must go as far north as Berlin to find a competitor in size, as far east as Bombay and as far west as the Americas to find its equal, and one may travel to the southern Pole without ever meeting its peer (Abu-Lughod 1971: 3).

Cairo was built within one mile of the 7th century Fustat (maSr), in 969 by the Fatimid dynasty. While Fustat served as a commercial zone, Cairo was built as the residence of the Fatimid princes (Abu-Lughod 1971). In 1983, the population of Cairo was estimated at 10, 500, 000.[2] That is almost a quarter of the population of Egypt. Cairo is by far the largest city in Egypt, and in Africa as a whole. It is the administrative, commercial, cultural, and manufacturing center of Egypt, producing cotton textiles, knit and leather goods, watches, liquor, perfumes, among many other manufacturing products. It is also the site of such major industries as oil refineries and heavy machinery. The physical and architectural shape of Cairo today is a combination of medieval Islamic and nineteenth century French architecture and planning. Commenting on both, Abu-Lughod states: "medieval Cairo has been incorporated into the modern metropolis as a living and still vigorous entity" (Ibid: 56).

Cairo is truly a city that never sleeps. Shops and restaurants remain open well after the sun goes down, and during the month of Ramadan, well after midnight. A tremendous amount of activity takes place in public spaces such as alleys and larger streets. There are street vendors, year-round outdoor cafés; people sitting on the stoops or chairs outside their homes watching their children play; some squatting on the ground and reading newspapers, others listening to the radio; still others

Methodology

ironing clothes, washing cars, or just smoking a cigarette and taking a break. This outdoor activity has contributed to one of the best features of city life in Cairo: its safety. The last statement might come as a surprise to some who consider all parts of the Middle East to be synonymous with political violence and perhaps with a general state of chaos. But Cairo as a city of more than ten million is quite safe. So much so in fact that in one of the publications of the American government called the Country Handbook series, this feature is found worthy of mention. Writing about Egypt in the 1980s, the Handbook Series states:

> Random violence in the commission of ordinary crime was not a common occurrence. Violence when it did occur was more likely to be associated with political crimes than ordinary felonies. [. . .] Less grievous crimes, such as minor thievery and pickpocketing, were rampant in the poverty-ridden streets of metropolitan Cairo, but these activities were rarely accompanied by violence (Nyrop 1983: 255).

In order to do interviews, I had to go to many unfamiliar neighborhoods. Most of the time I was not accompanied by anyone. The infrequency of random and violent crime in Cairo, and the fact that streets are always filled with people, allowed me to accomplish this task virtually at any time of day or night. Cairo is not unique among Middle Eastern cities in this respect. But this is a feature which distinguishes it from other speech communities studied such as New York or Detroit.

Chapter Two

Details of Fieldwork: Contacting and Sampling Speakers

The speakers interviewed for this study do not comprise a random sample. On the one hand, as Royal (1985) and others explain, detailed and up-to-date census data on Cairo's residents are not available. On the other hand, it is culturally more appropriate to contact people, not as a stranger, but as a friend or acquaintance of one of their own friends or relatives. As such, my contacts with speakers were strictly through introductions and friendship networks.

I was referred by friends to their families, who in turn introduced me to their neighbors, friends, and acquaintances. Since I was interested in a stratified sample, I described the kinds of people I needed for my interviews and, for the most part, my contacts were able to locate such people for me. In one case, a friend took me to her aunt's house on the other side of town. I interviewed the aunt, her children and her maid. Through my newly acquired friendship with the maid, I later went to her house and interviewed her children and her neighbors. In this way, I was able to broaden the range of speakers in my sample. In another case, a friend who owned a small business let me interview his employees. Soon my social networks grew. A year after my fieldwork was complete, my initial contacts in Cairo were repeatedly surprised to find that I had interviewed relatives and acquaintances they had not directly introduced me to. One last example which helps illustrate the many ways one is able to meet people in Cairo, is my search for an apartment in the second month of my stay. I contacted three women who were real estate agents to see some apartments. One of them who was in her mid 50s came to pick me up in her car with her husband. I did not take the apartment but she invited me to her house for dinner to meet her daughters. Since we remained in touch, I was able to interview her and her husband a few months later. One crucial advantage of going through social networks was that by the time I

Methodology

would go to someone's house for an interview, I had already met them at least once; and sometimes we had already become friends by the time of the interview.

Perhaps the ease I experienced in meeting people was partially due to my particular background. I am an Iranian and a Muslim. From the point of view of appearance, I was recognized as an Egyptian. I come from a similar cultural and religious background. Egyptian and Iranian cultures share many fundamental cultural domains.[3] These factors provided me with a cultural fluency which helped much in my interactions. Lila Abu-Lughod who studied a community of Bedouins in Egypt found her "Muslim identity" to be central to the way in which she was perceived and received by the community: "Many times during my stay I was confronted with the critical importance of the shared Muslim identity in the community's acceptance of me" (Abu-Lughod 1986: 13). During my stay in Cairo, I had countless encounters including many that were with taxi drivers, where my identity as a "fellow Muslim" was commented on positively. Also important was a perception of me as a very young student, far younger than my actual age. Older women in particular acted quite protectively towards me, offering many invitations for lunches and dinners, advice, and friendship. Most reassuring was the way they would tell me to get this "homework" done fast so I could enjoy my stay in Cairo more.

Being from a similar cultural and religious background also helped with my language abilities. There are a number of Arabic expressions that are used in many Muslim countries regardless of the latters' particular native language(s). Expressions such as *Haraam, ʃeeb, inšaa'allaaH* are culturally quite central and are used frequently in everyday interactions. Knowing when and how to use these (and the many other Arabic borrowings into Persian) contributed to my recognition as an Egyptian in shorter interactions. However, in longer interactions, it was clear that I was not a native speaker and therefore could not be Egyptian. A few times, I was perceived as being from another Arab country. But often by the time I went to someone's house for an interview, they knew that I was Iranian. In one case, I went to interview a young woman who lived with her husband and her parents. The first thing she said with much surprise when she opened the door was: *danti miš xawaagah!*, 'but you're not a foreigner!' She had been told that I live in America and had assumed that I was therefore American.

My language training has been both in Classical and in Egyptian Arabic. I studied Classical Arabic in the States and Egyptian Arabic in Cairo through intensive private tutorials with a professor at the American University in Cairo. Though my Egyptian Arabic is certainly not native, my cultural background helped me appear more fluent than I really was. Frequent positive comments on my language were generally that I sounded like I had been living in Egypt for years. One negative comment came from an actor who in criticizing a film director for casting a "non-authentic," urban Egyptian actress in the role of a peasant girl, stopped in mid-sentence and said: "Well, it's like if he had cast *you* in that role!"

In explaining the purpose of the interview to the speakers, it proved important to emphasize that I was not seeking any particular or technical information. The reason is that some speakers would exclaim that they "did not know much" and would name someone else as "more knowledgeable." After this initial experience, I began to use the expression *dardaša* to describe the purpose of the interview. This word, which is close in meaning to the word 'chat' in English, implies a friendly conversation without a particular agenda. It is furthermore a very common word and thus helped simplify the task of explaining the purpose. Indeed, the best

Methodology

interviews I could hope for would be those that came closest to a chat. I also said that I was interested to find out about life in Cairo from all kinds of residents, and in the way Cairenes talked. I added that this was an assignment which I had to do in order to finish my studies. A few times by the time of the interview, our contact had already explained the purpose of the interviews. With only one exception, I was never pressed for long explanations, nor was this activity perceived as suspicious or even odd. The exception was a woman in her mid 30s who was a writer. In an earlier encounter, we had had a rather heated discussion regarding her views on language.

Finally, I asked every speaker permission to use a tape-recorder. Contrary to my expectations, little justification was needed for its use. Being aware that in such long conversations speakers may recount things on tape that they may later regret, I would explain at the beginning that if that happened they could either erase those parts, or keep the tape themselves. Although some speakers, especially younger women sometimes spoke of personal matters, no one asked for these to be erased, or for the tape.

Some sociolinguists carry out their own interviews, while others use assistants for that purpose, and still others do a combination. Assistants are employed for a variety of reasons including their status as a native speaker of the speech community, while the researcher may not be a native speaker. According to some, the advantage of local assistants is that the speech of the interviewees is not potentially affected by the foreign interviewer. Such a reasoning though, would have to be applied to any type of behavior in which case it would suggest that social scientists can only do fieldwork in their own communities. In addition, there is as yet no evidence that when speakers talk to (relatively fluent) foreigners, their speech is radically altered. In any case, it is not clear how one would do *sociolinguistic* analysis without being present, and actively so. I did seek the help of an assistant to do some interviews, but this decision was largely based on time-constraints, and in part on wishing to find out about potential differences in speech patterns where the interviewer is male. It is also the case that having others do interviews helps broaden the range of the speakers in the sample.

The most important criterion for choosing speakers was that either they had to have been born and raised in Cairo, or had to have lived in Cairo since their childhood. Eighty-seven speakers were interviewed, 50 women and 37 men. Sixty of the interviews were carried out by myself, two by my Arabic teacher, and twenty-five by an assistant. The latter are both male native speakers. The total number of speakers interviewed during my fieldwork is in fact higher. A few times, I interviewed speakers that I did not tape-record; and at other times there were interviews during which either electricity was cut off, the tape-recorder batteries ran out, or the background noise was too high. Therefore the total number does not reflect all the interviews that were carried out.

Janet Abu-Lughod (1971) divides the population of Cairo into "three main types: (1) rural; (2) traditional urban; and (3) modern or industrial urban" (Ibid: 218). The sample in this study only includes the last two types, as my focus was the dialect of Cairo, and I was not concerned with the urban–rural dimension. A last point about sampling and Cairo's population should be mentioned here. Cairo is ethnically quite homogeneous. It therefore does not present the same problems in terms of sampling that ethnically heterogeneous speech communities such as New York do. As far as the Egyptian residents of Cairo are concerned, there are religious minorities such as Copts. But Copts are not considered as a different ethnic group.[4] The census of Cairo does not have an entry for ethnic groups. It does, however, provide data on religious minorities and

Methodology

agaanib, 'foreigners.' The distribution of residents according to religion is as follows: 89% Muslim; 10% Christian Copt; .007% Jew; .03% 'other religions' (CAPMAS 1978: 381). And finally, there are 98.9% Egyptians in Cairo vs. 1.1% non-Egyptians. In short, in terms of language, ethnicity is not a social category which differentiates the kind of Cairene one speaks, again as compared to New York, where Italians, Jews, African-Americans, etc. all speak their variety of the New York dialect. Thus although the sample of speakers here is neither random, nor is it claimed to be representative, it does reflect Cairene Arabic as it is spoken by a variety of its speakers in different social classes and educational levels.

Details of Fieldwork: General Pattern of the Interviews

Doing sociolinguistic interviews for this study was essential in order to provide an empirical outline of Cairene Arabic. The average length of interviews was an hour long, with the shortest ones lasting 40 minutes and the longest ones lasting two hours.[5] The majority of the interviews were on the longer side, i.e. somewhat longer than an hour. The 87 interviews comprise about 130 hours of speech. With a few exceptions, all interviews took place at the speakers' homes. I used several of the modules (conversational resources) developed by the Linguistic Change and Variation Project (Labov 1980), and added a few of my own. From the former, topics such as childhood games along with rhymes for counting out, school days, family, dreams, danger of death and so on were used. The modules that I developed for this fieldwork covered such topics as aspects of religious beliefs and practices, falling in love, comparing parents' personalities, and local customs and ceremonies such *muulids* 'saints' birthdays'; *šamm ilnasiim* 'Spring solstice' celebrations, the significance of the number seven, and so on. Several speakers were also asked to read a word list. The primary aim of this list was to obtain data on reading style and to see whether speakers avoid palatalization in reading. This list contained three kinds of words: foreign borrowings such as 'video' and 'radio,'; non-foreign words which are most commonly palatalized; and words designed to disguise the pattern which were interspersed between the target words. Clearly, this list was included in the interview only with speakers who had completed at least a few years of schooling.

Three experiments were carried out with adults and one with children. The adult experiments were concerned respectively with the production of Classical Arabic, its comprehension, and a subjective reaction test focusing on palatalization. The child language experiment aimed at finding out how early children learn lexical items that have the sound [q] in them; and whether boys and girls differ in this respect. The experiments were not carried out with all 87 speakers for a variety of reasons mostly having to do with lack of time on the part of the speaker. Most interviews were already quite long so that it was not really possible to ask for still more time. To redress this problem, the experiments alone were carried out with six additional individuals. The children's experiment was carried out with 27 children between the ages of 5 and 12. Since two of the experiments will not be reported on in this study, I will only describe the last two, that is one experiment with the adults, and one with children.[6]

After the first few interviews, it became clear that starting the conversation by asking about childhood games is a highly successful beginning. The main reason, I believe, was that the speaker became more confident that this was in fact going to be a 'chat.' This topic did much to break the initial tension created by the setting of the interview and the presence of the tape-recorder. In answering questions about childhood games, the speaker generally described several. When a game was mentioned that involved several players and a counting out system, the

Methodology

speaker was asked how he/she decided who would be "It." For example, the most frequently described game was /ʔustuɣmiyya/⁷ 'hide and seek.' So the question asked was:

> iyzzay ixtartuu il waaHid illi laazim yistaɣamma?
> 'How did you choose the one who has to cover his eyes?'

One of the rhymes which I had learned early on turned out to be useful not only in eliciting more examples, but also as a source of data on palatalization. This rhyme was the one most frequently sung by the speakers:

> Haadi baadi
> siidi muHammad il buɣdaadi
> šaaluu HaTTuu kulluu ſalaa di.

If the speaker had gone to school, as 80 out of 87 had, questions about school days were asked. The culmination of this topic was always a question about experiences with a mean teacher who had done something unjust to the speaker. These two sections which took about half an hour comprise the beginning of the majority of the interviews.

The topics which followed were pursued to varying degrees depending on the interest of the speaker. The most frequently employed topics were: family rules, work, fear (danger of death), dreams, literature, religion, love, marriage, and equality of the sexes. It should be kept in mind that speakers quite often brought up topics that were pursued for as long as they cared to discuss them, whether or not I had planned on bringing up those particular topics. These had to do with international politics (the war between Iran and Iraq); comparing different cultures (American, British, French, etc.); what Egyptians are like, and so on.

Chapter Two

Questions about parents' education and occupation, the speaker's age, his/her occupation, and possibly about grandparents were dispersed throughout the interview and were never asked either at the beginning or all at once. Following this section, language attitude questions were asked. Depending on the amount of time available and the interest of the speaker, this section sometimes took as long as 20 minutes. As was mentioned earlier, speakers were asked to read a word list after the language attitude section was complete. The list of the target words is as follows:

Target Words	**Gloss**
[stodyo]	'studio'
[mædiina]	'city'
[vidyo–fidyo]	'video'
[Inti]	'you, feminine singular'
[radyo]	'radio'
[næDiif]	'clean'
[Dyuuf]	'guests'
[da ʕaadi]	'that is normal'
[nadya]	'female name'
[sadaati]	'ladies (and gentlemen)'
[tælatiin]	'thirty'
[mušahidiin]	'viewers'
[dilwæʔti]	'now'
[di Hæyaati]	'this is my life'
[di mamti]	'this is my mother'
[gidiidæ]	'new, feminine singular'

Experiments

After the attitude questions, some or all of the experiments were carried out. The two experiments which will be discussed here were a subjective

Methodology

reaction test concerning palatalization; and an experiment with children. The aim of the subjective reaction test was to find out how speakers evaluate this variable; and at what stage of progress is it: below the level of social awareness, stereotyped, stigmatized, etc. This experiment was modeled after Labov's subjective reaction tests (Labov 1966) which were inspired by the work of Lambert and his colleagues (Lambert et. al 1960). With the assistance of my Egyptian Arabic teacher, we composed a passage in Egyptian Arabic which concerned the announcement of a new program on television. It provided several environments for palatalization which appear in bold face. The text is as follows:

> siyyidaa**ti** saadaa**ti di** ʔawwil Halaʔa maʃa il barnaamag il **gidiid** talaa**tiin** ma**diina** wa da barnaamag biyTuuf bi il mušahi**diin** fi mudun maSriyya muxTalifa min xilaal zikrayaat baʃD il nuguum illi itwaladuu fiiha wa il nuguum **Dyuuf** il barnaamag miš Hayuʔafuu fi zikrayaathum ʃand il makaan laakin HayuwaSluu riHlat zikrayaathum li Hadd laHzat extiyaar il fann ka mihna wa dilwaʔ**ti** nastaDiif ʔawwil il nuguum il muguu**diin** maʃaana fi il stu**dyu** il nigm il kumi**di** ʃaa**dil** ʔimaam

> 'Ladies and Gentlemen: This is the first installment of the new program "Thirty Cities." This program takes the viewers to different cities in Egypt through the (recounting of the) memories of some of the (film) stars who were born there. The guest stars of this program will not simply describe their memories of these cities, but will take us in their travels through their memories to the moment (in their lives) when they chose their art as a career. And now we invite the first star of the program

here with us in the studio, the star of comedy ſaadel Imaam.'

Since palatalization is a phonological variable which is first and foremost gender based with women leading far ahead of men, a female native speaker was chosen for the recording of this passage once without palatalization and once with it. Speakers were told that there are two women who want to become television announcers; in their opinion is one more suitable for the job or are both the same? Once speakers answered this question, they were asked to provide reasons for their choice. Finally, they were asked whether one appears to be more educated than the other and whether one is from a higher social class than the other.

Children's Speech and The Use of the Qaf

The aim of this experiment was to find out how early children learn words that contain the sound [q]. In some educated adult speech, there seem to be several examples of such words which have gradually become well integrated into Egyptian Arabic, for example /aſtaqid/ 'I believe, I think'; /qarrar/ 'to decide'. Thus the interest in this experiment was to gain an understanding of the process of this integration which also probably entails a lessening of the formality of such borrowings.

Five colorful pictures were drawn and bound together with a green cover to look like a book.[8] A brief description of each picture with target words in bold face, is as follows:

1. A peasant boy is walking towards his village (**qarya**);
2. He is sitting in his house watching television and on the screen is a woman reading (**tiqra**);
3. He is standing next to the television and changing the channel (**qanaa**);

Methodology

4. His father, looking happy, walks into the room;
5. He and his father are in a bus going to Cairo (**qaahira**); in the background the Tower of Cairo (burg il **qaahira**) and the Pyramids can be seen.

The children were told they were going to see some pictures and would be asked to describe each one to me. In number two above, the verb 'to read' was included not because it is generally pronounced with a [q], but to see if in the context of other qaf words, children would attempt to pronounce it with this sound. In number 5, the Tower of Cairo was used since the name *il qaahira* to denote 'Cairo' has mostly survived in such place names. To refer to Cairo itself *maSr* is used in most all cases.

Procedurally, I began this experiment with a short chat, asking the children about their schools, favorite subjects, the games they played, and whether they would like to tell me a story or sing a school song. Some were disappointed when the interview was over, volunteering more stories and songs, while a few thought that they were somehow being examined and wanted to be done with it as fast as possible. The latter were fortunately in a minority. I was able to do this experiment with 5 children and my assistant conducted it with 22 children.[9]

Social Class Distribution in Cairo and in the Sample

For Cairo as a whole, only crude indices of social class are available.[10] To provide rough estimates of the percentage distribution of social classes in Cairo, I will use the 1976 census data (published in 1978) on occupation and education. Tables 1 and 2 below provide this information. As can be seen, it is not possible to provide accurate percentages of the distribution of social classes in Cairo on the basis of these indices alone. However, the upper strata do not seem to comprise more than 15% of the total population; whereas the lower and lower middle classes comprise a much

Chapter Two

higher percentage. Table 1 shows that the percentages of women and men acquiring education are quite comparable, in some categories there are more women than men.

Table 1:
Distribution of Cairo residents according to level of education (in percentages)

Educational level	Men	Women	Total population
University	13.81	8.80	11.02
Diploma (2 year colleges)	0.46	0.65	0.65
Secondary	17.01	16.67	16.86
Preparatory	21.80	22.59	11.15
Primary	47.57	51.48	49.32
Total	100.00	100.00	100.00

source: CAPMAS 1978: 33.

Table 2 shows some surprising percentages. In the highest occupational level "Professional," the percentage of women holding such jobs is 28.2 while that of men is 12. There seem to be two explanations for this difference. One, explained to me by a project director at CAPMAS, is that in the lower occupational categories such as "Agriculture" women are not counted as accurately as are men—they are better counted in higher occupational categories. What the actual percentages would be if this problem were corrected is unknown. In addition, the percentages are arrived at separately for men and women so that the total number of women in this category is divided by the total population of working

Methodology

women. There are 58303 women in the Professional category. This number is divided by the total number of working women which is 206991. Table 3 below provides the distribution of speakers according to social class in my own sample. Speakers who are most under-represented are upper-class men. I was able to interview only one man in this category. As it turned out, the husbands or fathers of the upper-class women that I interviewed were generally quite busy and it was difficult to ask them for an hour or two of their time (see Appendix 1 for a brief description of each speaker).[11]

Table 2:

Distribution of Cairo residents according to occupation (in percentages)

Occupation	Men	Women	Total population
Professional	12.0	28.2	14.3
Managerial	2.6	2.3	2.5
Clerical	13.2	27.4	15.3
Commercial	4.2	10.9	10.0
Services	13.2	11.5	12.9
Agriculture, fishing & animal husbandry	1.1	0.4	1.0
Industrial workers, transport	41.4	8.5	36.7
Unclassified	5.6	17.5	7.3
Total	100.0	100.0	100.0

source: Central Agency for Public Mobilization & Statistics (CAPMAS), Cairo Governorate. Vol. 1, 1978: 34.

A composite index of social class was constructed to stratify the speakers.[12] Although most sociolinguists would agree that the construct of "social class" is far more complex, simplified categorizations such as the one used here do turn out to be useful for the particular purposes of correlating linguistic variation and change with rough points along a hierarchy of social groups. Four factors are taken into account. In order of importance, they are: father's or mother's occupation; whether the speaker attended a private language school (madrasa il luɣa), a private Arabic school (only two speakers had attended such schools), or a public school; the speaker's neighborhood; and his/her occupation. Each factor receives between 1 to 5 points, with 1 being the highest and 5 the lowest scores. The weight of each factor is respectively, 0.5, 0.25, 0.15, and 0.1; and the index of a person who receives 1 in all categories is: (1 x .5) + (1 x .25) + (1 x .15) + (1 x .1) = 1.

Table 3:
Distribution of speakers according to social class in this study (in Percentages)

Social class	Men	Women	Total
Lower Middle Class	30	32	31
Middle Middle Class	38	16	25
Upper Middle Class	30	34	32
Upper Class	2	18	12
Total	100	100	100

Sample of Speakers Analyzed for Each Sociolinguistic Variable

In Chapter 3, the social characteristics of palatalization are analyzed. Since I had decided to code a minimum of 200 tokens per individual, the

Methodology

main criterion I used here was the length of the interview. Of course, the overall aim was to have as equal a representation of social features as possible in each category. Tables 4, 5 and 6 provide the distribution of speakers according to sex, age, education and social class, for palatalization. A total of 49 speakers were analyzed, 25 women and 24 men.

Table 4:

Distribution of speakers according to age and sex (in raw numbers)

	Women	Men
below 30	12	9
30-50	9	11
above 50	4	4

Table 5:

Distribution of speakers according to education and sex

	Women	Men
No education	4	2
High school	12	10
College	4	7
Beyond college	5	5

Chapter Two

Table 6:

Distribution of speakers according to social class and sex

	Women	Men
Lower Middle Class	8	7
Middle Middle Class	6	7
Upper Middle Class	9	9
Upper Class	2	1

In choosing a sample for an analysis of the social characteristics of the qaf, which appears in Chapter 4, the overall aim was to select speakers from a variety of educational backgrounds. Among the more educated speakers, I selected those who discussed the more formal topics at some length. According to many researchers, the incidence of learned words increases in discussing such topics. Furthermore, I included a fourth category 'beyond college' which has generally not been looked at in other studies concerned with the influence of education on the use of Classical Arabic features. A total of 32 speakers were analyzed with 16 women and 16 men. Tables 7 and 8 show the social distribution of the speakers analyzed in Chapter 4.

Table 7:

Distribution of speakers according to sex and education

	Women	Men
No education	2	2
High school	4	5
College	6	6
Beyond college	4	3

Table 8:

Distribution of speakers according to sex and social class

	Women	Men
Lower Middle Class	2	3
Middle Middle Class	5	8
Upper Middle Class	5	4
Upper Class	4	1

In the next chapter, we begin our analysis of stylistic variation in Cairene Arabic by a close look at the variable of apical palatalization.

---

1. Not all neighborhoods in which speakers were interviewed appear on the map. See Appendix 1 for a complete listing of all the neighborhoods in which speakers were interviewed.

Chapter Two

2. The data provided in this section are taken from: *Atlas of the Middle East*, 1988, Macmillan Publishing Co., New York.

3. Three brief examples of what is intended here by 'cultural domains' are: humor; deference to elders; and the importance of proper greeting style. Both in Iran and Egypt, as compared to the United States, greetings are supposed to be expansive, lengthy, and accompanied by appropriate verbal expressions. A 'simple hi' is strongly disliked, and may be interpreted as a sign of impoliteness, lack of interest, and so on. This is a subject of much comment by Iranians and Egyptians who come into contact with Europeans and Americans.

4. The Copts that I interviewed were surprised at the question and said that they do not consider themselves as a separate ethnic group.

5. A different sample of speech was obtained by recording television and radio programs. Men and women program announcers were recorded as well as group discussions, the news, soap operas, children's programs, news conferences, commercials advertising different products and so on. It should be mentioned here that by far the majority of program announcers on television are women. Only in the nightly news program is there always a male broadcaster either in conjunction with another male or as is often the case with a female partner. This sample will not be analyzed here, except for a few general observations which will be mentioned where appropriate.

6. At first, I intended to design experiments that would add to our understanding of what constitutes speaking *fuSHa* from the point of view of *different* speakers. However, the question is so complex that I came to mistrust the utility of any "experiment." One of the most obvious problems has to do with the inescapable artificiality of any test passage that would be composed by a researcher. Which co-occurrence restrictions does one follow, and whose? If all, then how does one decide to what the speakers are reacting? For these and similar reasons, I did two experiments with more modest goals. One asked speakers to recount a story that they heard on tape in Egyptian Arabic, in *fuSHa*. Another had to do with comprehension of instructions of use that are written on commercial products.

7. Badawi and Hinds (1986: 631) give ʔustuyummaaya or ʔistuyummaaya. I have transcribed it according to the most frequently used pronunciation that I heard.

8. The idea for this experiment was taken from Karmiloff-Smith, 1981. She had a different focus, but I found the idea useful for my own purpose.

9. Since he carried out this experiment with nineteen of the children in various *group* sessions, only three of these which were conducted with each child separately will be used.

10. I contacted a demographer who was a project director at CAPMAS. He told me that no such data on social class is available for Cairo and suggested the use of the census data on occupation and education.

11. The one upper class man that I did interview is a physician. I had an appointment with him at his house at 4:00 in the afternoon. I waited until 9:30 when he showed up very tired. Out of politeness, he did the interview although I offered to come back another time.

Methodology

12. An Egyptian demographer and an Egyptian sociologist helped with coming up with the four factors, and constructing the index. Their help is gratefully acknowledged here, as in the acknowledgments.

Chapter Three
Palatalization: A Non-classical Stylistic Resource of Cairene Arabic

Part I: Linguistic Characterization

In all speech communities, speakers use lexical, phonological, syntactic, and prosodic features for stylistic purposes. Cairene speakers draw on the resources of Cairene and Classical Arabic, and on those of other languages. In the speech of any given speaker, the relative frequency of forms belonging to one of these sources depends on the complex interaction of many factors. The present chapter is concerned with patterns of social differences in the use of one stylistic resource—palatalization—whose spectrum of choices does not involve the classical language. Palatalization is one of the many resources of Cairene Arabic for stylistic variation, whose origin does not lie within the linguistic system of Classical Arabic. Its detailed treatment in this chapter aims to a) add to dialectological studies of Arabic; b) demonstrate the insights that can be gained into sociolinguistic dynamics by examining variation in a non-classical variety; and c) to substantiate the general claim of this study that variation in Arabic-speaking speech communities is not limited to the use

Palatalization: A Stylistic Resource of Cairene Arabic

of forms originating from Classical Arabic, but involves crucially other resources of non-classical varieties as well.

The data on which this chapter is based consist of 49 interviews with 25 women and 24 men (See Chapter 2 for a discussion of this sample). A total of 8011 tokens were extracted. Two women and two men, whose speech contained frequent and advanced palatalization were chosen to be coded first in order to establish the envelope of variation. Their interviews, three of which were nearly two hours long, were coded in their entirety. More than 400 tokens were extracted from each. On the basis of the speech of these four individuals, the rest of the interviews were coded impressionistically, for six phonetic environments which will be described in the section on 'Coding Procedure'.

Among the many phonological variables that exist in Cairene Arabic, apical palatalization is one of the most prevalent. It can be heard in very frequently used words, such as:

/inti/	'you, fem. sing.'
/di/	'this, fem. sing.'
/mamti/	'my mother'
/faaDi/	'empty'
/naadi/	'club'
/tuHuTTi/	'put, fem. sing.'
/gidiid/	'new'

Palatalization in Cairene Arabic affects allophones of the dental stop phonemes /t, d/, /T, D/ called, respectively, "plain," and "emphatic." The "emphatic" stops of Cairene Arabic are produced with accompanying pharyngealization, where the root of the tongue is backed. According to a number of morphophonemic rules, various consonants can be geminated. Thus words with the geminates /tt/ and /dd/ also undergo palatalization.[1]

In Cairene Arabic, there is what may be termed 'strong' palatalization, and 'weak' palatalization. The major basis for this distinction is that a strongly palatalized segment becomes an affricate, while such is not the case with a weakly palatalized segment. That is, in strongly palatalized segments we have *affrication*, and in weakly palatalized ones, we have *frication*. Thus, for any given segment involved in this process, it may not be palatalized at all, it may be weakly palatalized, or strongly palatalized. We will come back to a more detailed description of weak and strong palatalization.

Articulatory Features of Palatalization from a Cross-linguistic Perspective

The palatalization of [t, d] in Cairene is similar both in phonetic environment and auditory effect, to palatalization of dental and alveolar stops in other languages, as described by Ladefoged (1975), Bhat (1978), Catford (1988), and Keating (1988a). To my knowledge, there are no detailed studies of palatalization, or X-rays of palatalized segments in Cairene Arabic. Thus we must look to studies of other languages to gain a basic understanding of what is involved in the articulation of palatalized segments. Two detailed studies of the articulatory features of palatalization will be reviewed in this section. These are Bhat (1978) and Keating (1988a).

Bhat 1978 is a detailed survey study of palatalization of apicals and velars. An examination of "120 instances of palatalization occurring in languages and dialects belonging to different families" is provided here. This study is unique in its scope. Bhat states that we may look at palatalization as a case of anticipatory place assimilation since the articulation of the consonant is affected by the high and front position of the tongue in the production of the following vowel. To be able to draw parallels between Bhat's findings with those of our study, we review them

Palatalization: A Stylistic Resource of Cairene Arabic

in the following order: articulatory features; favoring phonetic environments; and the effect(s) of palatalization on the segment.

Bhat argues that there are three different processes involved in palatalization: tongue fronting, tongue raising, and spirantization. These processes can occur alone or in different combinations "to produce instances that have been denoted under the cover term, palatalization" (Ibid: 50). Of particular concern to us is Bhat's discussion of apicals. He states that when apicals are palatalized, it is the blade of the tongue and not its apex which is the articulator. In this way, a large part of the tongue makes contact with the alveolar ridge or the hard palate. In Cairene Arabic, it seems to me, palatalization involves all three processes. For example, in producing [ınči], the tongue is both raised and fronted, and we have the affrication of the underlying [t].

According to Bhat, the most common environments for palatalization are a following front vowel and a following palatal glide, (which he calls a "yod"): "a following yod is more effective on apicals, whereas a following vowel, especially stressed, is more effective on velars" (Ibid: 60). In Cairene Arabic, a following palatal glide, and the high front [i] are indeed the two most favored environments for palatalization, with a palatal glide somewhat more favored than a high front [i].

Finally, Bhat finds that apical stops are most often changed to affricates as a result of palatalization (Ibid: 71). This is again the case with the palatalization of dental stops in Cairene which are changed to the voiceless palatal affricate [č] and its voiced counterpart [dž].

Keating 1988a is a study of the exact articulatory features of palatals based on X-ray evidence from a number of languages, including Czech, Polish, Russian, Mandarin, and German. She argues for considering palatals as "complex segments" and criticizes earlier studies which variously described palatals as "one of many places of articulation";

or defined acoustically as "acute and compact"; or as coronals since they are made with the front part of the tongue (Ibid: 77). By studying a variety of X-ray pictures from these languages, she attempts to locate: (1) the point of contact, the "narrowest passageway"; (2) the part of the tongue and palate which are involved in this contact; (3) where the tip and front of the tongue are; and (4) the general shape of the tongue body. First, she establishes that there is a "very long contact between the entire front of the tongue and much of the hard palate." This length, states Keating, shows us that the articulation of palatals does not involve one point of articulation as is the case with other consonants. Secondly, the tongue tip is generally down; and the shape of the tongue body is high and front (Ibid: 87).

For Cairene Arabic, based on my own imitations of palatalized segments, there seems to be a difference in place of articulation between weak and strong palatalization. A weakly palatalized segment is articulated more front in the mouth than a strongly palatalized one. Secondly, in the articulation of the latter the tip of the tongue is up, while for the former (weak) it is down. Finally, the length of contact is shorter for a weakly palatalized segment.

Although Bhat does not examine X-rays, his findings on the articulatory features of palatalization are corroborated in Keating's study. It is likely that such articulatory features also characterize palatalization of [t, d] in Cairene. However, since the segments [T, D] are supposed to be underlyingly pharyngealized, the exact articulatory process of their palatalization may be different. We will come back to a full discussion of this issue in the section on 'Palatalization of Pharyngeal Segments' below.

Palatalization: A Stylistic Resource of Cairene Arabic

Spectrographic Analysis

Approximately thirty examples of words containing various environments for palatalization taken from my interviews were spectrographically analyzed in order to determine the distinctive acoustic properties of strongly palatalized as opposed to weakly palatalized stops. There were two main cues. First, the duration of the release burst and aspiration is longer for strongly palatalized segments than for weak ones. Second, the spectrum of the noise during the release and aspiration is higher in frequency for strongly palatalized than for weakly palatalized stops. Also, the release of palatalized segments may be more gradual than for non-palatalized or weakly palatalized segments. Spectrogram 1 shows a weakly palatalized realization of the word *Hayaati*, 'my life.' The time scale is in seconds. The duration of the noise between release and voice-onset time was measured at .056 sec. On Spectrogram 2, which is a strongly palatalized realization of the same word, the duration of frication was measured at .106 sec. Moreover, the strongly palatalized realization shows a higher frequency spectrum, with the energy dropping off below about 4500 Hz, as compared to the weakly palatalized one which falls off in energy below about 3000 Hz. The gradualness of the onset of frication at the stop release is a subtle cue which can be seen only on a high-quality spectrogram where fine gradations of amplitude are visible. Because these spectrograms are printed in black-and-white rather than a continuous scale of shades of gray, this difference does not appear. Royal (1985) seems to have measured palatalization in Cairene Arabic in the same way: "If the 'noise' portion was limited to a mere spike on a spectrogram, its duration could approach zero; but friction could also be, and often was, prolonged to 60 msec. and more" (Ibid: 150). The focus of Royal's study was measurement of pharyngealized segments. As such, she does not comment further on the acoustic features of palatalization, or the distinction we are making between weak and strong cases. Based on the words which were spectrographically analyzed in the present study, (and taking into account articulatory features mentioned earlier), there seem to be three dimensions along which weak and strong palatalization can be differentiated: (a) duration of the release burst and aspiration; (b) the frequency of the release and aspiration; and (c) shift (or lack) of the primary place of articulation.

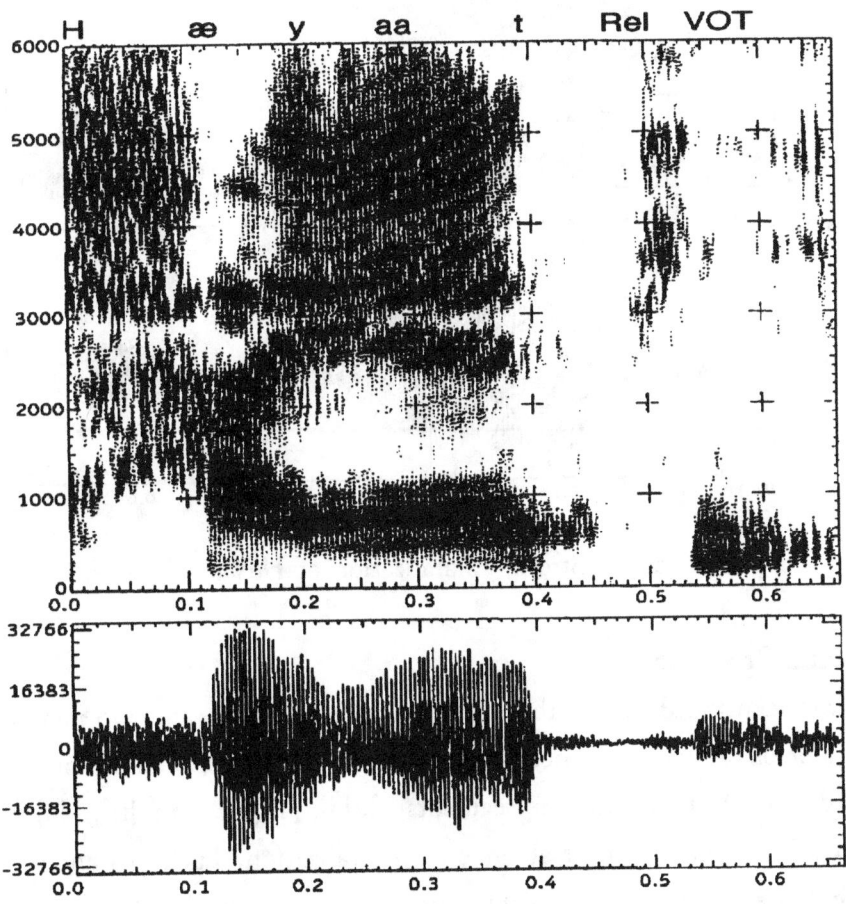

Spectrogram 1: Weak Palatalization of *Hayaati*, "my life"

Palatalization: A Stylistic Resource of Cairene Arabic

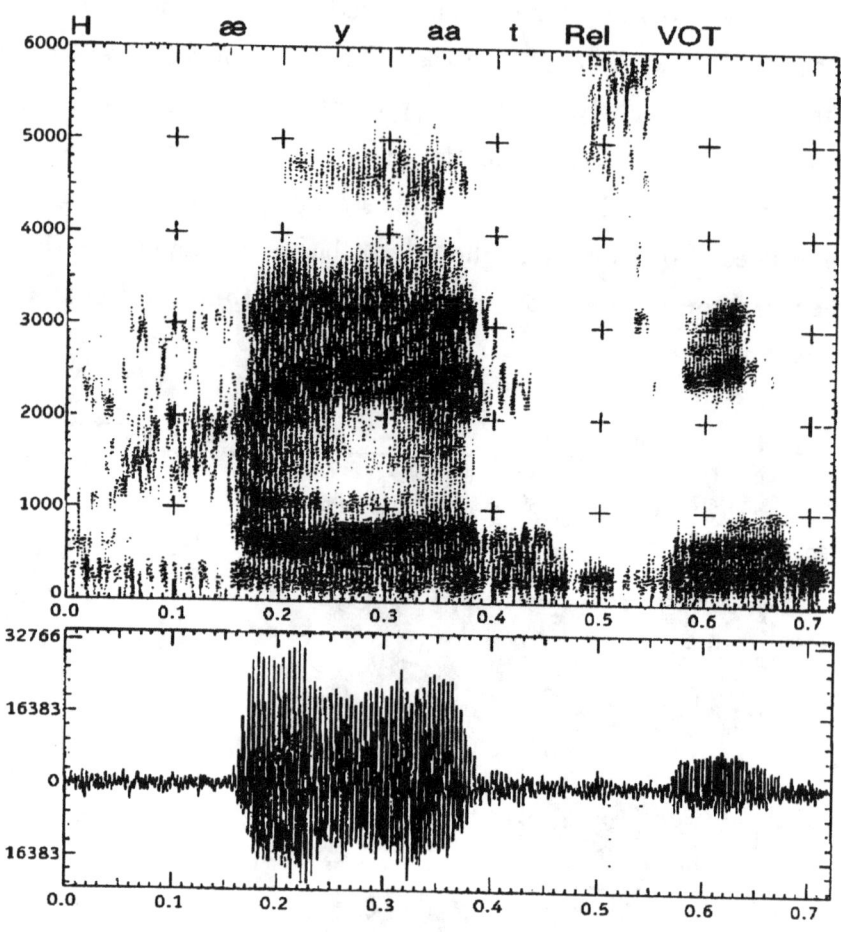

Spectrogram 2: Strong Palatalization of *Hayaati*, "my life"

Coding Procedure

As was mentioned earlier, the interviews of two women and two men who are four of the most advanced speakers with regard to palatalization, were coded first. On this basis, the segments [t], [d], [T], [D], and [tt], [dd] were coded for weak, strong, or absence of palatalization. Each instance of a potential environment for palatalization was noted, whether inside a word, or across word-boundary. If palatalization occurred, this was analyzed as application of the rule of palatalization to that segment; and weak or strong palatalization were distinguished. Second, the phonetic environments favoring palatalization were noted as follows:

Following Environments

a. short high front vowel (word-final) [i] /faaDi/ 'empty'
b. non word-final (initial; medial) [-i-] /tiktib/ 'you write, masc.'
c. long high front vowel [ii] /gidiid/ 'new'
d. long mid front vowel [ee] /sanateen/ 'two years'
e. palatal glide [y] /nadya/ 'female name'
f. epenthetic vowel /ruHt gibt/ '(I) went and bought' (lit.' brought')

g. other vowels /uskutuu/ 'be quiet, plur.'
h. consonant /sitt ʔawi/ 'woman very'
i. pause

A few of these environments bear explanation. The high front /i/ was coded separately depending on whether it occurred word-finally, or word-medially, e.g. /ʕaadi/ 'normal', versus /tiktib/ 'you write, masc.' Some studies distinguish only two allophones for /i/, and refer to them as word-final and non-final. The reason is that the latter term would also include word-initial [i]. In keeping with this terminology, I will use the term non-final, instead of word-medial to refer to all allophones of /i/ which are not word-final. The long [ii] belongs to a separate phoneme.

A following glide occurs most often when the following word starts with a glide, as in /bizzaat yaʕni/ 'in essence meaning...'; but it also occurs in words such as /nadya/ 'female name', /vidyu/ 'video', and so on. An epenthetic vowel is inserted when there is a sequence of three consonants (Broselow 1976), as in /ʔu<u>mt ba</u>ʔollaha/ [ʔomtəbæʔollæ hæ], lit: 'I got up tell

Palatalization: A Stylistic Resource of Cairene Arabic

her; I turned around and told her.' This environment then turns out to be a potential one for palatalization. The quality of the epenthetic vowel is variable. Some speakers pronounce it as a short high front [ɪ], others pronounce it as a lower schwa [ə].

Turning now to the last three environments, we should mention the following. Although in the vast majority of cases, palatalization takes place before a high front vowel (or glide), there were a few instances where the vowel was low front. The actual examples in my data are:

[bɪtæʃmɪlha]   'she does it'
[bæʃD æyyɪ]   '...each other any...'
[bɪtæʃii]   'mine'

There were also three tokens, all repetitions of the same word, where palatalization took place when the following vowel was a high back [u]. The actual word was:

/uskutuu/ → [oskočuu] 'be quiet, plural'

All three palatalized tokens occurred during an interview with a mother whose children were being noisy and were preventing her from talking. It may be that the environment for palatalization is becoming more general, embracing not just high front vowels, but also low front, and high back vowels. We should also mention that the above instances of advanced palatalization involving [æ], and [u] were all uttered by women.

Palatalization occurs, though rarely, when the segment is followed by a pause: /bint/ → [bɪnč]'girl.'[2] Finally, when the following segment is a consonant, palatalization occurs but again, rarely:

/itrabeet fil/ → [ɪtræbeeč fɪl]. '(I) was brought up in.'

There are also examples in the data of sequences of three consonants which are not, as would be required by the phonotactics of Cairene, broken up by an epenthetic vowel. Yet in this environment, palatalization takes place:

/sitt ʔawi/ → [sɪč ʔæwi] 'woman very'[3]

Two other linguistic factors were coded for: domain of application of palatalization (word-internal; and across word boundary); and the grammatical status of the word. Grammatical status was taken into account to show that unlike its importance in the distribution of qaf lexical items (see Chapter 4), it plays no role in palatalization. All tokens were coded in detail according to their part of speech: adjectives, nouns, verbs, active participles, and early statistical runs showed that grammatical status of the lexical item does not play a role. I also added the factor 'negated verb/preposition' to this factor group. The reason for adding this factor is that in negated forms, palatalization rarely takes place, perhaps due to a dissimilation process that discourages the occurrence of two fricatives or affricates in the same word. As will be seen, the linguistic features which characterize the distribution of the qaf, such as the importance of lexical and grammatical status of the word, turn out to be unimportant for palatalization.

Results of Statistical Analyses

The programs of Goldvarb 2.0 and Varbrul 1.2 were used for a multivariate analysis of the data (Rand and Sankoff 1990). The results reported on in this section are based on examples, or tokens of strong palatalization, i.e. where palatalization resulted in the affricates [č, dž]. We will, however, compare the results of weak and strong palatalization later in this chapter. In the following statistical runs, all and only the linguistic factors were included.

Palatalization: A Stylistic Resource of Cairene Arabic

As can be seen from Table 1, all the voiceless segments have higher probabilities for undergoing palatalization than do their voiced counterparts.

Table 1:
Percentages and probabilities of application of palatalization for dental stops

segment	percentage	probability	N
t	22	.58	3857
T	17	.53	185
d	18	.43	3313
D	15	.36	221
tt	11	.38	106
dd	10	.36	329
			8011

Concentrating on the first four segments, we also see that the plain [t, d] have higher probabilities than the pharyngeal [T, D], respectively. What is surprising is that the pharyngeal [T] has a higher probability than the plain [d]. One might expect that a pharyngealized segment would be less likely to undergo palatalization than a non-pharyngealized one. We will take up this issue in the following section. The geminate segments [tt] and [dd] will be dropped from later discussions since they are not involved in this process to any appreciable degree. Together they comprise a little more than 400 tokens.

Chapter Three

Palatalization of Pharyngeal Segments: Contradictory Processes?

Keating (1988b) surveys a variety of studies which have proposed phonological feature systems. She states that palatals are classified as [–back], and pharyngeals as [+back], among other features used to classify these sounds (Ibid: 7). That is, while for pharyngeals the tongue root is retracted, for palatals it is fronted (see also Royal 1985). This contradiction in features is what renders the results puzzling: How can the same segment be both front and back at the same time? Below, I will provide evidence to suggest that phonemically pharyngeal segments are often articulated without pharyngealization. Thus when these segments are palatalized, they are probably produced without pharyngealization in the first place.

Royal (1985) is a detailed acoustic study of pharyngealization in Cairene Arabic. Her data base includes 57 speakers with 29 women and 28 men. Royal found that pharyngealization is a variable process in that the "strength of pharyngealization" present in an articulation varies:

> One of the points of our argument will be that pharyngealization is not an 'on or off' phenomenon, but rather a gradient one, with possibilities of stronger or weaker pharyngealization available to the speakers over a considerable range (Ibid: 101).

Secondly, it has long been noted that the pharyngeal quality of the consonants in Arabic can best be seen on the adjacent vowels. Specifically, according to Royal, studies of pharyngealization on a number of Arabic dialects have found that: "[i] is the one vowel which is not backed next to a pharyngealized consonant..." (Ibid: 99). This is exactly the environment which we have found to favor palatalization regardless of the 'plain' or pharyngeal nature of the underlying segment.

Palatalization: A Stylistic Resource of Cairene Arabic

More evidence comes from Kahn's acoustic study of pharyngealization based on data from the speech of five native speakers of Egyptian Arabic; two Palestinians; one Lebanese; and six Kuwaiti and Saudi Arabians. Interestingly, when Kahn compared the Egyptians with the other speakers, she found that they had comparatively weaker pharyngealization: "Statistically . . . there is a substantial difference between the Egyptian and other dialects." (Ibid: 48).

On the basis of the data in Table 1, I carried out a chi-square analysis of [t] versus [T]; and [d] versus [D]. For [t] versus [T], the chi-square is 3.25 with $p < .10$; and for [d] versus [D], the chi-square value is .75, with $p < .50$. Therefore the differences between the two segments of each pair are not statistically significant.

A final piece of evidence comes from Badawi and Hinds' *Dictionary of Egyptian Arabic* (1986).[4] Looking up some entries for the pharyngeal /T/, /D/, and /S/, alternative entries with the plain counterparts of these segments are cited.

/T/	ʃiTr / ʃitr	'perfume'
	TurTa / turta	'large fancy cake' (Italian *torta*)
	TišT / Tišt	'shallow basin used for laundry' (Persian *tašt*)
/D/	Diiq / diiq	'narrow'
	Dmn / dmaan	'helm, steering'
/S/	Saaɣ / saaɣ	'to work fine metals' (also Siiɣ / siiɣ)
	Sanduuq / sanduuq	'box, container'

The above list is by no means exhaustive and other examples from the Dictionary may easily be cited. One may assume that Badawi and Hinds found speakers for whom the unmarked pronunciation of these and similar lexical items is a non-pharyngealized one.

Given the preceding evidence, I conclude that the reason [T] has a higher probability than [d] is that the former loses its pharyngealization variably, and becomes a plain [t]. And as we can see from Table 2, a [t] has the highest probability for undergoing palatalization. Probably some allophones of the pharyngeal phonemes are merging with the non-pharyngeal phonemes.[5]

Effects of Following Environment

The three following environments which have the highest probabilities for palatalization are: a palatal glide [y]; a high front [i], and a long high front [ii], as shown in Table 2. From an articulatory point of view, these results are expected: as we saw earlier, all studies of palatalization indicate that the position of the tongue in this process is high and front, assimilating to the tongue position for the following vowels.[6] Thus the highest favored environments for palatalization are high front vowels. In this way, it is not surprising that the last four environments, that is, [ee]; any other vowel; a following consonant; and pause, show very low probabilities.

There are, however, two puzzling findings in Table 2. The first is the difference between the two allophones of /i/. Word-final [i] (/faaDi/ 'empty') has a probability of .68, while non-final [i] (/tiktib/ 'you write masc.') has a probability of .28. In addition, there is a considerable difference between word-final [i], and [ii], on the one hand, and non-final [i], and [ii], on the other (e.g. the previous examples, vs. /gidiid/ 'new').

Palatalization: A Stylistic Resource of Cairene Arabic

Table 2:

Percentages and probabilities of application of palatalization for following environment

Environment	percentage	probability	N
[y] glide	29	.68	489
[i] (word-final)	24	.63	3703
[ii]	18	.51	1239
[ɪ] epenthetic	21	.49	344
[i] (non-final)	10	.28	1573
[ee]	3	.10	113
other Vowel	6	.19	128
Consonant	5	.13	280
Pause	4	.12	142

Why should there be a difference between long and short [i]? To discuss these questions further, let us first take a look at the entire Cairene vowel system.

The Cairene Vowel Phonemes

```
        i       u           ii      uu
                            ee      oo
            a                   aa
```

This chart is taken from Broselow (1976) which is also based on Mitchell (1956). As can be seen, there is no phonemic short /e/ (or short /o/). In Table 2 we saw that the following vowel has to be high (and front) for palatalization to take place. What are the articulatory features of the allophones of /i/? Are all of its allophones equally high?

It seems to me that what crucially distinguishes the allophones of /i/ is *height*: word-final [i] is higher than non-final [i]. The latter is closer in quality to a mid-front [e]. For example, in a word such as /babtidi/ 'I begin', the syllable [di] is more likely to undergo palatalization than [tɪ]. Using the program of Textsort, I made a file of all tokens that have /abtidi/ and its various conjugations e.g. /biyibtidi/ 'he begins', /bitibtidi/ 'she begins', etc. and obtained the frequency of palatalization for both [tɪ] and the [di]. In Table 3, we see that the segment with a following word-final [i] undergoes palatalization more frequently, even though a [d] is less likely to do so than a [t] due to the presence of voice, as we saw in Table 2. We may also compare [ii] and [ee] whose probabilities are: .51 and .10, respectively. These two vowels differ only on the basis of height. This is further evidence that vowel height is an important factor in explaining why a word-final [i] is a more favored environment than non-final [i].

Table 3:
Percentage of application of palatalization for medial [tɪ] versus word-final [di] in conjugations of /biyibtidi/ (n=79)

	[di]	[tɪ]
strong palatalization	20	5
strong and weak palatalization combined	42	20

Mitchell (1956) states that the vowel /i/ has a "different" quality when it occurs word-finally. He likens a non-final [i] as in the word /bint/ 'girl', to the English vowel in 'bit'; but a final [i] he states, is similar to the

English 'beet' (Ibid: 10). Thus Mitchell seems to be making a tense/lax distinction where [i] is tense word-finally, and lax elsewhere.[7] He mentions that more tension is used in the pronunciation of word-final [i] (Ibid: 10). It may indeed be the case that tenseness plays a role, especially since tenseness often seems to be associated with fronting—or movement to the periphery.[8] Thus pending instrumental analysis, it may turn out that this dimension is involved in the palatalization of dental stops in Cairene Arabic. Blanc (1974) distinguishes between the "high, tense, short vowels (i and u) and lower, laxer, short vowels (e and o)" (Ibid: 208). His transcription makes basically the same distinction as we make here in our coding, distinguishing between word-final [i] and other [i]'s in terms of height.

There is another issue to consider in this regard, and that is the potential role of stress. To address this issue we would have to compare, for example, stressed word-final [i], with stressed non-final [i]. In my data, the only lexical item in which the [i] is word-final *and* stressed, is the feminine demonstrative /di/ 'this'. Otherwise, the rules of stress as described by Broselow (1976) do not result in its placement on the final syllable of a word.

For all other lexical items which have final [i], e.g. /ʕaadi/ 'normal', /inti/ 'you, fem.', /mamti/ 'my mother', etc., the penultimate, (or the antepenultimate) syllable receives primary stress. Leaving aside the word /di/, we have a group of tokens which all have final, unstressed [i], and a group of tokens which have both stressed and unstressed non-final [i]. Since I did not code for stress in my original coding, I cannot provide a full answer to this question. Bhat (1978) found that in apical palatalization, unstressed front vowels are a more favored environment than stressed ones. If this is the case, then the difference between word-final [i] which has a far higher probability than non-final [i], may also be due to the fact that the former tokens are unstressed. Still, the evidence presented above shows that height is crucial in predicting the application of palatalization.

The role of stress brings us to the second question posed above: why is there a difference between [ii], on the one hand, and both allophones of /i/, on the other? Clearly, here we are also dealing with vowel length as a potential factor. But length, in itself, does not discourage palatalization as a comparison of [ii] with [ee] shows. So we should look at other factors. The difference between [ii] and word-final [i] may be explained by the fact that in Cairene Arabic long vowels are always stressed regardless of their position within the word. Thus [ii] is always stressed, whereas word-final [i], as described above, is not. On the other hand, comparing non-final [i] with [ii], we would have to note that while [ii] is always stressed, the stress of non-final [i] depends on its position in the word. But if as Bhat states unstressed vowels favor palatalization more, we would expect non-final [i] to show a higher probability and not a lower one than [ii] which is always stressed.

Wahba (1991) did an acoustic analysis of long and short vowels in closed syllables in Egyptian Arabic. He found that long [ii] is significantly *higher* than short [i] (Ibid: 4). This finding strongly supports our claim that the crucial dimension which explains the difference between all the high front vowels is height.[9]

Other Linguistic Factors

As was mentioned earlier, the data were also coded for domain of application. The small difference in probability between word-internal palatalization versus across word boundary: .51 versus .46, shows that it is unimportant. This is consistent with a variety of other phonological rules in Cairene Arabic such as High Vowel Deletion, I Epenthesis, etc. in which the presence or absence of word boundary does not affect the form and application of the rule (see Broselow 1976: 1–24).

As for the occurrence of palatalization in negated forms, the probability of application turned out to be very low: .07. This can be explained in terms of dissimilation. The discontinuous, negative morpheme in Egyptian Arabic is /ma...š/. Thus we get, e.g. /maruHtiiš/ 'you fem. didn't go.' By dissimilation I mean that the presence of the palatal fricative [š] discourages palatalization which would create a palatal affricate. Bhat (1978) discusses a similar dissimilation process in Moroccan Arabic: "no morpheme containing s or z contains also š and ž anywhere within its bounds, nor does s or z ever occur in morphemes with š or ž" (Ibid: 64). Ohala (1981) considers palatalization as one of many processes which "participate in dissimilation," where the dissimilation can affect adjacent segments or be "at a distance" (Ibid: 193). Thus this kind of dissimilation seems to occur in other languages as well.

Before we proceed to a sociolinguistic analysis of this variable, we should address one other question, namely, whether weak and strong palatalization are two separate phonological processes or one. The linguistic evidence points more strongly towards one process though not wholly conclusively, whereas the sociolinguistic evidence shows clearly two processes at work. Diachronic data showing real-time distribution are crucially needed here. In the absence of this kind of data, I will offer the less convincing apparent-time data showing the speakers' use of weak and strong palatalization according to their age. We will begin with the linguistic evidence.

Weak and Strong Palatalization: One Process or Two?

First, let us note that the term 'palatalization' is a cover term embracing a number of phonological processes. In this regard, Bhat (1978) states that this varied usage makes it difficult to come up with a satisfactory definition which would include all kinds of palatalization. But, he goes on to say that one of two conditions have to be present in order to be able to classify a phonological process as palatalization.

> The conditions are: (1) the environment that induces the change must be a 'palatalizing environment' (i.e. it must be a front vowel, a palatal semivowel, or a palatal or palatalized consonant), and (2) the sound that results from the change must be palatal or must have a secondary palatal articulation. [. . .] In most of the instances that are included under the term palatalization, however both the above conditions would be present (Ibid: 49).

Since both of these conditions are satisfied in the case of weak and strong palatalization, we may use one term, as we have done so far. Bhat criticizes earlier works which have considered palatalization as a single process and argues that the three processes of fronting, raising, and spirantization can occur alone and for this reason, they should be considered as "independent entities" (Ibid: 51). At this point, it seems to me that all three processes are at work in the palatalization of dental stops in Cairene Arabic. Thus there is no reason to separate them. We can, however, compare weak and strong palatalization in terms of the segments involved along with favoring following environments to explore this question. Let us first add to the distinctions we have made so far between weak and strong palatalization, by noting the way Bhat distinguishes the two:

Palatalization: A Stylistic Resource of Cairene Arabic

There are evidently two different ways in which palatalization could affect a consonant: (1) it could modify the primary articulation itself, and (2) it could add a secondary palatal articulation to the consonant, leaving the main articulation unaltered (Ibid: 67).

It is the second effect that describes weak palatalization in Cairene Arabic. Namely, we have a dental stop to which is added a secondary palatal articulation. In strong palatalization, there is a shift of the primary place of articulation to a point further back towards the palate. In terms of its auditory effect, weak palatalization in Cairene sounds similar to the variable palatalization in Parisian French which occurs in words like [rad^{y}o] 'radio'.

We can compare the probabilities of the dental stop involved in both kinds of palatalization to see if there are any differences. Results of Varbrul analyses, once with weak palatalization as application; and once with strong palatalization as application, are presented in Table 4 below.

Table 4:
Comparison of weak and strong palatalization

Segment	Percentage		Probability	
	weak	strong	weak	strong
t	13	22	.48	.58
T	12	17	.48	.53
d	18	18	.52	.43
D	9	15	.35	.36

The most important difference between weak and strong palatalization in terms of segments is that whereas for the latter, [t] has the highest probability, for weak palatalization, it is [d]. This difference is statistically significant ($p<.001$). However, the other differences are quite small and do not affect the order of the segments involved. The two kinds of palatalization appear remarkably similar with respect to following environment as can be seen in Table 5.

Table 5:
Comparison of following environments for weak and strong palatalization

	Percentage		Probability	
Environment	weak	strong	weak	strong
glide	22	29	.69	.68
word-final [i]	19	24	.57	.64
[ii]	15	18	.53	.51
epenthetic [ɪ]	8	21	.40	.49
non-final [i]	8	10	.37	.28
[ee]	7	3	.28	.10
other vowels	2	6	.12	.19
consonant	2	5	.17	.13
pause	9	4	.45	.12

The order of environments in terms of their probabilities is similar for both weak and strong palatalization. The only large difference has to do with the probability for the category 'pause' which is .45 for weak and .12 for strong palatalization. There are a total of 142 tokens in this category. Some speakers release their final dental stops and when this stop is voiceless, there is considerable aspiration in the release. This aspiration is similar to the one for weakly palatalized voiceless segments and I coded them as such. This, I believe, is why 'pause' has a much higher probability. Other than this difference, which I consider to be minor, there are no major differences which would argue for considering weak and strong palatalization as two separate processes. Thus at this point, we do not have sufficient reason to separate the two.

For a more detailed view of the data, Table 6 which is a cross tabulation of segments with following environments is provided. I conclude tentatively that we are dealing with one process. Namely, we have a gradient variable with three variants: those that are not palatalized at all, those that are weakly palatalized, and those that are strongly palatalized. The interesting question which is difficult to answer is whether weak palatalization either for the speech community as a whole or for each individual, came into existence before strong palatalization. In other words, was weak palatalization a step towards strong palatalization?

Table 6:
Cross-tabulations of dental stops and following environments for applications 0, 1, 2 (respectively)

	t		T		d		D	
	N	%	N	%	N	%	N	%
glide	95	50	5	26	90	46	23	52
	39	21	5	26	48	24	7	16
	56	29	9	47	58	30	14	32
[i]	659	50	11	41	1307	60	41	76
	243	18	8	30	431	20	6	11
	422	32	8	30	449	21	7	13
[ii]	423	62	41	84	315	71	27	84
	98	14	3	6	80	18	3	9
	161	24	5	10	49	11	2	6
[ɪ] ep. V	165	68	3	60	24	75	4	57
	14	6	1	20	6	19	0	0
	65	27	1	20	2	6	3	43
-[i]-	649	82	63	85	197	83	50	82
	45	7	4	5	26	11	3	5
	91	11	7	9	14	6	8	13
[ee]	27	79	2	50	73	97	0	0
	5	15	2	50	1	1	0	0
	2	6	0	0	1	1	0	0

Palatalization: A Stylistic Resource of Cairene Arabic

Part II

An Innovation of Women: Sociolinguistic Characterizations

We will begin our discussion with the most outstanding feature of the social distribution of the data. Palatalization, perhaps more than any other aspect of the Cairene phonology distinguishes the speech of men and women: women have frequent and advanced palatalization, while men have little palatalization in their speech. Table 7 below shows the magnitude of this difference. Due to such large differences, most of the data in this section will be presented for women and men separately. This is also in keeping with the suggestions made in Eckert (1989b) and Labov (1990).

Table 7:

Probability and percentage differences of application of palatalization between men and women

	Weak		Strong		Total
	Prob.	%	Prob.	%	Tokens
women	.60	18	.77	31	4418
men	.38	10	.18	5	3593

Labov states that multivariate analysis of the kind sociolinguists use most, namely Varbrul, assumes independence among factors and was designed primarily for *linguistic* analysis where independence can be expected. For social factors where we can expect interaction, separate runs for men and women are required; and the use of cross-tabulations to locate possible interaction. I will use cross-tabulations to report on the results.

Chi-square tests are used to assess the significance of any apparent differences.

Coding the Social Factors

For the category of age, I first grouped speakers into 5 different categories: below 20, 20-30, 30-40, 40-50, and above 50. More clear patterns could be seen when these 5 groups were reduced to three: below 30, 30-50, and above 50. These are therefore the three categories I will be reporting on. Similarly, for the factor of education, I originally divided the speakers into the following categories: no education; some elementary school; some high school; high school; college and beyond college. However, since the differences between the first two categories; and the second two turned out to be either non-existent, or very small, I grouped them together. Thus we will look at four educational levels: no education; high school; college, and beyond college.

The factor of 'style' was coded as follows: narrative; non-narrative; response to questions; and word list. Tokens which were part of the personal narratives related by the speakers were coded as 'narrative'. Non-narrative was defined as those stretches of speech where the speaker volunteered a discussion which was neither a narrative, nor a response to a question. Tokens which were part of the first two sentences of an answer to a question, were coded as 'response'; also all tokens which occurred during discussions on language, literature, and the section on experiments were put in this category. Some speakers were asked to read a word list (see Chapter 2), therefore, all tokens obtained from this reading were categorized as 'Word List' style. Finally, since the majority of the upper middle class and all of the upper class Cairenes in this sample had attended private schools where a language other than Arabic is the medium of instruction, I compared those who had attended such schools

Palatalization: A Stylistic Resource of Cairene Arabic

with those who had attended public schools where the medium is Classical Arabic. Only private schools which used a language other than Arabic as the main medium of instruction were counted as 'private.'

Is Palatalization a Sound Change in Progress?

Two questions need to be answered with regard to the status of palatalization: 1) how recent is it; and 2) is it a sound change in progress in the sense that it has neither gone to completion, nor stopped completely in its track due to overwhelming stigmatization. To answer the first question in the absence of real time data, we would have to show that palatalization was not present during the childhood or adolescence of the oldest speakers we have data on. Graph 1 shows the use of strong palatalization among three age groups. Neither men nor women above 50 have any strong palatalization. But in the next age group, there is a jump from 2% to 28% for women.

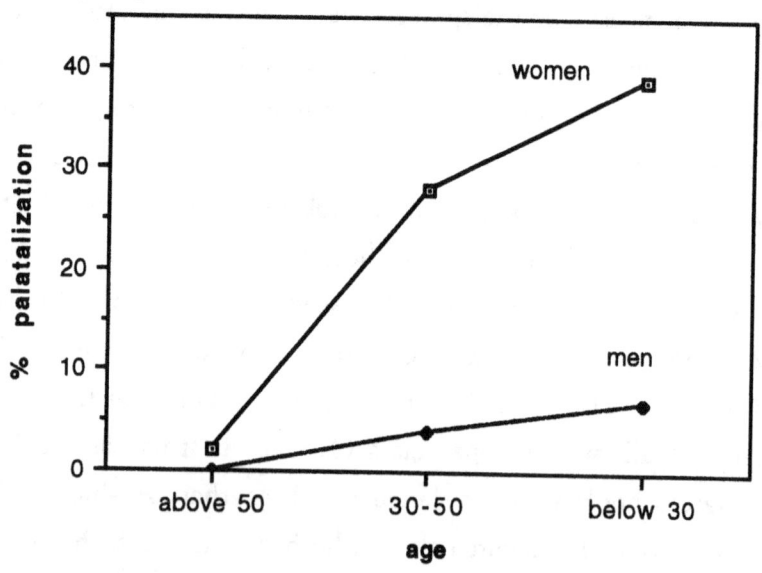

Graph 1: Percentage of strong palatalization in three age groups

This frequency goes up to almost 40% in the youngest age group. Differences between the three age groups are significant at the .001 level. Although the frequency differences between the three male groups are very low, they are all significant at the .001 level.

The pattern in Graph 1 shows that strong palatalization probably did not exist for speakers above 50, when they were children or adolescents. In other words, it was not part of the phonology of Cairene Arabic in the 1920s or 30s. In addition to a reference to palatalization in Royal (1985), Blanc (1974)[10] mentions a Jewish Cairene woman, born and raised there, whose "dental stops are strongly prepalatalized before i, ii, and y, a feature very commonly to be heard both in Cairo (SC as well as NSC) and Alexandria.." [SC=standard Cairene; NSC=Non-standard Cairene](Ibid: 217). This speaker was born "about 1910" and was interviewed in 1972. So she was around 62 years old at the time. Blanc does not elaborate further on this point. I interpret his designation "prepalatalization" rather than palatalization to be the same as what I have been calling weak palatalization. Blanc's speaker would be among our group of "above 50" who have weak palatalization in their speech. Still, we cannot conclusively determine just how recent is palatalization.

As for the second question, the systematically differentiated distribution of palatalization (both strong and weak) among women in particular shows that palatalization is a change in progress. As will be seen below, in addition to the data presented in Graph 1, data on education and social class also support this claim.

The pattern for weak palatalization is presented in Graph 2. What is interesting about this distribution is that both for men and women, those in the 30–50 age range (that is the generation with whom strong palatalization probably started), show the highest amount of weak palatalization. Moreover, for both men and women the differences between this age group and the other two are significant at the .001 level.

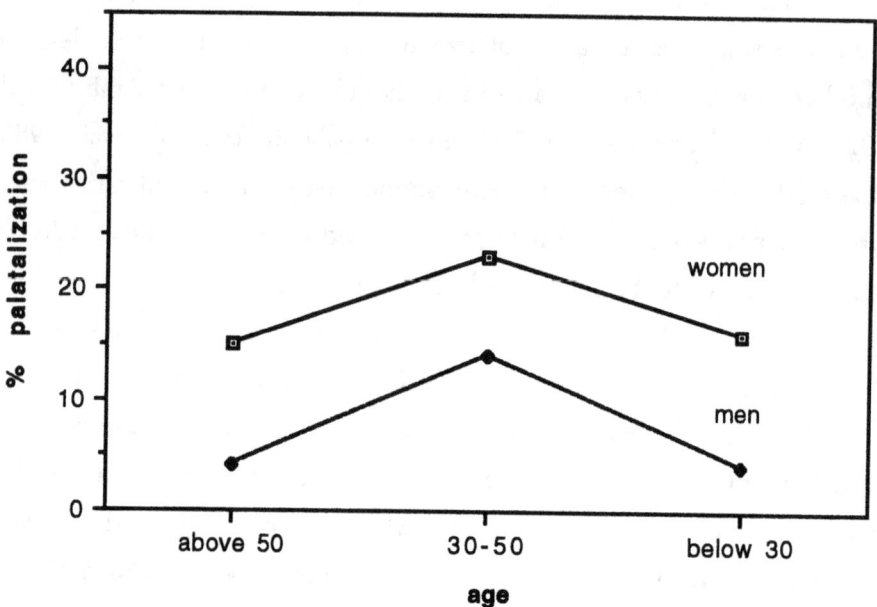

Graph 2: Percentage of weak palatalization in three age groups

Also, comparing Graphs 1 and 2, the youngest women have twice as high a frequency of strong palatalization as weak palatalization. More importantly for us, the oldest age group has 15% weak palatalization for women and 4% for men. Based on the linguistic behavior of the oldest group in terms of weak and strong palatalization, it seems that weak palatalization preceded strong palatalization. Blanc's data also lend support to this conclusion. In this age group, the difference between weak and strong palatalization is significant at the .001 level.

Graph 3 provides a more complete picture by showing the age distribution for both kinds of palatalization. Again, to be able to locate when weak palatalization came in, we would need diachronic data, and speakers in their 70s and 80s.

Graph 3: Weak and strong palatalization in three age groups

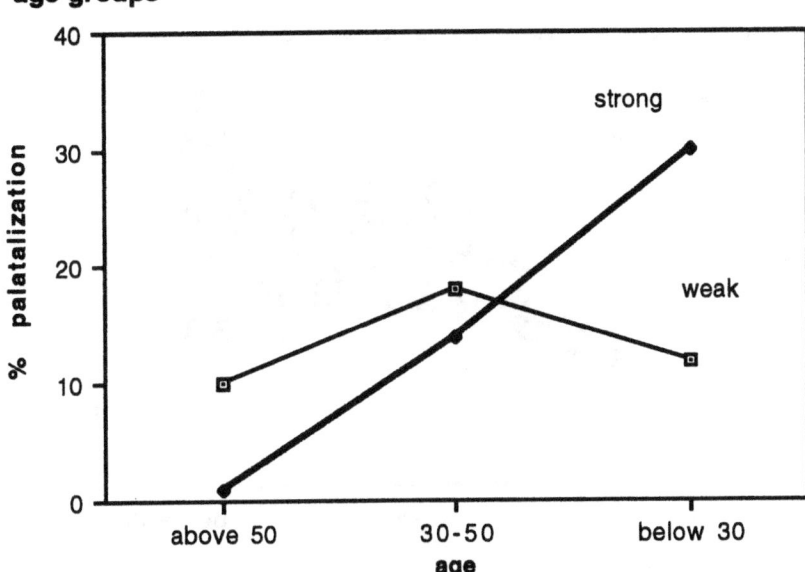

Restating the conclusions reached so far, it seems that palatalization is a sound change in progress; and that it started in the form of weak palatalization. Graph 4 shows that strong palatalization is replacing weak palatalization for the youngest age group.

Locating the Innovators: Gender and Social Class

Graph 5 shows the distribution of weak palatalization among women of four social classes (see Chapter 2 for categorization criteria). Here we see that Upper Middle Class women have the highest frequency of weak palatalization, almost twice as high as women in the Lower Middle Class and Middle Middle Class categories. Chi-square analysis shows the difference between LMC and MMC women is not statistically significant ($p < .80$). However, all other differences between the social classes are significant at the .001 level.

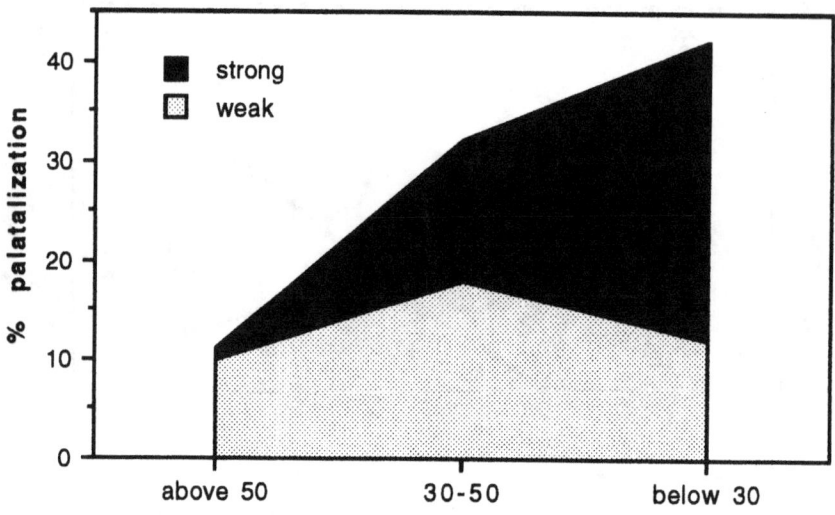

Graph 4: View of weak and strong palatalization in an area graph

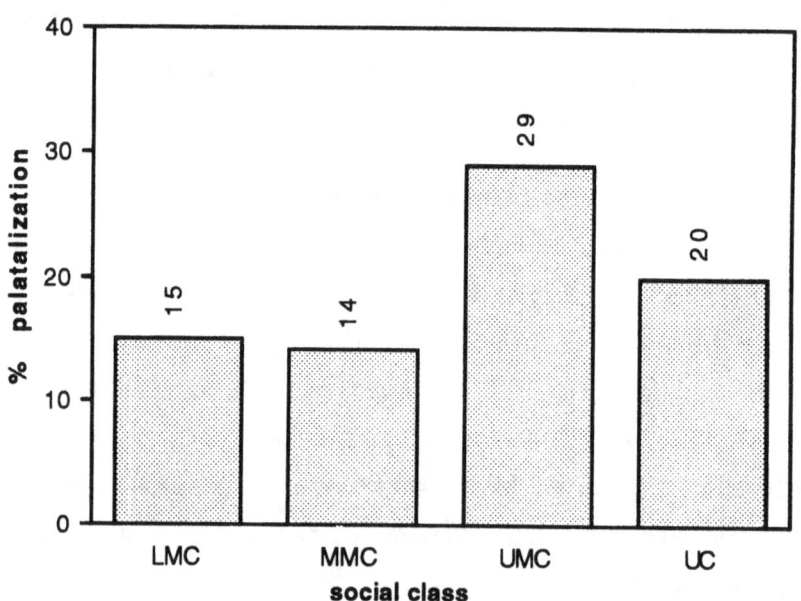

Graph 5: Percentage of weak palatalization among women in four social classes

On the other hand, the data on *strong* palatalization show that it is LMC and MMC women who have the highest frequencies. This can be seen in Graph 6 where weak and strong palatalization among women in the four social classes are compared. It seems that LMC and MMC women took weak palatalization a step further both in terms of going from frication to affrication and in terms of frequency.

The evidence thus suggests that palatalization is an innovation of women. If weak palatalization came in first, then it was an innovation of upper and upper middle-class women. Writing on lack of variability in the speech of women and "illiterate" speakers, El-Hassan (1977) states that:

> [I]nherent variability is indeed characteristic of many features (phonological, grammatical and lexical) in the speech of educated Arabs in contradistinction to the speech of illiterate, older Arabs (notably women) who, by sheer necessity rather than design, tend to be committed to a fairly homogeneous colloquial which exhibits little or no variation at any one time (El-Hassan 1977: 122).

It is clear that the limited conceptualization of stylistic variation in Arabic discussed in Chapter 1 results in claims that run counter to the actual linguistic practices of many speakers. Variables such as palatalization seem to go unnoticed and unacknowledged because they do not originate in the classical language.

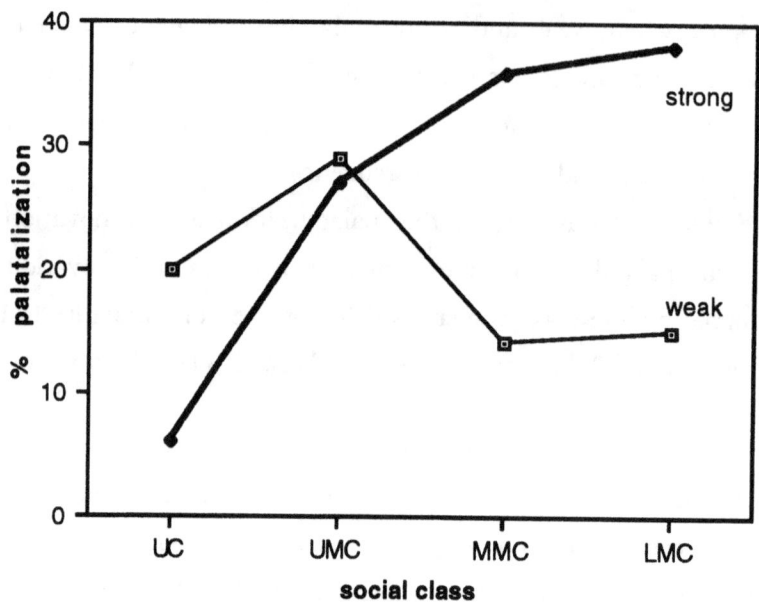

Graph 6: Percentages of weak and strong palatalization compared for women in four social classes

The relation of style to social class has been discussed by a number of researchers including Labov (1966, 72), Bell (1984), and Holmes (1992). Where a new, "non-standard" variant is concerned, its use has been found to decrease in more formal styles. However, in the case of weak and strong palatalization, its use increases in Word List style as can be seen in Tables 8 and 9. While there is little consistent stylistic differentiation, the clearest pattern is that the highest amount of weak palatalization is used in Word List style. Chi-square calculations show no significance between the first three styles ($p < .70$), but they are all different from Word List style at the .05 level. The same pattern can be seen among men.

Table 8:

Percentage of weak palatalization in four styles among women and men

	Women	Men	N
Narrative	18	12	426
Non-narrative	19	8	496
Response	17	9	205
Word List	25	21	54

Table 9:

Percentage of strong palatalization compared in four styles

	Women	Men	N
Narrative	31	4	519
Non-narrative	31	5	676
Response	29	3	267
Word List	54	11	237

In Tables 10 and 11, the same data are provided according to social class. In both Tables, LMC and MMC tokens are combined since we have found no statistically significant differences between the two groups so far, though this does not mean that their linguistic behavior is always the same. In Table 11, we see that MMC (and LMC) women have almost twice as high a percentage of weak palatalization as in other styles; and UMC women have a higher percentage than the former groups. The "non-standard" status of the palatalized variants seems to be over-ridden by some other social meanings.

The innovators of most sound changes studied so far have not been from the upper classes. In the case of weak palatalization that seems to be a change from above the social hierarchy, its status as an "upper class" way of talking is perhaps a factor in its increased usage in the most formal styles.

Table 10:

Cross-tabulation of social class and style for weak palatalization among women (percentages)

	Narrative	Non-N.	Response	Word List
MMC	12	16	15	21
UMC	31	29	24	33
UC	32	16	15	—

LMC and MMC combined.

In Table 11, we see that UC women seem to disfavor strong palatalization and UMC women have less strong palatalization in the two formal styles. The general pattern is that whereas weak palatalization is associated with women in the upper classes, strong palatalization is a feature of the speech of women in the (lower) middle classes.

Chapter Three

Table 11:

Cross-tabulation of social class and style for strong palatalization among women (percentages)

	Narrative	Non-N.	Response	Word List
MMC	34	38	36	68
UMC	30	32	16	17
UC	7	6	3	—

LMC and MMC combined.

This generalization can be seen quite clearly in Graphs 7 and 8 where the UC category is eliminated for lack of data in the Word list style, and where LMC and MMC women's tokens are combined.

It could be argued that lack of consistent stylistic patterns is due to the fact that palatalization is still below the level of social awareness and therefore has not received conventionalized and established meanings.[11] However, for a sound change to be below the level of social awareness does not mean that its use has no social meanings. Matched guise tests have demonstrated that people judge the speech of others without being able to pinpoint the reasons for their reactions. The lack of linear and predictable patterns of usage as reflected in the data on style show that consistent usage patterns are more often features of *stable* variables or those that are clearly associated with groups on the lower rungs of the social hierarchy. The social meanings of stable variables become conventionalized and established. On the other hand, the social meanings of sound changes in progress are multiple, changing, and *variable*. The data here show that if it is the case that all sociolinguistic forms acquire widely agreed upon and conventionalized social meanings through time, this process is not complete for palatalization (see below).

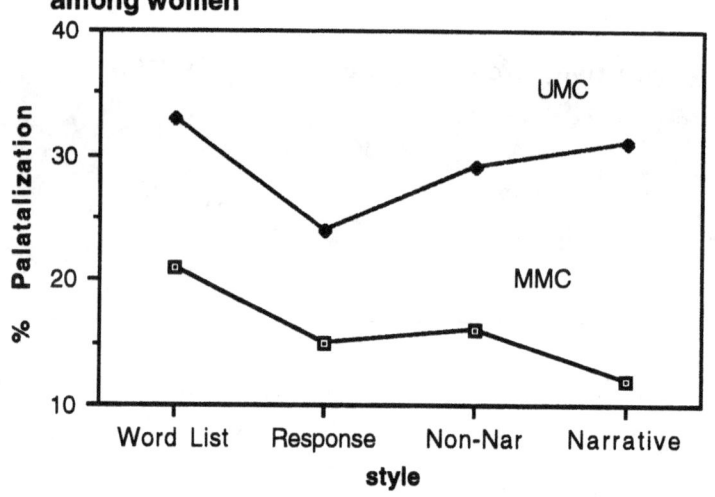

Graph 7: Social class and style for weak palatalization among women

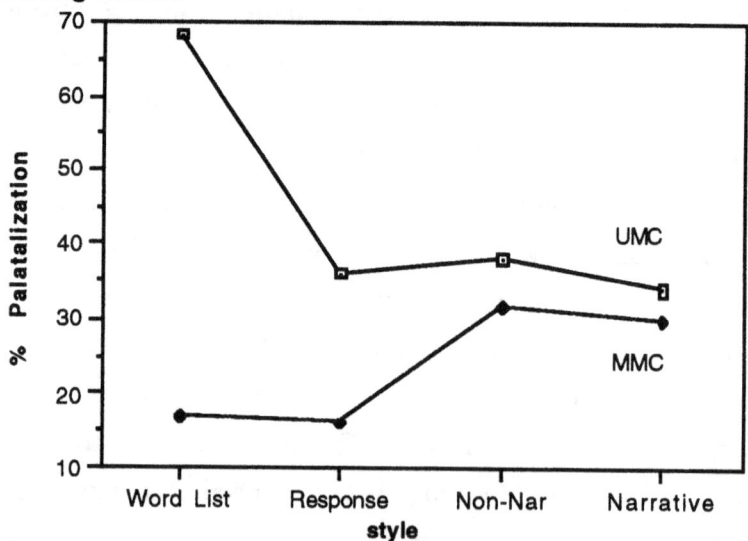

Graph 8: Social class and style for strong palatalization among women

Chapter Three

For the sake of completeness and comparison, the same data on men are provided in Tables 12 and 13. There is little social or stylistic differentiation among men. However, men in the LMC category in both Tables have their highest frequencies in Word List style. There is only one man in the UC category and so we cannot be sure that his relatively high percentages are generalizable to other men in the same social class.

Table 12:

Cross-tabulation of style and social class for weak palatalization among men[12]

	Narrative	Non-Nar.	Response	W L
LMC	9	10	7	22
MMC	11	6	12	11
UMC	16	7	7	28
UC	30	19	18	—

Table 13:

Cross-tabulation of style and social class for strong palatalization among men

	Narrative	Non-Nar.	Response	W L
LMC	8	11	8	31
MMC	3	3	0	6
UMC	2	1	1	0
UC	7	9	6	—

Finally, in order to obtain an overall picture of the contour of this sound change from no palatalization to weak and then to strong palatalization, Graphs 9 and 10 are provided. Graph 9 shows a two stage

Palatalization: A Stylistic Resource of Cairene Arabic

sound change, similar to the lenition of (ch) in Panama City described by Cedergren (1973). Strong palatalization is replacing weak palatalization for women below 50 who are in the Lower Middle Class and Middle Middle Class groups.

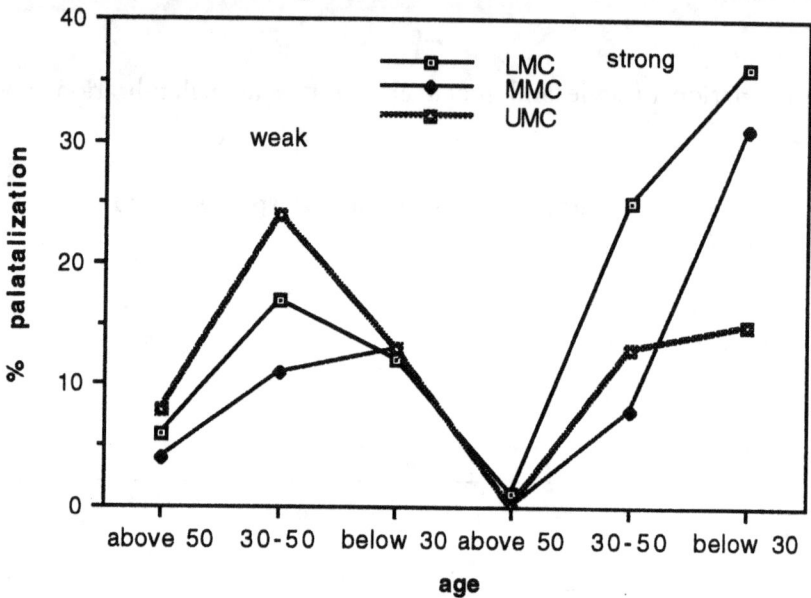

Graph 9: Weak and strong palatalization according to age and social class among women

Graph 9 also shows that women in the UMC are not following this lead. Graph 10 provides the same data for men. Here however, it is only LMC men who show any participation in the use of strong palatalization. In both graphs I have highlighted the UMC to show better the probable origin of this sound change.

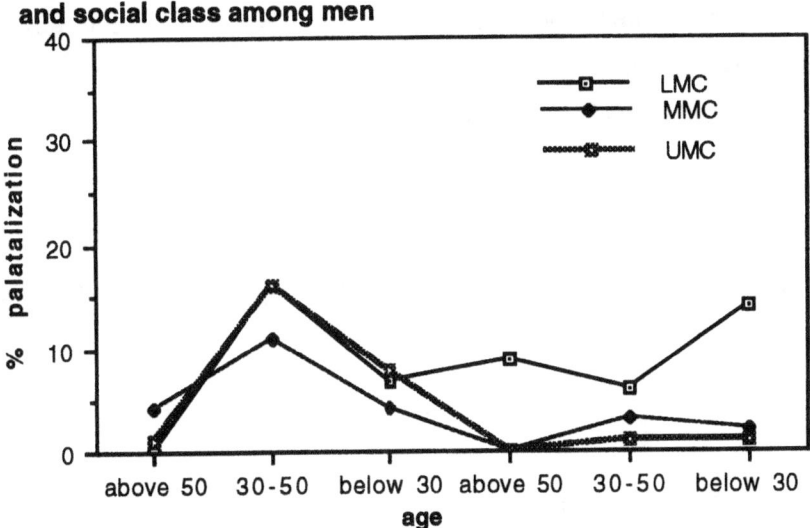

Graph 10: Weak and strong palatalization according to age and social class among men

Education and Type of School

One other piece of evidence which supports our conclusion that palatalization was an innovation of UMC women should be brought forth at this point. In the present sample, with the exception of one UMC woman and three UMC men, all of the UMC and UC speakers had attended private schools. None of the men and women in the other social categories had gone to such schools. If we can show that those who attended private schools have a significantly higher frequency of weak palatalization, then our claim about the source of this innovation is further confirmed. Table 14 below shows that women who attended private schools have twice as high a frequency of weak palatalization as those who attended public schools.

The frequency of weak and strong palatalization is reversed depending on the type of school the speaker attended. For strong palatalization those who went to public schools have a higher frequency than those in the private school category. This is almost a replication of our data on social class, but not completely since four speakers in UMC here are in the public school category. But this factor, I believe, has some explanatory power in the differentiation of class-based linguistic differences that we have observed.

Table 14:

Percentage of weak and strong palatalization by private and public schools for women

	Weak	Strong
Public	13	42
Private	28	15

Table 15:

Percentage of weak and strong palatalization by private and public schools for men

	Weak	Strong
Public	10	5
Private	13	4

Differences between the private versus public school are significant both for weak and strong palatalization at the .001 level. Table 15 shows the same data for men. Although men in private school have the highest amount of weak palatalization, these two categories do not seem to be relevant for them in terms of their palatalization. Chi-square calculations show little statistical significance (p < .10) for weak palatalization; and for strong palatalization (p < .20).

Graphs 11 and 12 present data on education for men and women. Graph 11 is reminiscent of Graph 6 on social class, since the pattern is reversed for weak and strong palatalization. That is, as the level of education goes up, so does the frequency of weak palatalization. Strong palatalization, however, *decreases* after "high school." Women in high school have the highest amount of strong palatalization; men in the same category have the highest amount of weak palatalization (see Graph 12).

What is interesting about both graphs is that those with no education are not the ones with the highest amount of palatalization in their speech. Nor is strong palatalization a feature of highly educated speech. This is also consistent with previous results: upper class women, i.e. generally those with more education than high school, have less strong palatalization in their speech than weak palatalization. Strong palatalization is a feature of middle and lower middle class, high school educated women.

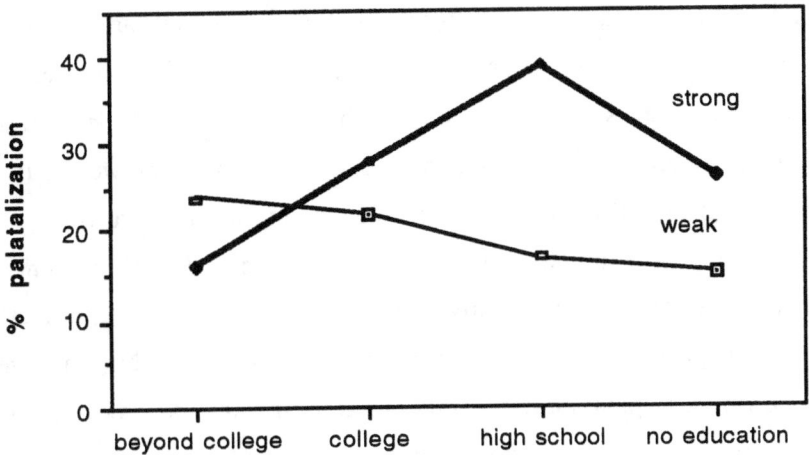

Graph 11: Distribution of weak and strong palatalization for women in four educational levels

Palatalization: A Stylistic Resource of Cairene Arabic

Such results explain better why the data on stylistic differentiation do not bear consistent patterns. Strong palatalization, for example, is neither a feature of least educated, nor most educated speakers.

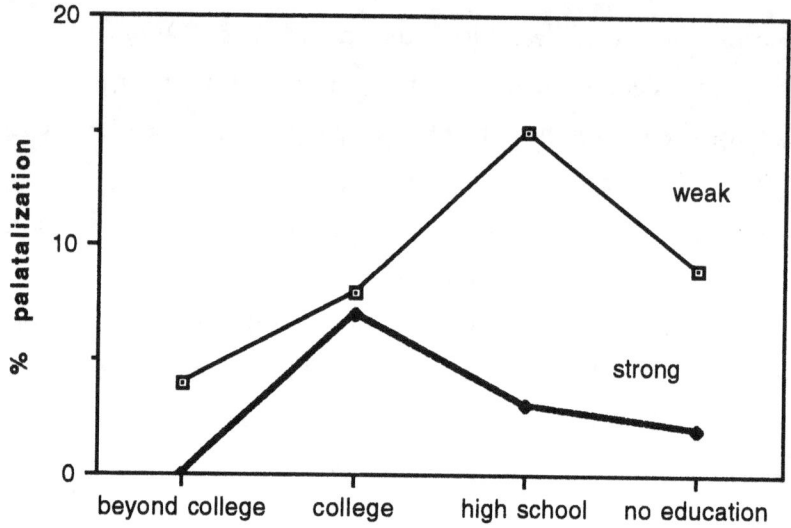

Graph 12: Distribution of weak and strong palatalization among men in four educational levels

Speakers' Reactions to Palatalization

I have provided evidence from a variety of social angles, that (weak) palatalization originated in the upper classes. All our results turned out to be consistent with this hypothesis. Thus, palatalization is in all likelihood a change from above the social hierarchy.[11] However, it is more difficult to establish palatalization as a change from above the level of social awarness as a linguistic process that people can directly comment on. Only five people out of the many that I met and/or interviewed directly commented on palatalization as a feature of women's speech. No one ever commented on weak palatalization, only on strong palatalization. I carried out a subjective reaction test which was designed to assess the speakers' evaluations of strong palatalization (no test was carried out for weak palatalization). A female native speaker of Cairene Arabic read the same passage twice, first without palatalization and then with palatalization. Speakers were told that the voices of two women who would like to become television announcers were recorded while reading the same passage. They were asked to tell me if they find both equally suitable or unsuitable; or one better than the other (for more details see Chapter 2). This test was carried out with 27 judges, 15 women and 12 men.[13]

Since the two passages were read by the same person, speakers were told that two women with similar voices were chosen so that differences in voice quality would not affect their decision. Three of the judges said that they thought the two voices belonged to the same person. However, most of the other respondents commented on the differences between the two voices, and how one was more "calm," or more "beautiful" than the other.

In Table 16 we see that the majority of women and men chose the announcer without palatalization as better suited for the job. The three women who chose the second one (with palatalization) all have palatalization, are in their early 20s, with high school education and of lower middle-class background. The three men who made the same choice are lower-class adolescents with one or two years of high school. The woman who found no difference between the two has very frequent and advanced palatalization in her speech. In fact, while reading the words on the word list and strongly palatalizing these words, she made fun of women's raising and fronting of /aa/ while maintaining full palatalization. Although a minority of men and women vaguely commented on the second announcer's pronunciation, speakers in general did not directly comment on it. They were asked to give reasons for their choice and provide examples of what they considered better pronunciation if they said that they liked one more than the other. Once they told me about their choice and we discussed it, I asked them if one of the announcers sounds better educated and/or of a higher social class. Most speakers answered in the negative to both of these questions. I also brought up the subject of (strong) palatalization with some women who have consistent weak palatalization and have strong palatalization only in some lexical items, e.g. /ʕaadi/ 'normal, everyday'. They said that they know what I am referring to, but that they do not do it and it is mostly lower class women who talk like that. They said all this while (weakly) palatalizing throughout. Those who did show some awareness of this process always referred to examples of strong palatalization only.

What I conclude from the foregoing discussion is that there is solid evidence that palatalization is a change from above the social hierarchy. But the subjective reaction test shows that it probably is not a change from above the level of social awareness.

Table 16:

Preferences: Results of subjective reaction test to strong palatalization (in raw numbers)

	Without Palatalization	With Pal.	No Difference
Women	11	3	1
Men	9	3	0

Differential Effects of Interviewers

A male native speaker carried out 17 of the 49 interviews in this sample, 9 with men and 8 with women; and I did the other 32 interviews. He interviewed LMC and MMC women, and one woman in the UMC category. To make the data comparable, I excluded from my interviews, data on men and women in the 2 upper class categories. Graph 13 shows differential effects on the frequency of palatalization. There is more weak palatalization with the female interviewer; and for MMC, there is more strong palatalization with the male interviewer.

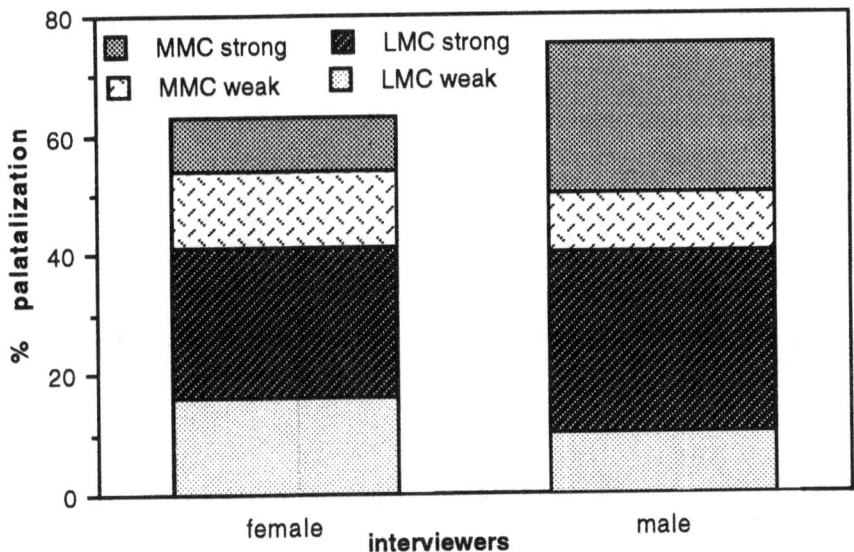

Graph 13: Weak and strong palatalization with different interviewers

The percentage frequency of LMC women does not change greatly according to this factor. Since palatalization is, among other things, a "female" variable, we will separate male and female interviewees to see the effect of the interviewer in more detail. Graphs 14 and 15 provide this information. Both men and women have a higher frequency of weak palatalization with a female interviewer. For LMC and MMC women, as well as for LMC men, all differences between the female and male interviewer are significant at the .01 level.

Palatalization: A Stylistic Resource of Cairene Arabic

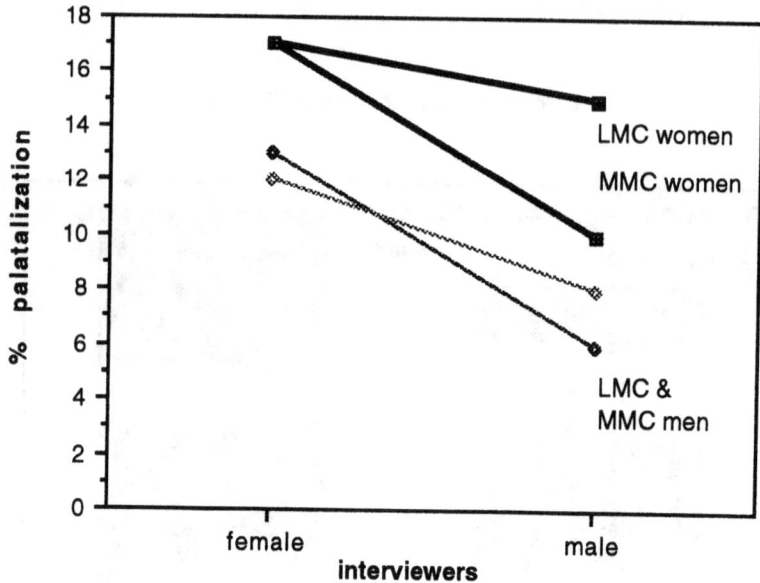

Graph 14: Weak palatalization according to sex of the interviewer and speaker

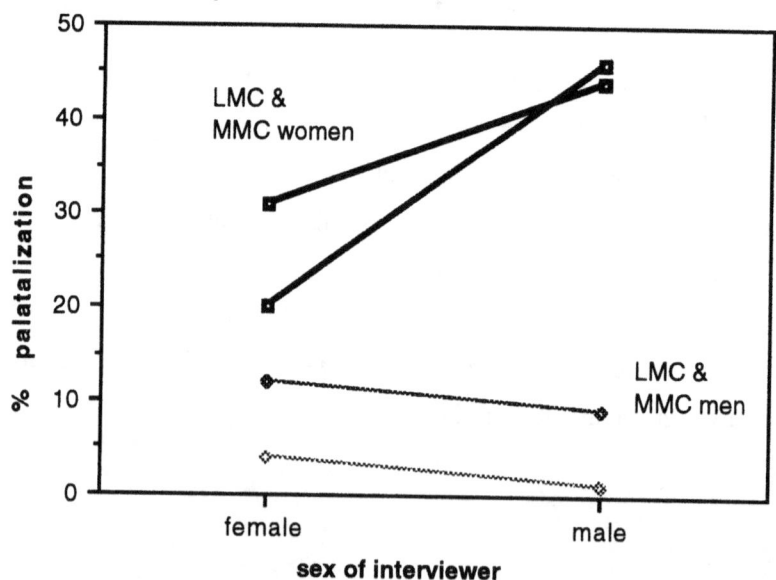

Graph 15: Strong palatalization according to sex of the interviewer and speaker

In Graph 15, we see that women in both social classes have higher frequencies of strong palatalization when talking to the male interviewer. The largest difference is for MMC women who have 20% strong palatalization with the female interviewer; and 46% with the male interviewer ($p < .001$). On the other hand, men have higher frequencies of strong palatalization when talking to the female interviewer. Although the differences here are small (LMC men 9% to male interviewer versus 12% to female interviewer; MMC men 1% versus 4%), they are statistically significant at the .001 level.

It is quite possible that what accounts for the differences is the sex of the interviewer. But interviewers are not simply "male" or "female"—they also have different personalities and come from various social backgrounds. In this case, two such differences had to do with their social class backgrounds, and the fact that one was a native speaker while the other was not. It should also be mentioned that neither had any palatalization in their speech. It is reasonable to assume that all of these were perceived by the speakers whose speech patterns seem to have been affected.

I will now turn to the last question posed at the beginning of this section, namely: What are the social meanings of palatalization?

The "Paradox" in Women's Linguistic Behavior: A Critique of Sociolinguistic Theory

More than a decade has passed since the controversial formulation of the linguistic behavior of women with regard to stable and changing variables. Sociolinguists following the formulation in Labov (1982) have repeatedly stated the rather paradoxical nature of a linguistic behavior which shows a preference for "standard variants" in stable variation; and one for "non-standard" variants in situations of linguistic change. Most recently,

Labov (1990) wrote that these two patterns are "difficult to reconcile to each other."

A number of shortcomings in sociolinguistic studies of the role of gender in variation and change are discussed in a recent review of the literature by Eckert and McConnell-Ginet (1992). In this section, I will discuss a problem that relates sociolinguistic treatments of social meaning to the "paradoxical" linguistic behavior of women. Unpacking some of the assumptions underlying the formulation could help resolve this controversy. The discussion touches directly on the "evaluation" and "transition" problems, the importance of which was stressed in two of the central theoretical treatments of sociolinguistics: Weinreich, Labov, and Herzog (1968), and Labov's follow up in "Building On Empirical Foundations" (1982).

To begin with, we must articulate the unstated assumptions in sociolinguistic theory that underly the evaluation of stable and changing variables in the same terms. That is, as we have stated before, variants of both kinds of variables are evaluated through such terms as "standard/non-standard"; "conservative/innovative." The identity of terms seems to render linguistic behavior with respect to stable and changing variables as seemingly comparable. Thus if women use the "non-standard" variants of a stable variable less than men; and the "non-standard" variants of a changing variable more than men, their linguistic behavior is seen as "paradoxical" since they are simultaneously using more and less of "non-standard" forms. But does "non-standard" in both cases mean the same thing(s)? Do speakers evaluate their status as "non-standard" forms in the same way? As may be recalled from Graph 8, (and other data on style), the use of strong palatalization increased in Word List style—that is, in the most formal style. In contrast, where the use of stable variables is concerned, the frequency of their "non-standard" variants *decreases* in the most formal styles. Instead of arguing that the increased use of palatalization in formal styles can be a sign of instability and chaos, there is more evidence to suggest that palatalized forms are evaluated in such a way by speakers that cannot be captured by a mere reference to their "non-standard" status.

The social meanings of the variants of a stable variable become stabilized, conventionalized, and often polar. That is, the range of the meanings becomes limited and ceases to be in flux. Here, perhaps, one is more justified in using binary values such as "standard/non-standard." Crucially, the "non-standard" variants of a stable variable come to bear negative associations, often being identified as markers of uneducated, lower class, casual, and "less correct" speech. These are forms in whose social meanings speakers have been socialized for generations—forms that writers in many genres exploit for "realistic" dialogue and "authentic" characters. In short, their social evaluations are largely known to the speech community, whether or not different groups agree with what they have come to represent. None of these, however, can be assumed to be applicable to the social meanings of the variants of changes in progress—they go through a period of variation. The meanings of new variants are constantly "negotiated" as they are used in a variety of situations by a variety of groups and individuals. Eckert and McConnell-Ginet (1992) make a similar point when they state that:

> Speakers develop linguistic patterns as they engage in activity in the various communities in which they participate. Sociolinguists have tended to see this process as one of acquisition of something relatively 'fixed'—like social identity, the symbolic value of a linguistic form is taken as given, and the speaker simply learns it and uses it either mechanically or

strategically. But in practice, social meaning, social identity, community membership, and the symbolic value of linguistic forms are being constantly and mutually constructed (Ibid: 14).

Depending on the stage of a sound change in progress, the "non-standard" evaluation of some of its variants may have yet to acquire all sorts of negative associations with low status groups and as forms to be avoided in formal styles. In fact, those who are vigorously propagating these new forms through their usage must be evaluating them in any number of positive terms. Hence the question that has so often been asked—why do women use "non-standard" variants in one case but not the other—is misleading.

I am thus arguing that attempts at understanding the linguistic behavior of any given social group will remain unsuccessful so long as the social meanings of all sociolinguistic variables are assumed to be known, given, and to be operating within the same "socially sensitive" dimensions. Sociolinguistics owes much of its success to a theoretical and methodological apparatus that makes it possible to observe linguistic change while it is in progress. But its preoccupation with understanding *change* seems to have meant a lack of attention to *variation in meaning* that accompanies variation in form while the change is still in progress. It has thus treated the social meanings of changing variables as given. But the transition problem cannot be approached without an understanding of the evaluation of linguistic forms. Works such as Trudgill (1983, 1986) and Chambers and Trudgill (1980) have added to our understanding of the mechanisms of transition. However, the repeated finding that variation that starts in the lower classes moves to groups higher in the social hierarchy remains at the level of theoretical generalizations in the absence of any examination of the specific social meanings that prompted the transition of such forms to other classes (see Kroch 1978; Milroy 1987, Milroy and Milroy 1992; Guy 1988).

In what follows I contrast group and individual behavior, to show the multiplicity of meanings that palatalization seems to have for different groups and individuals. Judging by the group data we have looked at, palatalization has a variety of social meanings. Perhaps the fact that this variable is gradient contributes to its multiplicity of meanings. So far we can say that it is clearly more a feature of women's speech; and it is associated with the upper middle class, and a high level of education when it is weak; with the middle and lower middle classes, and a high school level education when it is strong. Based on my observations while doing fieldwork, I might add that palatalization is also "cosmopolitan" and urbane. Although evaluations of linguistic forms appear conflicting, we cannot assume that from the point of view of those who use palatalization, they are in fact contradictory. Nor can we assume that speakers are only influenced by a consistent set of values. Guy (1990) asks us to pay more attention to the "existence of conflicting evaluations of innovations" (Ibid: 8). For example, one meaning we can be sure of is that palatalization is "female." Does this make palatalization also 'feminine,' 'soft,' 'refined,' etc.? Labov (1990) states that: "If the advancing change is associated with female behavior, it is not unlikely that working class men will withdraw from it..." (Ibid: 234). Certainly, the evidence presented so far on *group* data justifies this assertion. But when we look at the linguistic behavior of individual men, we have to reconsider our automatic association of "female led changes," such as palatalization, with some other putative female attributes that are claimed to keep men from using them. Though the latter has been claimed by a number of scholars, the exact reasons for the claim have not been explicitly articulated.

Palatalization: A Stylistic Resource of Cairene Arabic

Varieties of Social Meaning: Individual Portraits of Speakers

Let us examine the speech of several men and women individually who use palatalization more frequently than the group averages we have seen so far. Graph 16 presents data on weak and strong palatalization for three men. The three are from lower middle class backgrounds. They all have between 20–30% *strong* palatalization.

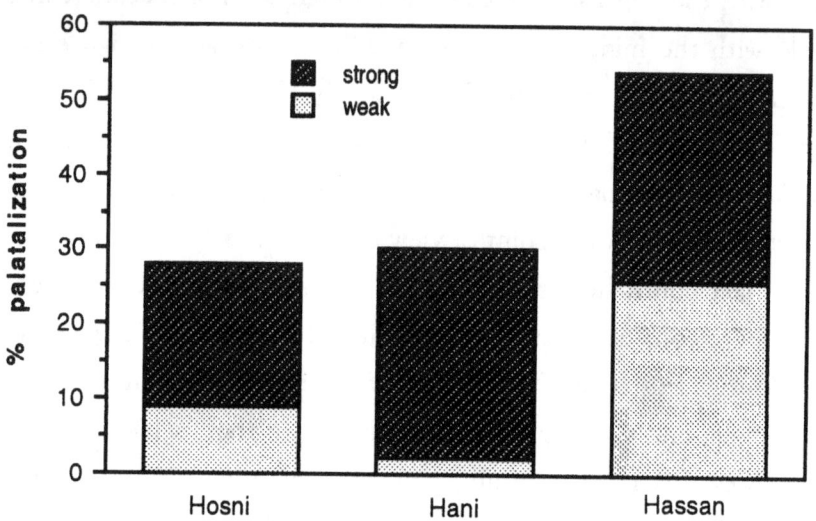

Graph 16: Weak & strong palatalization in the speech of three men

The first speaker, Hosni, is 40 years old. He is married and has four children. He has some high school education, and he is what Egyptians call an [ækseswaar], (< Fr. *accessoire*), that is, he is in charge of props and costumes in a large popular theater in Cairo. He is a rather large stocky man of medium height. According to other employees at the theater, Hosni intimidates potential trouble makers within and outside the theater with his appearance and demeanor and often acts as a bouncer. My own impressions of him during the interview were similar. He is in a word far from 'effeminate'.

Chapter Three

The next speaker, Hani, is a skilled laborer who works at a white gold factory. He is 38, divorced and says that he has the equivalent of a high school education since he taught himself how to read and write. At the time, he was writing regularly for the factory newspaper. Like Hosni, he is a large, stocky man. He told me that when the parents of the girl he loved, refused to let them marry, he ran home and asked his mother to arrange a wedding for him in two days with any girl of her choosing. The mother complied and he in fact got married two days later.

The third speaker in Graph 16 is Hassan. He is 17 years old. His father who was a taxi driver, has been dead for some time. Hassan lives with his mother now and while attending high school works part-time. During summer vacations he says he never takes time off as he feels responsible towards his mother and always works full time. Hassan shows some tension during the interview when his interviewer, a man of 33 and an engineer, implies that Hassan is still a child. Hassan responds that his *Tofuula*, that is, his childhood ended a long time ago, probably with the death of his father.

What are the social meanings of palatalization for these men? Even if we assume that they evaluate palatalization as "non-standard," we must ask what "non-standard" means to them. It would be reasonable to speculate that an aspect of its meaning has to do with its use by women. But for these men, that association seems to entail other positive associations. As far as speakers such as Hosni, Hani, and Hassan are concerned, we have no evidence that they either want to appear effeminate, or more importantly evaluate 'female' as entailing meanings that are to be avoided. The women who use (strong) palatalization the most, are forceful, extrovert, quick, urbane, with a dazzlingly fast and snappy way of talking. We would be at a loss to explain the linguistic behavior of these men were we to assume a) that the "non-standard" status of palatalized forms

Palatalization: A Stylistic Resource of Cairene Arabic

means what the "non-standard" variants of a stable variable would; b) that for them palatalization is solely associated with "femaleness," and c) such an association always entails meanings that men from the lower classes in particular would want to avoid. In any case, for these men the association of palatalization with women does not appear to be something negative, as seems to be the case with (working class) men studied in other speech communities.

If high frequency of use is evidence for positive evaluations of an innovative form, then data from women with the most advanced palatalization confirm that its "non-standard" status is not comparable to "non-standard" stable variants (see Graph 17).

Graph 17: Weak and strong palatalization in the speech of four women

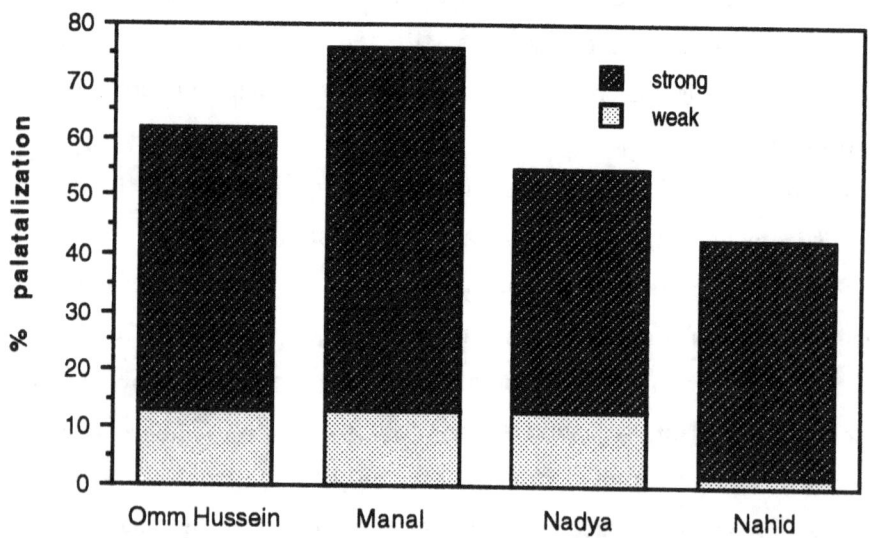

The first speaker, Omm Hussein is a burly 45 year old woman who looks much older than her age. She is divorced, has six children and never went to school. She is the breadwinner, indeed the head of her large

Chapter Three

household which has her own children and their children. Although she has grown sons and daughters, most of them are dependent on her income and on her general management both within and outside of their household. She is a maid/cook/caretaker in the home of some American residents of Cairo. In a two-hour interview with Omm Hussein, she told me many personal stories. At least three of them had to do with arguments which had ended up in physical fights.

The second speaker, Manal, is 30 years old, is married and has five children. She has a high school diploma and has worked at many different jobs. She began working in the middle of high school because her father died and the family needed her income. From what she told me of her life, she has consistently challenged her husband, her parents, her brothers and her community on the restrictions they have wanted to place on her life-style; and has taken them to task when they have exhibited double standards regarding the proper behavior of men and women. Most of the time, her husband is simply not around and she is the one who takes care of the needs of her children, their education, and their upbringing.

Nahid is a very lively and energetic 25 year old accountant who works in a small company. She has a high school diploma from a public school. Although there are pressures on her to get married, she prefers to first establish her economic independence. She says that she is closer to her mother because she finds it impossible to have a discussion with her father who usually tries to impose his views on her without a willingness to negotiate.

Again, we may ask, what palatalization means to these women? If I were to look for a set of adjectives common to these speakers, I would say that they have strong characters, are independent, and in general have 'tough' personalities.[14] Based on this discussion and the quantitative data, I conclude that palatalization, being a change in progress is "innovative" and "non-standard" from the standpoint of the history of Cairene Arabic, but what these mean to the speakers needs far more ethnography than what sociolinguistic methodology generally entails.

With respect to palatalization, gender thus plays a central role in the dynamics of language change in Cairene Arabic. Formulating the linguistic behavior of women and men with respect to palatalization according to general practice, we will say that women are the innovators of palatalization, using the "non-standard" variants more than men. This replicates findings in many other speech communities, as we mentioned earlier. However, as we also tried to demonstrate, palatalization and probably all sound changes in progress have a far larger range of meaning, depending on their stage of development. Thus with reference to the "paradoxical" nature of the linguistic behavior of women, and problems involving the reconciliation of their patterns of usage, I would argue that there is only a need for "reconciliation" when we show that the social meanings of stable and changing variables with respect to their "non-standard" variants are comparable and operate along the same dimensions of evaluation. Otherwise, it would be difficult to substantiate the claim that women's or any group's linguistic behavior is "paradoxical."

Summary and Conclusion

A large number of sociolinguistic studies in diverse speech communities have found that women are often the innovators of sound changes. We have shown here that palatalization in Cairene Arabic is an innovation of women in the upper classes in its weak form. In the case of Arabic, all *non*-classical forms are automatically considered as "non-standard." Accordingly, in the case of palatalization, whether a form is not palatalized at all, weakly or strongly palatalized, it would always be "non-standard" so long as it belongs to Cairene Arabic and not to Classical

Chapter Three

Arabic. It is clear that the automatic equation of Classical Arabic with "Standard Arabic" is problematic as was discussed at length in the first chapter (see also Ibrahim 1983, 1986, 1989). The dialect of Egyptian Arabic that is spoken in the capital has itself a "standard" variety so that variants of palatalization are "standard" and "non-standard" with respect to Cairene Arabic. Forms that are palatalized are "non-standard" and forms that are not, are "standard." The social differentiation in the use of palatalization and the fact that the spectrum of its variants only involves Cairene Arabic, demonstrate it to be a stylistic resource of Cairene Arabic. One aim of this detailed look at palatalization was to show that stylistic variation in a non-classical variety such as Cairene Arabic is possible without a necessary recourse to forms that originate in Classical Arabic.

In the next chapter, we will examine the kind of stylistic resource that has come into existence due to sociolinguistic interaction between Egyptian Arabic and Classical Arabic. The sociolinguistic variable we have chosen is a borrowing from Classical Arabic that is used by a variety of Egyptians for stylistic purposes. As will be seen, unlike palatalization, this variable is used more frequently by men.

---

1. Parts of this chapter were published in an article that appeared in *Language Variation and Change*. See Haeri 1994.

2. In this environment, gemination of the final consonant also occurs frequently, i.e. [bɪtt] 'girl'. The possible interaction of these two processes is not explored here.

3. It is not clear to me what happens to the initial glottal stop in /ʔæwi/ 'very'. It may be that it gets elided and we get [sɪčæwi]. Broselow (1976) states that glottal stops which are historically "derived" from the /q/ are "always present no matter what the environment." (p. 24). That is, they do not get deleted or are "never elided." (p. 25). On the other hand, a geminate followed by another consonant might not be considered as *three* consonants.

Palatalization: A Stylistic Resource of Cairene Arabic

4. I was quite fortunate to have this dictionary at my disposal. It had just recently become available and to my knowledge it is the first comprehensive dictionary of Egyptian Arabic. It goes far beyond previous ones which were often intended for tourists or foreigners and were quite lacking in scope.

5. In Column 4 of Table 1 the raw number of tokens is presented. Lexical items containing the segment [d] are by far more frequent than those with [T]: 3313 vs. 185, respectively. Thus one comes across the palatalization of [d] more often.

6. In words like /inti/ 'you, fem.', the final [i] is sometimes devoiced. There also seems to be a lowering rule being applied to the [i] *after* palatalization has taken place. Only in lexical items with a final [i] where palatalization occurs, does final [i] sound to me to be lowered. If palatalization does not apply, the lowering does not take place either.

7. I would like to thank Ellen Broselow for her comments on an earlier version of this section.

8. Labov, personal communication.

9. Long [ii] occurs most frequently in closed syllables. Tokens of the form /šoftiih/ 'you fem. saw him/it' where the final vowel is long, stressed, and in an open syllable were very infrequent in my data.

10. I had been looking for references to palatalization for quite some time both in the literature, and by asking Egyptian linguists. Until quite recently, Royal's study was the only one I had found. The mention of palatalization by Blanc in an otherwise unrelated article on the imperfect was found by Kirk Belnap who called my attention to it. I thank him greatly for this small treasure.

11. See Chapter 5 for a more complete discussion of the distinction between changes from above and below social awareness.

12. There is only one person in this category. Men in this category were often quite busy and it turned out to be very difficult to ask them for a one to two hour "chat."

13. One of the women and four of the men are not part of the larger interview sample for this study. Since my interviews were generally quite long, I often had to forego the subjective reaction test or any of the other experiments that I had designed. To help this situation, I chose some speakers with whom I only carried out the experiments.

14. It is interesting that Bhat (1978) characterizes palatalization as "rough": "It may be possible to specify articulatory features as 'rough' and 'fine' such that the rapidity of speech would tend to strengthen (or newly introduce) the former, whereas it may weaken or delete the latter. Palatalization would belong to the "rough" class (p. 65).

Chapter Four
The Re-appearance of a Classical Sound: The Qaf

Part I

Diachronic and Synchronic Analyses

This chapter is concerned with the linguistic and sociolinguistic ramifications of the disappearance and later re-appearance of a Classical Arabic sound—the *qaf*—a voiceless, uvular, stop. But where we speak of the "disappearance" of a phoneme in the course of linguistic change, we should first pause to make a number of points. We know that the merger of the qaf with the glottal stop (*hamza*) resulted in the disappearance of the qaf as a phoneme in oppositional relations to other phonemes (Trubetzkoy 1969 [1939]) in the phonology of what we call "Egyptian Arabic." However, as may be recalled from Chapter 1, the qaf is an example of a Classical Arabic sound that continued its existence for some speakers in restricted domains. For those who engaged in religious or other scholarly studies, the qaf remained present in the texts they read and wrote, and perhaps in some of their conversations to each other. For the majority of speakers outside of this reading-writing elite, the qaf most probably remained in their recitations of daily prayers, and of the Quran; and was heard in sermons and public speeches. Exactly how Egyptians have been reciting their prayers throughout the centuries is not a question that we can

The Re-appearance of a Classical Sound: The Qaf

answer with any certainty. We can speculate that features of Classical Arabic phonology such as the qaf could have survived in this way in the daily lives of "ordinary" speakers. Thus, on the one hand, the hamza replaced the qaf in all environments, but on the other, the qaf continued to exist, not as a phoneme, but as a sound. In these and similar ways, the qaf also must have continued to have symbolic meanings and associations, which through time and for different speakers have evolved and transformed. It should be mentioned that there are a number of other Classical Arabic phonemes such as the interdental fricatives and the "jiim," that could theoretically have followed the path of the qaf. But in my data from Egyptian Arabic, such sounds almost never occurred. The qaf seems to be unique in this sense (in the case of Egyptian Arabic), and while there may be a number of reasons for why that should be the case, the sheer preponderance of lexical items with a qaf as compared with those containing other classical sounds might be a factor (see Badawi and Hinds 1986).

One of the most fascinating and most difficult questions with regard to the co-existence of Classical Arabic with non-classical Arabic languages is the variety of ways they have come into contact with each other. Through what means in any given historical period and at present, do classical and non-classical varieties make contact? As important as the concept of "diglossia" has been, it seems to have prevented inquiries into this question. Diglossia has rarely been investigated through the framework of means of contact. Clearly, different speakers come into contact with the classical language through different means—friends, teachers, books, radio, television, the mosque, prayers, recitations, and so on. How do different means and frequencies of contact affect the consequences of diglossia? The exact processes through which the qaf "re-appeared" in the speech of Egyptians is difficult to determine without archival and ethnographic study. It will be sufficient here to make the generalization that the spread of mass education must have played a crucial role in widening the influence of Classical Arabic on non-classical varieties so that whereas before mass education it was only the reading-writing elite that had access to borrowings from the classical language, mass education made such borrowing possible for a larger number of people. Simultaneously, the use of Classical Arabic in mass education, in the bureaucracy, non-religious writings, and so on, widened its contexts of usage.[1]

Bearing in mind the qualifications discussed above, what follows is an attempt at describing and analyzing the co-existence of the voiceless, uvular stop /q/ with the glottal stop /ʔ/. The presence of the qaf in the urban dialects requires explanation because according to various accounts, sometime between the 11th to the 15th centuries, this phoneme merged completely with the glottal stop, i.e. /q/ → /ʔ/ (Garbell 1978 [1958]). It is likely that if Classical Arabic had not been chosen as the medium of secular mass education (and writing), the qaf would have only remained in the restricted domains we mentioned above. However, the qaf has "reappeared" not only in lexical items used by highly educated scholars, but also in the speech of others. Although the number of qaf lexical items in the speech of those interviewed for this study is low, the phenomenon itself justifies detailed attempts at explanation. Of all stylistic resources that are borrowings from Classical Arabic, the use of qaf lexical items is by far the most prevalent.

Diachronically, there is ample evidence that the qaf has been reintroduced into the non-classical dialects through a process of lexical borrowing. Synchronically, the question is whether such lexical items are borrowed "in whole," or whether one sound is substituted for the other? Because there are some lexical items that can be realized with either a glottal stop or a qaf, this alternation has given rise to analyses that are modeled after the sociolinguistic variable rule. Such analyses view the alternation as *phonological* variation, positing unconditioned phonological rules which change one segment to another. Thus the choice is said to be not between two lexical items, but between phonological segments. What kinds of evidence can we put forward in support of these alternative analyses?

As will be seen later in this chapter, there is more evidence in support of the lexical analysis. But regardless of which analysis we chose, the fact that the origin of the spread of qaf lexical items lies, not in a sound change, but in borrowings discourages a straightforward application of the variable rule model. This is a central point of the present chapter. Some of the linguistic consequences of diglossia may be unique, while some are similar to other settings where classical and non-classical varieties, "standard" and "non-standard" ones, or learned and "vernacular" varieties co-exist and influence each other in many intricate ways. The specificities of the sociolinguistic setting in Egypt and other Arabic-speaking speech communities promise to enrich the existing models of variation once they are carefully delineated.

History of the Glottal Stop and the Qaf

There is general agreement among dialectologists and historical linguists about the changes that these two phonemes have undergone within the sedentary Arabic dialects. Due to lack of historical documents, no information on the possible *phonetic conditioning* of the merger is provided. For the same reason, the exact dates of these changes cannot be ascertained. Moreover, as Garbell explains:

> A special difficulty with regard to the dating of phonetical and/or phonological changes in Arabic dialects in general is

caused by the constant—and in recent times increasing—borrowing of lexemes from the literary language (Garbell 1978: 204).

Even so, her study is one of the few which provides approximate dates and we will discuss these below.

Let us first locate the place of the Cairene dialect within the entire group of Arabic dialects. Cowan (1960) in his study entitled *A Reconstruction of Proto-Colloquial Arabic*, divides the Arabic dialects into five major branches:

Western Arabic
North Africa
Spain
Malta
Sicily

Eastern Mediterranean
Egypt
Greater Syria

Peninsular Arabic
Bedouin dialects
Yemeni dialects

Mesopotamian
Iraq
Northeastern Arabic

Central Asian
dialects of Soviet Uzbekistan

The Re-appearance of a Classical Sound: The Qaf

What is important to bear in mind as we proceed with our discussion of historical developments is that whether we posit a koiné Arabic as the ancestor of the modern dialects or Classical Arabic, the direction of the sound changes affecting the phonemes /q/ and the /ʔ/ within the *sedentary* dialects, have been either the same or similar (Ferguson 1957, 1959a). We will first discuss the glottal stop since this phoneme underwent changes long before the qaf merged with it.

In his 1946 study of Classical Arabic, Cantineau summarizes sound changes that the glottal stop has undergone as follows:

> Voici en gros ce qui se passe: (a) entre consonne et voyelle, le 'ʔ' tend a avoir pour realization 'zero': *marʔat-* par ex. etant prononcé *marat-*; (b) entre voyelle et consonne ou entre deux voyelles, le 'ʔ' tend a avoir une realization vocalique: *raʔs-* etant prononcé *raas-*, [. . .]. En somme il y a une tendence a la neutralisation des oppositions 'ʔ-a', 'ʔ-i', 'ʔ-u' (Cantineau, 1946: 108).

Thus, according to Cantineau, in prevocalic position, the [ʔ] merged with zero; in preconsonantal and intervocalic position, the same thing happened but with the preceding vowel becoming lengthened, e.g. /raʔs/ → [raas] 'head'.

Birkeland (1952) is a diachronic study of the evolution of Egyptian Arabic. Regarding the glottal stop, he states: "As a final consonant after a long vowel it was elided as early as in Stage II. Within the word [. . .] it must have been elided in stage IV. As initial consonant it has no function and is pronounced very feebly" (Birkeland 1952: 53). He does not date his stages, though, I believe they are similar to Garbell's which will be provided below.

Garbell (1978 [1958]) is a detailed historical study of sound changes in the Eastern Mediterranean dialects that also includes analyses of Egyptian. According to Garbell, in Stage I, which is from the 7th–8th centuries, the glottal stop merged with zero in final position. In medial position, especially intervocalically, it became a semi-vowel, either a [y] or a [w], with the preceding vowel becoming lengthened. In Stage II, from the 9th–10th centuries, it was further weakened in word-initial position. Many more phonetic details regarding the glottal stop are offered in this study, but they are not of direct relevance here.

Barbot (1981) is a two volume study of Syrian Arabic. Like Garbell and Cantineau, Barbot provides a detailed analysis, where he considers each position within the word separately, and provides many examples. (cf. p. 436-464). His statements along with those of the other authors can be summarized as follows:

Summary of sound changes affecting the /ʔ/

Stage I (7-8 AD)	Stage II (9-10 AD)
$ʔ \to \emptyset\ /\ -\ \#\#$	$\#\#\ ʔ \to (\emptyset)$
$ʔ \to y, w\ /\ V_1\_\_V_2$, where $V_1 \to VV$	$ʔ \to ʔ\ /\ \infty$

Cantineau (1960) starts his discussion of the qaf by noting that Semitic had a triad of 'dorso-palatal and velar occlusives':

$$\begin{array}{c} k\text{———}g \\ | \\ q \end{array}$$

In what he calls "arabe ancien," this triad did not exist. Instead there was a pair k–q without the /g/, where, "l'element **k** est postpalatal sourd et l'element **q** velaire emphatique" (Cantineau 1960: 64). The qaf was

The Re-appearance of a Classical Sound: The Qaf

apparently voiced in "Old Arabic." Within the nomadic dialects the opposition q–k was one of voiced–voiceless with no difference in place of articulation (Cantineau 1960; Blanc 1964). However, the qaf became voiceless in the sedentary dialects, and the opposition became one of a difference in place of articulation:

> Au contraire, dans les parlers de sédentaires et notamment de citadins, c'est la localisation qui est pertinent: 'q' est toujours realisé plus en arrière que 'k': velaire si 'k' est postpalatal, postpalatal si 'k' est prepalatal . . . (Cantineau 1946: 104).

The distinction between the nomadic dialects and the sedentary ones, according to Cantineau, is natural as the former represent the older stage of the language, where the opposition was one of voice.

Thus the first sound change to affect the qaf was its change from a voiced to a voiceless phoneme in the sedentary dialects. The question is how did this voiceless qaf merge with the glottal stop? Diachronic studies often state that there are almost no historical records which would help shed light on the exact phonetic conditioning of the process of this merger. We do not have a way of finding out whether this merger was in fact phonetically unconditioned, as is often said to be the case. If it was, this would support the thesis that the merger was due to substratum influences. This hypothesis will be discussed separately in the next section. Secondly, the articulation of the qaf is believed by some to have included a concomitant closure of the glottis (Cantineau 1960: 68). On this point, Cantineau states:

> [. . .]quoique non absolument prouvée, cette assertion est vraisemblable; elle rendait compte de l'assourdissement du phonème, car tout occlusion de la glotte, empêchant les vibrations

Chapter Four

> des cords vocales, est incompatible avec le sonorité (Cantineau 1960: 68).

If glottal closure was present, the passage of the qaf from a voiceless uvular articulation with simultaneous glottal closure to one of only glottal closure is perhaps more phonetically plausible than it would appear at first glance.

Barbot's 1981 study provides several examples on the basis of which one might speculate on the phonetic causes of this merger. He gives the example of the triconsonantal root qʕd 'to sit.' Derivations of this root include /qʕoːd/ 'imperative, masc. sing.', and /qʕodu/ 'imp. plural'. According to Barbot, in many of the modern urban dialects, this initial qaf has entirely disappeared.

/qʕoːd/ → [eʕoːd], [ʔeʕoːd] 'sit, masculine'

Note that here the initial consonant cluster consists of a voiceless uvular stop [q]; and a voiced laryngeal stop [ʕ]. Judging from the other examples Barbot provides, it may be possible to make the following generalization: where qaf was a member of a word or syllable-initial *consonant cluster*, the cluster was simplified with the qaf completely disappearing as in the example he provides: qʕd → ʔeʕd, eʕd where an initial vowel would be preceded by a glottal stop. It is possible that this simplification first took place only in initial position, especially where the qaf preceded another back consonant. Such tendencies were present in Arabic as evidenced by the example of consonant dissimilation provided by Cantineau (1960) where an initial [q] became a [k] when followed by a front consonant such as a [t]:

The Re-appearance of a Classical Sound: The Qaf

> Un *qaf* ancien peut se dissimuler en **k** devant un **t**. Dans beaucoup de parlers, tant orientaux que maghrebins, le verb 'tuer', cl[assique]. *Qatala* est passé a or[iental] *katal*; maghr[ebin] *ktal*...(ibid: 70).

Subsequently, this process may have been generalized to all other positions regardless of what kind of consonant followed. It should be emphasized that the above is at best an educated guess at the possible phonetic causes of the merger of the qaf with the glottal stop. This speculation suffers from certain inaccuracies. For example, there is not exactly a consonant cluster since some unstressed short vowel occurs between the two consonants. It should be noted though that among the most frequently used qaf lexical items taken from my interviews, there are none that contain a consonant cluster with qaf as a member.

In any event, the qaf thus merged with the glottal stop in all positions sometime between the 11th and the 15th centuries (Garbell 1978: 211). Ferguson believes, however, that such changes occurred much earlier (Ferguson 1959a). While Birkeland provides a date for the merger of qaf with /g/ in Upper Egypt (14th century), he states that we cannot do the same for the change of q > ʔ in Cairo (Ibid: 54).

Disappearance of the Qaf: A Case of Languages in Contact?

Several authors have noted substratum influences as possible reasons for this and other linguistic changes in Arabic. Since many of the areas the Muslim armies conquered spoke languages other than Arabic, the latter came to be spoken by large populations of non-native speakers (Cantineau 1946, 1960; Barbot 1961, 1981; Versteegh 1984). Speaking of the 'Syrolibanais' urban populations, Barbot states that this population was mostly Aramean and as a result of this fact, Arabic underwent many transformations and continues to do so (Barbot 1961: 175). He characterizes the centuries immediately following the conquests as "cette periode féconde en 'primo-infections' linguistiques" (Ibid: 175). One major sound change in Arabic which was the change of the interdental fricatives to stops is described by many to be a result of contact with Aramaic:

> It has been assumed (chiefly by German scholars and Cantineau) that the merger of the interdental fricatives /θ/ and /ð/ with the dental plosives /t/ and /d/ respectively occurred under the influence of Aramaic (Garbell 1978: 208).

Cantineau (1946: 104) seems to attribute the cause of the merger of /q/ with /ʔ/ to the Aramaic substratum: "On ne doit pas oublier que dans beaucoup de regions de sédentaire et dans beaucoup de villes l'arabe repose sur un substrat (en général araméen)" (see also Cantineau 1950: xxvi).

Fleisch (1974), in a dialectological study of Lebanese Arabic, also cites the Aramaic substrate as an important factor among the causes of sound changes in Arabic. However, he disagrees with Cantineau on the role of the substrate in this particular merger: "précisement c'est dans ce 'noyau' [where Aramaic speakers live], cette region soi-disant privilegiée, que le *qaf* s'est conservée le plus longtemps." (Ibid: 136).

Barbot (1981) reiterates his 1961 position in which he cautiously agrees with Cantineau (Barbot uses ' for [ʔ]).

> La realization ' du q, si elle n'est pas a coup sur un trait du substrat arameen, représenté du moins une caractéristique d'un parler ultra-sédentaire qui, dans notre domaine, correspond tres exactement à une région de substrat araméen (Ibid: 444).

My purpose in including a discussion of substrate influences is not to investigate which author is correct. The interest here is to provide some

The Re-appearance of a Classical Sound: The Qaf

information on the socio-historical context which makes our understanding of the social values attributed to the use of the /q/ and the /ʔ/ more profound. For the dialectal division sedentary/nomadic also corresponds to several other important sociological divisions. For example, as Barbot points out in this passage, the glottal stop was a feature of the "ultra-sedentaire." Therefore the glottal stop was a characteristic of the speech of the urban centers. Blanc (1964) states that while the sedentary population included Muslims, Christians, and Jews, the Bedouin population were Muslims. He also points out that the Arabization of the non-Muslim populations took place along with the founding of cities by the Muslim armies:

> From the seventh century, when Arabization began as a result of the Muslim conquest, until the 10th century, when centralized governments began to decline, Arabization and urbanization went hand in hand. Cities were founded, became populated and prospered. The non-Muslims adopted the Arabic speech of the Muslim townsmen (Blanc 1964: 169).

Thus areas with large numbers of non-native speakers were the seat of many linguistic changes. These changes of which the change of the qaf to the glottal stop is perhaps one example, came to be associated with the more culturally and politically dominant urban centers. The qaf was a feature of dialects that were considered more "correct" and "pure," but simultaneously it represented the speech of groups who lacked the status of urban speakers. Fleisch (1974: 136, fn. 3) gives the example of several families in a Maronite village (Bajje) in Lebanon where the [q] is still pronounced "dans quelques familles á l'interieur de la maison et l'on s'en abstient dans la rue, sous peine de faire rire de soi." In this example, we can see that the purity and correctness of the qaf was not sufficient to protect those who use it from ridicule. Ferguson (1988) also mentions Cantineau's 1936 study of Palmyra where the /q/ was giving way to the glottal stop: "The important point here is that MSA [Modern Standard Arabic]–Classical /q/ was yielding to local prestige norms at that time and place as it is now doing in large areas of the Arab world" (Ibid: 127).

The foregoing socio-historical context argues strongly against a blanket assignment of "prestige" to Classical Arabic and its features. Specifically, where the latter come into conflict with other varieties that have a number of positive associations through their identification with urban centers and their milieus. The point is not that Classical Arabic lacks status, but that the contents of this status need to be specified. Attributing unambiguous, timeless, and unchanging "prestige" to Classical Arabic and its features is historically inaccurate, and portrays a dichotomous, black and white sociolinguistic situation in which there seems to be no ambivalence (see Ibrahim 1983, 1986). Holes (1987) found that where the features of the prestigious Sunni dialect in Bahrain come into conflict with those of Classical Arabic, Sunni speakers generally do not "correct" towards the norms of Classical Arabic. One could certainly not argue that the Sunni speakers do not revere Classical Arabic, nor that they would consider their dialect as more "correct." But clearly there seem to have emerged competing and conflicting pressures on language use that need to be investigated rather than ignored. We will return to this discussion again in Chapters 5 and 6.

Review of the Literature: The Lexical Borrowing Model

To characterize the use of lexical items that contain the qaf, a variety of linguists have used terms such as "borrowing" (Garbell 1978); "classicism" (Ferguson 1959b; Blanc 1960); and "literary borrowing" (Al-Ani 1976). It goes without saying that such terms have been used interchangeably by these and other linguists (e.g. Cantineau 1960; Fleisch 1974; Birkeland 1952).

Among the studies cited above, Blanc 1960 is perhaps the first detailed, data-based study of the oral use of Classical Arabic in more or less spontaneous conversation. Among the features Blanc discusses, he notes the use of [q] instead of its modern reflexes by the speakers. He points out the difficulty in drawing a line between "classicizing via phonemic modification" on the one hand, and "lexical suppletion," on the other. However, in his analysis, he chooses the latter, namely lexical suppletion, in particular due to the presence of lexical items which *lack dialectal equivalents*, e.g. /taqaddum/ 'progress', where there is no */taʔaddum/.

Al-Ani (1976) investigates the use of the /q/ and its reflexes in Iraq. In Baghdad and Basra /g/ is the modern reflex of /q/, whereas in the northern dialects the /q/ is retained. Al-Ani uses an Iraqi-English dictionary and finds a total of 1302 lexical items, 672 of which are cited with a [q], and 630 with a [g]. He divides those lexical items with [q] into 'dialectal' versus borrowings where the former category comprises lexical items that have always had the qaf and continue to do so. This is in contrast to other lexical items with a qaf that are more formal and appear to have been borrowed from Classical Arabic. Al-Ani concludes his investigation with the following remark:

> It should be noted that the large number of items that appeared as a result of my investigation should not give the impression that the Baghdadi dialect is adopting the /q/ instead of the /g/. It seems to me in examining the items containing /q/ that the majority of them are generally not replacing the sound /g/ but are determined by the literary influence on this dialect (Al-Ani 1976: 108).

Thus, although Al-Ani does not explicitly pose the question of phonemic replacement or lexical suppletion, he describes the situation in terms of borrowing. In these studies, then, there is general agreement about the reasons for the co-existence of [q] with its modern reflexes: namely there is a process of lexical borrowing from Classical Arabic into the dialects, and not one of replacement where every non-classical reflex would change to a qaf.

Review of the Literature: Variationist Studies

Most of the studies reviewed in this section are pioneer sociolinguistic studies of Arabic. They document the ways in which the phonology of Classical Arabic has influenced various non-classical Arabic varieties. Specifically they provide data on the use of Classical Arabic features and their reflexes in the present-day dialects in the speech of different groups of speakers. Describing and analyzing these influences are a very important part of Arabic sociolinguistic settings. However, the model of a sociolinguistic variable was developed primarily for urban speech communities in the United States, and other similar communities. Care must be taken in applying this model to Arabic, without at the same time exaggerating the latter's uniqueness. As we will see below, modifications of this model are required to take into account sociolinguistic variables that are created as a result of contact with Classical Arabic, and other variables that show more similarity to those studied in other speech communities.

The following review of the literature is limited to studies that have specifically investigated the use of the qaf. We will review studies of Cairene Arabic (Schmidt 1974; Schultz 1981); Palestinian Arabic (Shorrab 1981); dialects of Jordanian Arabic (Abdel-Jawad 1981; Owen and Bani-Yasin 1987); Bahraini Arabic (Holes 1987); Qatari Arabic (Al-

The Re-appearance of a Classical Sound: The Qaf

Muhannadi 1991); and one brief article that analyzes the speech of Arab speakers of different origins talking to each other (Sallam 1980).

One of the earliest sociolinguistic dissertations on a dialect of Arabic is that of Schmidt (1974) written on Cairene Arabic. The data on the use of the [q] is based on 28 interviews, sixteen of which were carried out with students at the American University in Cairo (eight men and eight women), and twelve were with men from the "working-class neighborhood of Al-sayida Zaynab" (Ibid: 32).

Schmidt provides two detailed classifications of the lexical items used by his informants. What we are concerned with in this section is his specific treatment of the co-existence of [q] and the [ʔ]. According to Schmidt, there is a rule which he calls "Q-Colloquialization" which changes a [q] to a [ʔ]. Although he notes the existence of a few words to which this rule "never applies" (e.g. /qaahira/ 'Cairo'), his measurements of the occurrence of the [q] in percentages indicates that he takes every lexical item with an etymological /q/ to be a potential domain for the application of this rule. He thus considers this alternation to constitute a "phonological variable" (Ibid: 77).

In view of the fact that the merger of the /q/ with the glottal stop took place centuries ago, the rule Schmidt describes is a diachronic one. If all /q/'s merged, there is no on-going process that 'colloquializes' lexical items with a qaf. In this regard, Holes 1987 comments on a similar alternation between [k] and [č] where the former is Classical and the latter is the Bahraini reflex:

> [. . .] while synchronic /č / arose in very many lexical items as a result of a historical k → č change in which /k/ was in contiguity with a high, front vowel, its present-day susceptibility to vary with /k/ has nothing to do with phonetic environment, to judge

from the data: susceptibility to variation is rather a question of the 'lexical status' of the word in which /k/–/č/ occurs (Ibid: 2).

Secondly, as will be shown below, the alternation is not realized in most lexical items in Cairene Arabic. There are, for example, doublets and new coinages. Finally, Schmidt found no internal conditioning for this rule:

> The majority of the colloquialization rules discussed in this thesis have not been 'inherently variable', that is, the rules themselves do not contain linguistic constraints of variable weight (Schmidt 1974: 128).

Schmidt both poses the question of phonemic modification or lexical suppletion which Blanc (1964) did, and asks the question of "whether most or all of the EC [Egyptian Colloquial] forms which are historically cognate with the CA [Classical Arabic] forms can be said to have underlying forms identical to the Classical Arabic underlying form" (Ibid: 59). To answer this question, Schmidt considers phonetic and morphophonemic data. It should be mentioned that Schmidt is interested in the question as a whole and does not limit it to the case of the two phonemes in question. As far as the latter is concerned, he considers phonetic data and finds no evidence in support of positing *common* underlying forms:

> One kind of evidence that would argue strongly for shared CA-EC [Classical Arabic-Egyptian Colloquial] underlying forms would be to show that certain low level phonological rules at play in EC must operate on underlying forms identical to or at least more similar to the CA forms. This kind of evidence does not seem to be available (Schmidt 1974: 188).

The Re-appearance of a Classical Sound: The Qaf

The second study of Cairo that analyzes the use of the qaf is that of Schultz (1981). This is an investigation of "formal spoken Arabic" in Egypt. The data consist of tape-recordings from a radio program in Cairo where such topics as poetry, medicine, the social sciences, festivals and plays were discussed and debated. Schultz used 19 hours of the recordings based on the speech of 49 men. No women are included in his data base. Schultz acknowledges the problem of deciding whether the speakers were reading from notes or talking spontaneously. However, he states that "it was not difficult to decide." The main aim of this study was to investigate the oral use of Classical Arabic. In his brief section on the qaf, Schultz states his agreement with Schmidt (1974) in characterizing the alternation as "Q-Colloquialization."

Sallam (1980) is a study of qaf usage which is based on twenty speakers, drawn from an original pool of forty. The latter are from five different countries: Egypt, Syria, Palestine, Jordan, and Lebanon. Sallam analyzed the speech that is claimed to result between Arabic speakers whose native dialects are different from one another. He describes the co-existence of the [q] and its various reflexes in such dialects as "phonological variation," where "the (Q)-variable has four alternates assigned either to regional differences or (intra)-personal variation" (Ibid: 78). This is the only study in which it is claimed that there is phonological conditioning governing the distribution of the [q] and its "variants." However, what his examples illustrate are often stylistic co-occurrence restrictions. (For a further critique of these examples, see Abdel-Jawad p. 197–99.)[2]

Shorrab (1981) is a dissertation which is entitled "Models of Socially Significant Linguistic Variation: The Case of Palestinian Arabic." Shorrab's data are from the speech of twenty-six Palestinians residing in Buffalo, New York—with thirteen men and thirteen women. A part of this study focuses on the qaf which is treated similarly as a phonological variable. Shorrab does not elaborate on this choice. He also does not find any phonological conditioning.

Ammani Arabic is extensively analyzed in Abdel-Jawad (1981). As compared to the previous studies, the data base here is the largest, consisting of 154 interviews and thirteen recordings of public speech events. These interviews were carried out with three groups: urban, Bedouin, and Fellah (rural). The data that will concern us here are from the urban speakers, of whom there were a total of 59, with twenty-four women and thirty-five men. Abdel-Jawad characterizes the qaf, as the previous authors have done, as a phonological variable whose variants are [q], [ʔ], [g], and [k], the last three reflexes belonging to urban, Bedouin, and Fellahi speakers, respectively (Ibid: 172). He states that linguistically the /q/ and the /ʔ/ are in free variation, except in a few items where the [q] has been maintained, as in /qurʔaan/, 'Quran'. He also investigates but finds no phonological conditioning.

In describing diachronic changes, three rules are provided which change a [q] to any one of the three reflexes. These are "colloquialization" rules, a term that Schmidt (1974) also used. However, for the present situation with a "newer and more complex process," where the use of the [q] is increasing, "Q-Standardization" is said to be more appropriate (Ibid: 173). The domain of this rule is considered to be any word with an etymological /q/: "With the exception of some isolated items, however, any lexical item with [q] in SA [Standard Arabic=Classical Arabic] can be realized as both [q] and [ʔ] in the urban dialects" (Ibid: 180). Such a possibility, however, entails lack of semantic changes for cognates in the intervening centuries, and that is unlikely. Namely, in the course of the centuries following the merger, many lexical items with an original [q] have undergone semantic changes. In order for there to be the possibility of

The Re-appearance of a Classical Sound: The Qaf

an alternation, the two cognate lexical items have to be semantically equivalent or near equivalent.

Abdel-Jawad views the original merger to have constituted a "phonetic change" since the number of phonemes before and after the merger remained constant (Ibid: 275). The merger of the qaf with the glottal stop has been one of the most sweeping phonemic changes that many dialects of Arabic have undergone. That the /q/ did not completely disappear is not evidence for the "phonetic" status of the change. On the basis of historical and dialectological studies, we know that the qaf "disappeared" from sedentary dialects and ceased as a phoneme that could function in oppositional relations with all other phonemes of the sedentary dialects at any given point after the merger. Members of religious and literary elites may continue to use archaic phonological forms (as Latin continued to be used in the church); and such forms may remain as parts of formulaic genres, names and proverbs. These and other similar social conditions mitigate sound changes in all languages. However, they do not render sound changes as merely phonetic change.

Finally, the co-existence of the two phonemes is analyzed as being due to a "reversal" of the original merger which is taking place where speakers are "reseparating the original segments without confusion or hypercorrection" (Ibid: 184). But such a claim implies that all speakers have a perfect knowledge of the etymology of all such words and hence know which [k], [g] etc. is a reflex of the qaf and which is not. In my data from Cairo, I did not search for hypercorrections, but one that particularly caught my attention was the following, said by a public high school educated man of 41 who prays regularly. He recited a very famous sura from the Quran (112: 4), substituting wrongly qaf for [k], where there is originally a [k]: "[. . .] walam yaqun lahu qufuwan aHad." The actual sura reads "[. . .] walam yakun lahu kufuwan aHad."[3] Notwithstanding this example, the acquisition of Classical Arabic, and its lexical items is highly dependent on education (secular or religious). Thus perhaps educated speakers are capable of changing all cognates to their original phonological forms, assuming semantic congruity. But it would be highly unlikely that those with little or no education would even *regularly* engage in this kind of "reseparation," in which case they would not run the risk of making mistakes, and therefore would not hypercorrect. Abdel-Jawad does state that the "reversal of the merger" has come about as a result of "lexical borrowing", but it is not clear how lexical borrowing has led to an "unmerger" (Ibid: 189). It is likely that this is an attempt to capture the different moments of the re-appearance of the qaf. Still, it seems to me that too literal an application of the sociolinguistic variable model to the co-existence of the qaf and its reflexes has not served the purpose of clarifying what is an admittedly complex situation. As mass education in Arabic spreads, there will be more people using learned lexical items. We may recall Al-Ani (1976) who describes the presence of the qaf in a number of lexical items in Iraqi Arabic noting that an increase in the number of literary borrowings does not mean that the [q] is replacing the glottal stop or its other dialectal reflexes.

Owens and Bani-Yasin (1987) is an article in which the "lexical basis of variation" in three rural dialects of Jordanian Arabic is explored. Although the focus of the article is not on qaf usage, they do provide some data of interest. The reflex of the qaf in these dialects is [g]. The authors do not consider any alternation that may occur as phonological variation. Out of 688 tokens, they find 8 [qaal] 'he said, to say' and 680 [gal]. The authors conclude that this "variation" is "lexically conditioned." But the degree of "variation" is so minimal that it seems unnecessary to speak of a process and what conditions it.

The Re-appearance of a Classical Sound: The Qaf

Holes (1987) is an extensive sociolinguistic study of three dialects of Bahraini Arabic. Holes' data base consists of 87 interviews with 44 men and 43 women, chosen from an original sample of 180 interviews. The three dialects are differentiated according to sect and region as well as on other dimensions such as rural/urban, and literacy. Holes provides one of the most comprehensive treatments of the /q/ and its various dialectal reflexes in Bahrain. His analysis of the alternate use of these segments is divided into two parts. In the first part, he considers this alternation as phonological variation. He emphasizes the importance of the condition of 'morpho-semantic' congruity; excludes from analysis all forms which show no variability; and redefines the term 'phonological variable' to make it applicable to the situation at hand:

> A phonological variable is defined as a point in the phonological structure of the B[ahraini] A[rabic] dialects in which their synchronic reflexes of what may have been an originally shared O[ld] A[rabic] form do not agree (Ibid: 44).

However, in the second part he rejects a 'phonemic replacement' analysis and argues for a lexical analysis. Positing variable rules which change a dialectal reflex to [q], he notes that such rules are not only "highly unnatural as *phonological* processes," but they also "do not convincingly account for the full complexity of the data" (Ibid: 100–101). The reason is that the change from a dialectal form to a Classical Arabic one does not simply entail replacing the segment in question. It entails other phonological adjustments. For example, Holes cites the Classical Arabic word /džumʕa/ 'Friday', whose dialectal cognate is [yimʕa]. Thus there has to be a concomitant vowel change from [i] to [u]. There are many such instances where the "variant realization of each lexical item respectively represents bundles of 'dialectal' phonological features, or bundles of 'standard' phonological features..." (Ibid: 101). Holes further argues that a phonological analysis would have to assume that speakers face the "enormously complex task" of learning "unnatural and ad hoc" rules whose applicability are often restricted to a few words. He therefore concludes by rejecting the phonological analysis and states that the variation is "describable in terms of alternative lexical representations which speakers have internalized through exposure to MSA [Modern Standard Arabic]" (Ibid: 103).

Finally, we will briefly review a sociolinguistic study of Qatari Arabic (Doha city) based only on the speech of women (Al-Muhannadi 1991). According to the author, there are four variants of the qaf in Qatari Arabic: [q], [ɣ], [g], and [dz]. The first two are said to belong to "standard pronunciation" and the last two are "characteristics of QA speech" (Ibid: 97). Lexical items are carefully categorized into four different classes based on the presence or absence of three main criteria: ± standard, ± written, and ± recent. The author sets out to measure "Qaf-Standardization" in the use of the first two variants, and "Qaf-Colloquialization" in the use of the last two. For lexical classes I, II, and and IV she does not find stylistic variability. Therefore she sets out to measure it in Class III only, namely [+ standard, +written, and − recent] (Ibid: 128). Here the author finds some very interesting results because she included two reading passages in her interviews, one that contains proverbs recognized as "colloquial," and another that has proverbs in "Standard Arabic." She finds that even though speakers are reading and that the orthography would discourage "colloquial" pronunciation, in fact there is a "near-categorical" use of the colloquial pronunciation" (Ibid: 129). Thus as the author rightly concludes, it is not the case that including reading material in interviews necessarily forces a "standard" phonology on the readers, though intuitively that would seem to be the

The Re-appearance of a Classical Sound: The Qaf

case. As with previous studies, Al-Muhannadi does not find phonological conditioning. However, the use of percentages is again problematic for reasons that were discussed earlier. Although it is clear that the author does not assume variability to be present for all lexical items, the use of percentages again implies the application or non-application of an unspecified rule.[4] But since lexical status was found to be of paramount importance in this study, we cannot use percentages to measure lexical variation (see section on "Measurement" below).

The studies reviewed above have highlighted some of the central issues in Arabic sociolinguistics. They have also helped bring out a number of questions for further investigation—what are the consequences of diglossia; what is the nature of variation in Arabic speech communities; what kinds of variation within these communities is similar to or different from other communities; and what kind of a "standard" variety is Classical Arabic? These and other questions will be pursued in the rest of this chapter.

The Qaf in Cairene Arabic: Linguistic Analysis

We will begin this section with some general observations. In Cairene Arabic, the reflex of [q] is a glottal stop. Alternation between qaf and the glottal stop does not occur in all lexical items. First of all, there are doublets—words in which the two segments stand in phonemic contrast to each other.

Three examples of such doublets are:

qarrar	'to decide'
ʔarrar	'to make someone confess'
mauqif	'position' 'opinion'
mooʔif	'stopping place' 'taxi stand'
qawi	'strong'
ʔawi	'very'

If this were a phonological variable, the semantic content would not change according to the choice of the "variant." As has long been recognized, doublets can be used to separate the results of sound changes from those of borrowings. Ferguson (1959b) uses the Indian grammarians' term "tatsama" to refer to these and other borrowings from Classical Arabic.

Secondly, there are lexical items with [q] which are either new coinages or terms referring to modern concepts and institutions introduced relatively recently into the Egyptian Arabic lexicon by the educational and literary establishments. These lexical items either did not exist at the time of the merger, or did not exist in the particular lexical combinations that have been coined. Therefore, again, the choice is not available in this group of words. Examples of coinages and recent terms are provided below:

qaizer	'kaiser roll'
qanaal il siwees	'the Suez Canal'
qiTaaʕ xaaS / ʕaam	'private/public sector'
il ʕilaqaat il ʕaamma	'public relations'

For instance, the word /qaizer/ ' kaiser roll' (a kind of bread) is a nativized, recent borrowing which lacks a pronunciation with the glottal stop. The same is true for the less recent borrowing /qanaal/ from French *canale*, that

The Re-appearance of a Classical Sound: The Qaf

is, there is no */'anaal/ (Badawi and Hinds 1986: 718). Similarly there is no *['itaaʃ xaaS]. Although the term /ʃalaaqa, ʃilaaqa/ 'relation' did exist in Classical Arabic, the term 'public relations' did not. Thus such terms are mostly realized with a [q] within the context of such expressions.

Thirdly, there is the large majority of lexical items which as a result of the merger have a glottal stop realization. These are very rarely classicized. For example, in my data, the Classical Arabic verb /qaala/ 'to say' was never realized as [qaala] except preceding quotations from the Quran. It always occurred in its Egyptian Arabic form ['aal]. Thus the majority of words which were affected by the merger do not seem to have a variant realization with the qaf *in usage*. Finally, there are some lexical items which can be realized with either sound: qaliil–'aliil 'little'; aqal–a'al 'less', and so on. But the bulk of qaf lexical items which are learned words do not have a direct dialectal equivalent with a glottal stop, as Blanc also pointed out. Treating the q – ʔ alternation as a phonological variable would leave unexplained the linguistic features discussed above.

Perhaps drawing a hypothetical parallel with English would bring the point closer to home. If English which has lost the contrast between /x/ and /k/ would now start regularly borrowing German lexical items which contain the sound [x], we would end up with similar consequences. (There are in fact some borrowings of this kind: *Bach* and *Achtung!*) There would be doublets; there would be no phonological conditioning; and for the majority of English lexical items, the /k/ would remain intact, as is the case with the glottal stop in Egyptian Arabic. Considering the foregoing discussion, it seems to me that the on-going process of borrowing from Classical Arabic has resulted in a kind of variation which is most often lexical rather than phonological.

Chapter Four

Borrowing from the Classical Language

In this section, I will present data in support of a lexical analysis. Forty-five minutes of each interview, amounting to approximately 24 hours of speech, were coded for 32 speakers, 16 women and 16 men. Every instance of [q] was recorded and counted. A total of 1168 instances of lexical items containing the [q] was obtained. Since I do not consider this alternation as consisting of any application or non-application of a rule, I have counted every instance of a lexical item with a [q]. As was discussed above, most other studies provide percentages or probabilities of *application of some rule*.

In their extensive research on the consequences of languages in contact, Haugen (1950) and Weinreich (1974 [1953]) state that in terms of grammatical category, nouns are the most freely borrowed. What is the distribution of grammatical categories across qaf lexical items? The **first** set of bars in Graph 1 show the percentage of qaf lexical items across different grammatical categories.

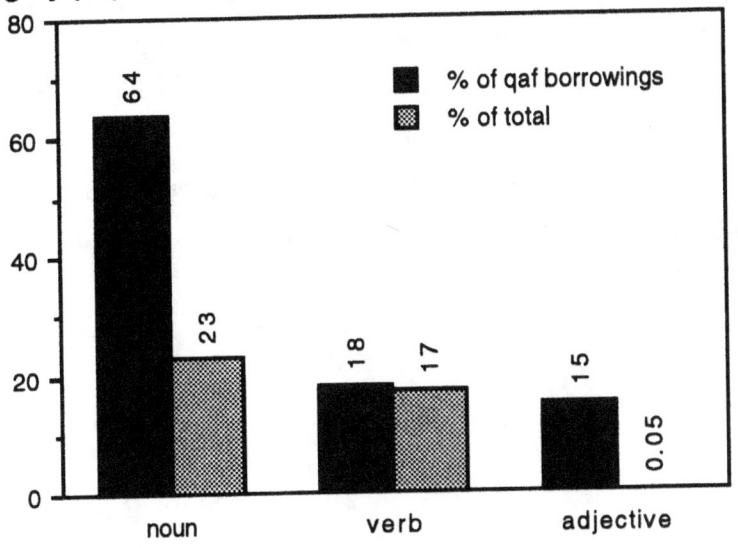

Graph 1: Distribution of Borrowings Across Grammatical Category (in percentages)

The Re-appearance of a Classical Sound: The Qaf

There are 750 nouns, that is 64% of all the recorded instances. The percentage of borrowed nouns is out of proportion to all other grammatical categories. That is, the percentage of nouns is three times that of the next highest category: 64% nouns, versus 18% verbs (209 tokens), and 15% adjectives (173 tokens).

To interpret these results fully, we need to compare the distribution of grammatical categories in qaf lexical items, to their distribution in lexical items without a qaf. To this end, one interview that had a written transcript was chosen at random and occurrences of the same grammatical categories in lexical times without a qaf were counted. Here the distribution is very different, as illustrated by the **second** set of bars in Graph 1: we have 23% nouns, 17% verbs, and .05% adjectives.

These results are strikingly similar to a study done by Poplack, Sankoff and Miller in 1988 on English words borrowed into the speech of French speakers of Ottawa and Quebec. The English borrowings: in French are compared with the Classical Arabic borrowings in Egyptian Arabic in terms of grammatical category. This comparison is presented in Graph 2. Poplack et al. compared this distribution of parts of speech to their distribution in monolingual French speech. Comparing the two distributions, they found that ". . .the predilection for borrowing nouns exceeds by more than a factor of five the frequency of this category in French" (Ibid: 63). Thus the overwhelming preponderance of nouns in qaf lexical items supports an analysis of a borrowing process, and hence a lexical analysis.

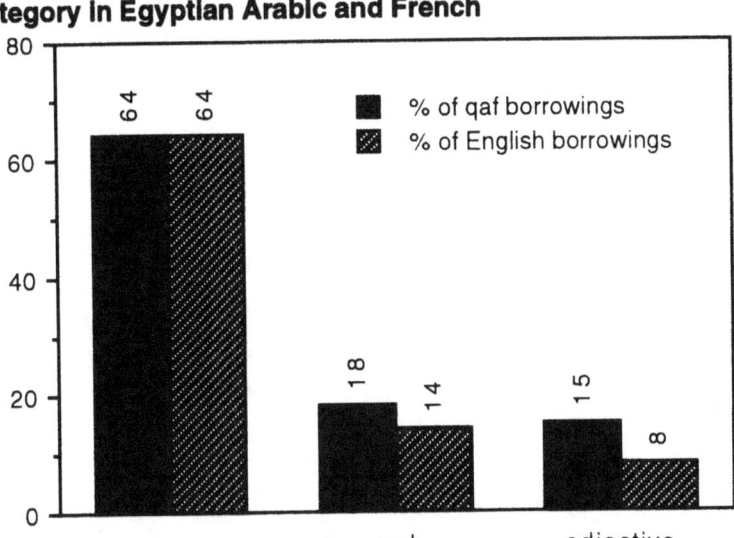

Graph 2: Distribution of Borrowings Across Grammatical Category in Egyptian Arabic and French

Types, Tokens, and Morphological Characteristics

In order to obtain an idea of the overall ratio of type to token, a lexical item was considered a type even when it occurred only once since this was frequently the case. For verbs, there were 56 different types, of which 35 occurred only once—that is 63% of the verb types were single occurrences. For nouns (active participles are included here), there were 153 types, of which sixty occurred only once, that is 39% of all nouns. Again, we can see that noun types outnumber verb types by more than a factor of 2-to-1. In Table 1 below, I have listed the ten most frequent nouns. The number of tokens in Table 1 represents all occurrences of the form in singular, plural, masculine and feminine. Together these ten nouns comprise 46% of all the nouns.

The Re-appearance of a Classical Sound: The Qaf

Table 1:

The ten most frequent nouns

Forms	#	Gloss
mooqif [< mæwqif]	77	position, opinion
ʕilaaqa	53	relation, relationship
qiSSa	52	story, tale
qaahira	37	Cairo
Sadiiq	32	friend
musiiqa	21	music
qism	19	section, department
qurʔaan	19	Quran
qiima	18	worth, value
quwwa	16	power, strength
TOTAL	344	

Fully 70% of the nouns and verbs in our data occurred in bare form without any morphological marking, that is, 675 out of 959. Of the total number of nouns and verbs which had morphological markings, there were 31 instances which had Classical Arabic morphology. Of these, 19 were inside quotations from the Quran. The low number of lexical items in this category is to be expected since borrowing a lexical item does not necessarily entail borrowing the morphological system. Haugen (1950) states that a sign of integration for borrowed words is that they are used with native morphology—that is, as opposed to being used in bare form. That 64% of all the lexical items are nouns and that 70% of nouns and verbs are in bare form, provide some confirmation that they have been borrowed; and many have not been integrated. These results reflect the fact that borrowing is a relatively recent process for the speech community as a whole considering that mass education in Egypt started in the early decades of the 20th century (Heyworth-Dunn 1968 [1939]; Aroian 1983). Thus, for the general population, a deeper familiarity with Classical Arabic spans only a few decades.

Quoted Names

A closer look at the data reveals that it might be useful to separate borrowings that may be called "quoted" from other. The latter category, for which the data were coded was defined as a word which is a:

- place name
- proper name
- name of an institution
- job titles
- direct quotations from religious and literary sources.[5]

The third and fourth categories above contain many neologisms and nativized borrowings. Table 2 shows examples of such words in these two categories. These lexical items are distinguished from the rest and treated separately here for several reasons. The first is that they have probably played a role in solidifying the re-introduction of the /q/, since as names, they are more likely to retain a [q] realization. Abdel-Jawad (1981) found that proper names had a probability of .60 to be realized with a [q]. Secondly, separating these words takes us closer to delineating the domain of *non-phonemic* alternation between the [q] and the [ʔ] since some of them do have a glottal stop realization.

Table 2:

Examples of quoted nouns among lexical items with [q]

Names	Gloss
gamiʕat il qaahira	University of Cairo
maktab il tansiiq	Student Placement Office
markaz il qoomi; qawmi	The National Center
kulliyat il iqtiSaad	College of Economics
niqaabit il mihna il tamsiliyya	Association of Theater Professions
wizaarat il ooqaaf; awqaaf	Ministry of Religious Endowments
qism il ʕilmi	Department of Science
qism il ingiliizi	Department of English
qism il falsafa	Department of Philosophy
muraaqib kabiir	Supervisor/Comptroller
il ʕilaqaat il ʕamma	Public Relations
ʕabd il qudduus	last name (also of a famous writer)

More importantly, we may ask whether the lexical items in this category which do have a glottal stop realization (often outside the context of such names), have acted as a model for the propagation of the alternation whenever the condition of semantic congruity is satisfied. Let us look at two examples from Table 2. The name /wizaarat il awqaaf/ 'Ministry of Religious Endowments' contains the word /awqaaf/ which due to its presence in the lexicon at the time of the merger, is also realized as [oʔaaf].⁶ Likewise, the proper name /ʕabd il qudduus/, being an old name, is also realized as [ʔodduus]. It is possible that such pairs provided some of the early examples of variant realizations of the "same" lexical item. In this way, such pairs could have acted as models for the further propagation of the *stylistic use* of the alternants. To become aware of this alternation, one need not be highly educated, as people from all social backgrounds and educational levels come into contact with such proper names. This awareness may remain passive as is the case with less educated or non-educated speakers, or it may become active.

Phonological Variation in the Ten Most Frequent Nouns

In Table 1, I listed the ten most frequent nouns. For these ten nouns, I used Badawi and Hinds' *Dictionary of Egyptian Arabic* to attest the presence or absence of alternate realizations. The dictionary entries are then compared to the data in my own interviews in Table 3.

Table 3:
Phonological variation in the ten most frequent nouns

Lexical item	Dictionary	Interview Form
1. qaahira	[q] only	[q] only
2. qur'aan	[q] only	[q] only
3. musiiqa	[q] only	[q] only
4. qiima	[ʔ] only	[q] only†
5. ʕilaaqa	[ʔ], [q]	[ʔ], [q] *
6. qiSSa	[ʔ], [q]	[q] only
7. Sadiiq	[ʔ], [q]	[q] only
8. mooqif	[ʔ], [q]	[q] only
9. qism	[ʔ], [q]	[ʔ], [q]
10. quwwa	/ʔuwwa/	/quwwa/
	/ʔiwwa/	/ʔiwwa/
	/qowwa/	

† I did hear [ʔiima] outside of interviews. * Occurred as [ʕilaaʔa] only once.

The Re-appearance of a Classical Sound: The Qaf

The first three of the forms in Table 3 have no realization with a glottal stop—that is, there is no variation here (although there is /mazziika/ 'music'). The fourth form, /qiima/ always occurs in my data with a [q], but in the Dictionary it is only cited with a glottal stop. The rest of the forms are all cited in the Dictionary first with a [ʔ] and then a [q]. As can be seen in column 3, that is not the case in my data except for three of the forms. Finally, forms 8, 9, and 10 are doublets or near doublets: /mawqif/ means 'position, opinion', but with a [ʔ], it means a 'stopping place' as in a 'taxi stand' (Badawi et al. 1986: 953). Likewise, while it is possible to use both /qism/ and /ʔism/ to mean the same thing, generally, the former denotes a 'section, department', while the latter denotes a 'police station, precinct' (Ibid: 699).

Judging from the results shown in Table 3, there is little phonological variation in my data. That is, there are not pairs of words which are semantically the "same" and in which there is actual variation between the qaf and the glottal stop. The citation forms in the Dictionary perhaps reflect inter-speaker variability. In my own data, those who use these forms with a qaf, did not show intra-speaker variability. But this could also be an effect of the limitation of the interview setting where the interlocutor of the speaker being recorded remains always the same. In any case, the absence of phonological variation argues against analyses based on application of a phonological rule.

Given the evidence in favor of a lexical analysis, we would like to measure lexical variation in the speech of the speakers. But how can lexical variation be measured? On the one hand, qaf lexical items often alternate with *non-cognates*. For example, /qur'aan/, 'Quran', alternates with /muSHaf/, 'a copy of the Quran'; /qaahira/ with /maSr/, 'Cairo, Egypt'; /Sadiiq/ with / SaaHib/ 'friend, masc.'; /Sadiiqa/ with /SaHba/, 'friend, fem.', and so on. One interesting example of non-cognate alternation is provided by the lexical item /qarrar/ 'to decide' used often by educated speakers. There were several speakers who never used this verb, nor its cognate /ʔarrar/ since the latter means 'to make someone confess'. Such speakers used the verb /yiʔuul/ 'to say' or /yiHibb/ 'to like, love', and a main verb, as in: /ʔult aruuH/, lit: 'I said I go'; or /Habbeet aruuH/, both meaning roughly 'I decided to go'. Similarly the verb /aʕtaqid/ 'I believe' is used frequently by educated speakers, but there is no */aʕtaʔid/. Instead verbs such as /aftikir/ 'I think, I believe' are used. The point is that once the variation is lexical, its domain cannot be fully defined. If this is the case, how can we accurately measure the amount of variation in the speech of individuals? Given such considerations, what I decided to measure is how frequently each speaker used lexical items with a [q]. The frequency of actual variation between the [q] and the [ʔ] in the 'same' lexical item, at least within the context of the interview was either non-existent or so low as to render pointless any attempt at measurement. But lack of alternation does not mean that the use of the qaf lacks social meaning. The social meanings of such lexical variation are not due to the implications of a "choice" between a qaf and a glottal stop, as is usually the case with the variants of phonological variables. The stylistic effects of lexical choices are achieved for a variety of reasons, partly having to do with the presence of synonyms, partly with the history of their usage, and in this case crucially related to what the use of Classical Arabic features mean, culturally, religiously, and politically.

Phonological Integration or Segment Substitution?

As Holes (1987) points out, since the merger of the qaf and the glottal stop, the dialects have undergone many other sound changes. Rarely is there a simple substitution of /q/ for /ʔ/. There are often other concomitant phonological changes. For example, the Classical /aw/ became /oo/ in many of the sedentary dialects. Thus for the word /mawqif/, 'position', we cannot simply substitute a [ʔ]: *[mawʔif] with no change in the vowel. There are many such examples which represent the co-occurrence restrictions on Classical and dialectal forms. In the same study, Holes states that he did not find any 'medial' or 'hybrid' forms in which, for example, only the [q] was substituted in the dialectal form without concomitant changes in vowel quality or phonotactic rules. He cited the absence of such forms as evidence that the alternation is lexical and not phonological. However, in my data from Cairo, there are a number of occurrences of forms which in all other respects conform to Cairene phonology: and phonotactic rules except that they contain a [q]. Some examples are provided in Table 4.

Table 4:

Examples of forms with Egyptian Arabic phonology and [q]

Classical Arabic	Egyptian Arabic	Gloss
/munaaqaša/	[monæqšæ]	'discussion'
/ʕalaaqat al (il)/	[ʕilaqt il]	'relation of'
/ʕalaaqati/	[ʕilaqti]	'my relation'
/iqtiSaad/	[iqtSaad]	'economy'
/aSdiqaa'/	[æzdiqaa']	'friends'

Another word which shows phonological integration quite clearly is the word [Sædiiq] 'friend' which is variably palatalized, palatalization being a phonological process belonging to Cairene Arabic (see Chapter 3). So we have: [Sædžiiq] or [SædYiiq]. Although such forms are not frequent, their occurrence provides some evidence for a segment substitution analysis.

Beyond such obvious examples, the issues become more complex. Given a word which has undergone rules of Egyptian Arabic phonology, except that it contains a [q], the question is: Was the word borrowed in its Classical Arabic phonological form and then integrated according to the phonotactics of Egyptian Arabic while retaining the [q]? Or was the [q] simply substituted for the [ʔ] in the Egyptian Arabic word? It is possible that given enough time, and increased awareness of semantically congruous pairs, this alternation will partly consist of segment substitution. Of course, where there is no semantic congruity and there are doublets or near doublets, such a substitution as a stylistic device is not available and the variation consists of lexical rather than phonemic replacement.

The more the number and use of qaf lexical items increase, the higher the likelihood that their status as highly formal terms will change. Frequency of usage along with an expansion in the kinds of contexts, and people who use them, will probably lessen their formality. Already, there are some which have become part of the everyday vocabulary of many educated speakers. One way to explore the process whereby qaf lexical items lose their highly formal and learned character is to look at the speech of school-age children to see how early they use any lexical item with a qaf.

Use of Qaf Lexical Items Among Children: An Experiment

Having listened to children speaking among themselves, and with adults, it seemed that interviewing them may not be the right technique in exploring their more formal vocabulary. I therefore designed a simple experiment to see whether any qaf lexical item at all is part of the vocabulary of children. If so, then the place of the qaf in the phonemic inventory of Egyptian Arabic would be further solidified. Care had to be taken in choosing words which are available within the context of children's daily lives and experiences. This experiment is described in

The Re-appearance of a Classical Sound: The Qaf

more detail in Chapter 2. For ease of reference, it will be briefly explained here again.

Five large and colorful pictures were bound together to convey the idea of a story book.[7] A description of each picture is as follows.

1. A peasant boy is walking towards his village (*qarya*);
2. He is sitting in his house watching television and on the screen is a woman reading (*tiqra*, or *tiʔra*);
3. He is standing next to the television and changing the channel (*qanaat*);
4. His father, looking happy, is in the room, saying something to him (*yaquul* or *yiʔuul* 'to say');
5. He and his father are in a bus going to Cairo (*qaahira*); in the background the Tower of Cairo (*burg il qaahira*) and the Pyramids can be seen.

The children were asked to describe what they saw in each picture. For example, for the first picture, the children started out by saying that a little *fillaaH* is walking towards his home. They were then asked questions such as: 'Is his home in the city? Where is his home?' This was done in order to get the desired response that his home was in the *qarya* 'village'. After having once described all the pictures, the children were told to tell the story again and that this time they were not going to be interrupted. The purpose was to see if additional lexical items would be used in this second version, and in general to get a better sense of the range of their vocabulary.

I tried to choose words which either lack exact synonyms in Egyptian Arabic or words which are as current as their counterparts in Egyptian Arabic. This was done to increase the chances of actually eliciting these words and to narrow the range of possible responses. The words /qarya/ 'village', /qanaat/ '(television) channel', and /burg il qaahira/ 'Tower of Cairo' fall into this category. The closest word to /qarya/ in Egyptian Arabic is /il riif/ which means 'countryside'. The word /qanaat/ is used quite frequently, though some speakers use /zuraar/ 'button' instead. I chose a proper name such as the 'Tower of Cairo' to make sure that the word /qaahira/ would be used.

Originally, I wanted the children to say that the boy and his father are going to Cairo /qaahira/ (Picture 5). However, this turned out to be difficult since they all said /maSr/ which means both 'Egypt' and 'Cairo'. I then added another question, asking what the name of the object (the Tower) in the picture was. Even so, most children gave the current abbreviation of that name which is simply /il burg/, 'the Tower'. We will come back to this problem later on.

One other word was included in this experiment. Picture 2 shows a woman on the television screen who is reading. The verb 'to read' is a Classical Arabic cognate /ʔaraa, yiʔra/. I wanted to see if children would attempt to replace the glottal stop in the Egyptian Arabic form with the [q], given the presence of the other words which have that sound. Picture 4 was included as a transition in the story and was not intended to elicit a word, except possibly the verb 'to say', /ʔaal, yiʔuul/ in Egyptian Arabic and /qaala, yaquulu/ in Classical Arabic.

Let us go back to the issue of eliciting these words. If the children did not use the desired words, they were prodded further with three or four questions. The words, from least to most difficult to elicit were as follows:

1. qanaat   '(t.v.) channel'
2. qarya   'village'
3. qaahira   'Cairo'

The Re-appearance of a Classical Sound: The Qaf

The first word was used spontaneously without any need for prodding, except for the one girl in these eight interviews. She used the word /zuraar/ 'button' and only with several further questions did she use /qanaat/. All the children at first used the word /il riif/ 'countryside' to describe the first picture. With further questions, almost all used the word /qarya/. The third word above, /qaahira/ was the hardest to elicit. Much prodding was needed for this word. They all used /maSr/ instead. This is also similar to the adult data, where /qaahira/ mostly showed up when I had to use it myself to make sure that the speakers were born and raised in Cairo, and not somewhere else in Egypt, since /maSr/ is potentially ambiguous. The other words, /tiʔra/ 'she reads', and /yiʔuul/ 'he says' were never realized with a /q/. The twelve year olds in this sample had the easiest time with this experiment. To give the reader an idea of the kind of language these children used, the uninterrupted version of one of the twelve year old boys' is reproduced below. The desired words appear in bold face, as well as every glottal stop which historically was a [q]:

il walad-da kaan min il **qarya**. wa huwwa kaan biysaaʃid baba masalan yaʃni. wa kaan biyitmaʃʃa fiiha wa biyizraʃ ʃaadi. il walad raaH baʔa il beet wa ʔaaʃid biyitfarrag ʃala tilvizyoon. fataHu. fataH il tilvizyoon wa daas ʃala il **qanaat** il taaniya. laʔa il bint **bitiʔra**. wa daxal ʃaleyh baba wa huwwa biyitfarrag ʃala il bint illi **bitiʔra** fi il tilvizyoon. wa baʃdeen ʔallu yallah biin iHna HanruuH il **qaahira** wa Hanʃuuf il burg wa il ahramaat.

'This boy was from a village. and he was, for example, helping his dad. and (he) was walking in it and working on the farm, like usual. the boy went home and sat watching television. (he) turned it on. (he) turned on the television and turned the channel to channel two. (he) found a girl (who was) reading. and his father came in while he was watching the girl read in the television. and then (he) told him let's get up and go to (we will go to) Cairo and (we) will see the Tower and the Pyramids.'

Table 5:

Occurrences of qaf in elicitation from children

WORD	AGE								occurrences
	12	12	12	10	10	9	8	6	
qarya	1	1	1	1	1	1	1	ø	7/8
qanaat	1	1	1	1	1	1	ø	ø	6/8
ti'ra	ø	ø	ø	ø	ø	ø	ø	ø	0/8
yi'uul	ø	ø	ø	ø	ø	ø	ø	ø	0/8
qaahira	1	1	1	1	1	ø	ø	ø	5/8
burg il qaahira	1	1	1	ø	ø	1	1	ø	5/8

The first three children who are twelve years old have all the [q] lexical items. Below this age, the number decreases. The last column belongs to a six year old who was just about to enter the first grade. He had none of the lexical items. Clearly, the role of education is crucial. Secondly, where there is *theoretically* the possibility of replacing a [ʔ] with the qaf—namely, where no semantic change would result and the concomitant phonological changes are minimal, as is the case with the words /ti'ra/ and /yi'uul/, no attempts at replacement were made. Again, this is similar to the adult

The Re-appearance of a Classical Sound: The Qaf

data where the influence of Classical Arabic as manifested in such phenomena as the re-introduction of the qaf, has not yet reached the majority of the lexical items with a glottal stop. On the other hand, most of these children did turn out to know and use some qaf lexical items. That some of these words are now used by children, and that the contexts in which they are being used are not formal (e.g. television channel), reduces the formal character of lexical items borrowed from Classical Arabic. The formality that the sound [q] itself conveys is mitigated also by its presence in the speech of children and in some of their everyday vocabulary.

Part II

In Whose Speech Has the Qaf Re-appeared? Sociolinguistic Analysis

The social matrices in which the use of qaf is embedded are quite complex. We will address the question of which groups of speakers use it, and how frequently. As will be seen, some patterns of usage are unexpected and require explanation. While I highlight some of the questions that need to be addressed with regard to the differential use of the qaf, I will take up potential explanations of these patterns in the next chapter.

The Qaf Index: A Problem of Measurement

Earlier on, problems of measurement and quantification of speakers' linguistic behavior were briefly discussed. In our linguistic analysis of the qaf, little evidence of phonological variation between the qaf and the glottal stop was found. We concluded that there is no rule which variably applies to glottal stops and changes them to a qaf (or vice versa). We cannot therefore measure percentages or probabilities of application of a rule in the speech of any given speaker or groups of speakers. The question is how then do we compare speakers—that is, what should we measure in their speech that makes comparisons possible?

In order to compare speakers, the following "qaf index" was constructed. For each speaker, the total number of lexical items with a [q] was recorded. Each and every instance was counted, even when the same word occurred more than once. To *normalize* the speakers, that is, to render their speech comparable, one has to take into account how many words per unit of time are uttered by each speaker. But if some speakers talk fast and some slow, any unit of time in itself would be meaningless. Therefore, I used written transcriptions and counted the number of all words used in 45 minutes of speech *for each speaker*. In this way, we arrive at a proportion for each speaker. The total number of qaf words was then divided by the total number of words that the speaker used. Since the number arrived at was very small, it was multiplied by 1000. For example, one speaker had 47 words with a qaf in 45 minutes of speech. The total number of words he used was 3930. Thus 47 was divided by this number, .012 and multiplied by 1000. Thus such a speaker would have around 12 qaf lexical items per 1000 words. It is this proportion, referred to here as the qaf index, which we will use to compare speakers. All chi-square calculations were carried out on the basis of number of borrowed words for each group, versus the total number of words, of which the borrowed ones were subtracted.

Differences Between Women and Men

Before discussing the data from Cairo, a summary of the results of several sociolinguistic studies carried out in various Arabic speech communities will be presented. Most of these are general investigations that included a consideration of gender differences with regard to the use of some Classical Arabic sounds and their reflexes in the modern dialects. Table 6 presents 5 such studies. All five found that men use the Classical Arabic segments

The Re-appearance of a Classical Sound: The Qaf

more than women. This finding has proved to be remarkably consistent across a variety of speech communities.[8] In the present study the same pattern was found as can be seen in Table 7. Men have a significantly higher qaf usage than women. Such patterns of usage with regard to classical and non-classical forms attracted much attention, since unlike patterns in "Western" speech communities, it was the men who turned out to use the "standard" (i.e. Classical Arabic) forms more frequently than women.

Table 6:

Five studies of sex differences

Speech community	Alternation CA–Reflex	Study
Cairo, Egypt	[q]–[ʔ]	Schmidt, 1974
Amman, Jordan	[q]–[ʔ]	Abdel-Jawad, 1981
Palestine[9]	[q]–[ʔ]	Shorrab, 1981
Damascus, Syria[10]	[θ]–[s,t] [ð]–[z,d]	Kojak, 1983
Basra, Iraq	[k]-[č]	Bakir, 1986

Table 7:

Differences in qaf usage between men and women[11]

	Women	N	Men	N
Qaf Index	4.48	273	7.58	555
			$p < .001$	

Chapter Four

We might recall from Chapter 1, the generalization that data from the Near East show a "reversal" of the pattern that had been found up to that point. But before we can address this issue, we need to look at the roles of education, and social class membership for both groups first.

Education and Social Class

Table 8 shows the correlation of qaf usage with four levels of education.

Table 8:
Education and qaf usage

	qaf index
No Education	0.88
High School	4.87
College	8.06
Beyond College	7.00

Leaving aside speakers in the 'beyond college' category, the results are presented in Graph 3, for women and men separately. Men have higher indices than women in all educational levels. What is striking, though, is that men and women are farthest apart in the college educated category. Abdel-Jawad (1981) found a similar pattern in Amman. The results are worth comparing. Data from Amman are presented in Graph 4 (Ibid: 254). Two interesting parallels can be seen. The first is that in both studies the widest gap is that between men and women in the highest educational level. We should briefly note here that differential access to education on the part of men and women would neither explain their relative closeness in the 'high school' category in Graph 3, nor why they diverge so much in the higher categories.

The Re-appearance of a Classical Sound: The Qaf

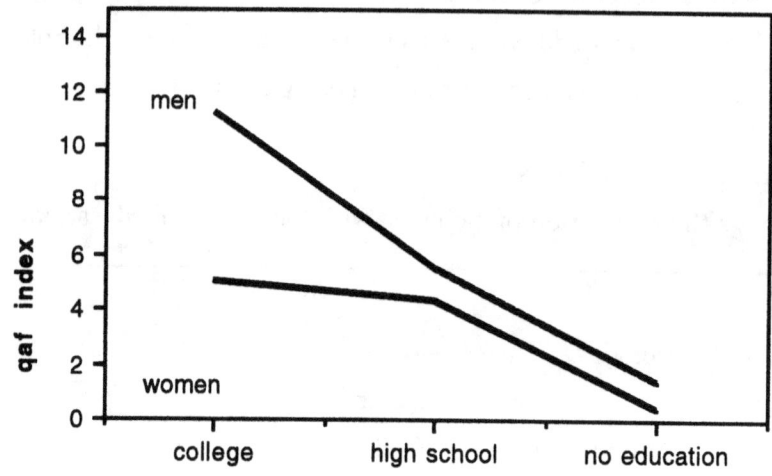

Graph 3: Comparing men and women in three educational levels in Cairo

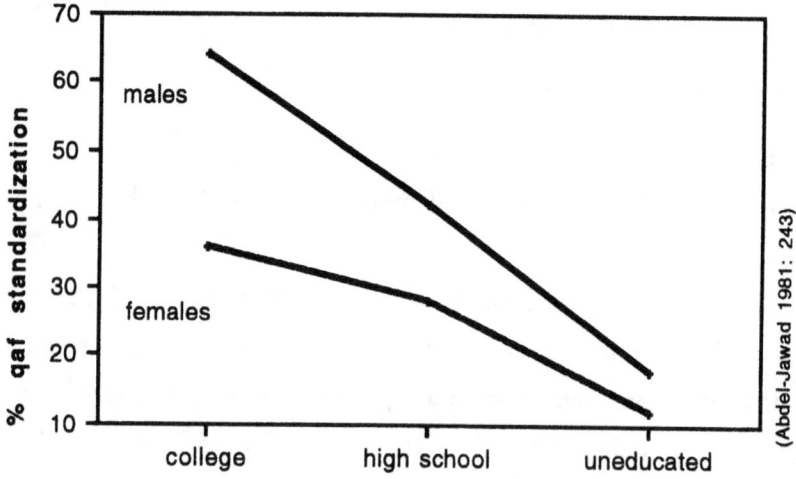

Graph 4: Comparing men and women in three educational levels in Amman

(Abdel-Jawad 1981: 243)

At both levels, men and women have had the same amount of education and yet, the gap in their use of this feature widens at 'college' level. The second interesting parallel is that both in Amman and in Cairo, the use of qaf remains rather constant for women from 'high school' to 'college'. Thus level of education seems to explain in part the difference between men, but not for women.

Previous studies have considered three educational levels. In the present study, we have included a fourth level, namely those speakers who have Masters or doctorates. Data on four educational levels are provided in Graph 5. So far, all studies have found a linear correlation between level of education and qaf usage. What we find here is that this relationship is maintained up to the level of 'college'. However, contrary to expectation, it does not remain the case beyond that level. In other words, those in the highest educational level are not the highest users of qaf.

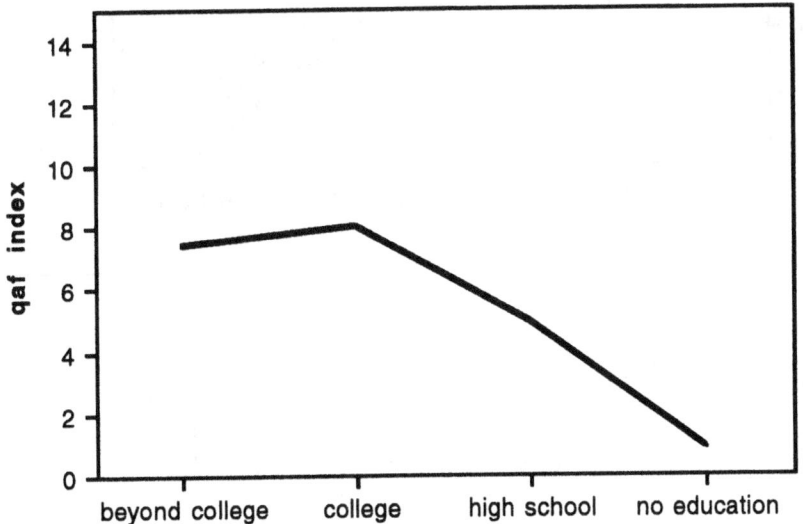

Graph 5: Qaf usage in four educational levels

When we separate men and women in Graph 6, we see that the usage of *both groups in that category* falls. Graph 6 is based on Table 9 below. All differences between the educational levels among women; and all those between men are significant at the .001 level, and the difference between the two highest levels is significant at the .01 level for women; but not significant for men (p < .10).

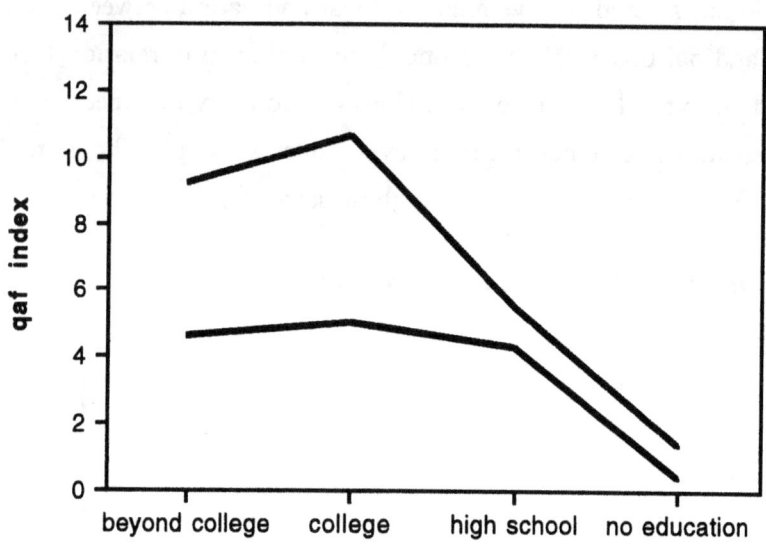

Graph 6: Comparing men and women in four educational levels

Table 9:
Education

	women	N	men	N
No education	0.37	6	1.39	14
High School	4.28	86	5.45	133
College	5.00	118	10.62	385
Beyond College	4.60	63	9.18	127

In the 'beyond college' category, for men as well as for women, their behavior is the opposite of that expected by their level of education. Why is it that those with the highest level of education are not the most frequent users of the qaf? Before attempting possible answers, the role of social class has to be explored.

Graph 7 presents qaf usage for all speakers in four social classes (indices are presented in Table 10). Speakers in the Middle Middle Class category are the highest users of qaf lexical items. The Upper Middle Class has lower scores and the Upper Class scores are still lower.

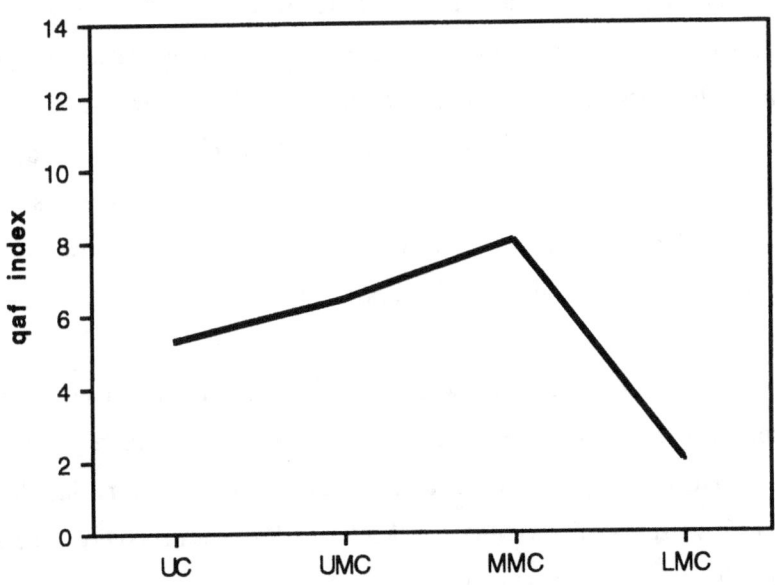

The Re-appearance of a Classical Sound: The Qaf

Table 10:
Social Class and qaf usage

	qaf index
Lower Middle Class	2.03
Middle Middle Class	8.04
Upper Middle Class	6.38
Upper Class	5.25

The pattern here is again contrary to expectation. Those in the highest social classes have lower frequencies of qaf usage. This is in sharp contrast to the findings of non-diglossic speech communities where the "standard" variants are used most frequently by the upper classes. Indeed, what is "standard" is defined by the usage of those classes. If the [q] is the "standard" variant, then what kind of a "standard" is it—what is it that bestows "standardness" on the variety it is a feature of? And how would we characterize the social dialect of the upper classes in Cairo—is it another kind of a "standard"?

Graph 8 shows men and women in the same social classes. For men there seems to be a linear relationship where those in the highest social category have the highest scores, and the differences are very small: 8.20, versus 8.59 versus 9.76 for MMC, UMC and UC, respectively. But since there is only one man in the upper class category, we cannot make any generalizations with regard to that class.

Graph 8: Qaf usage of men and women according to social class

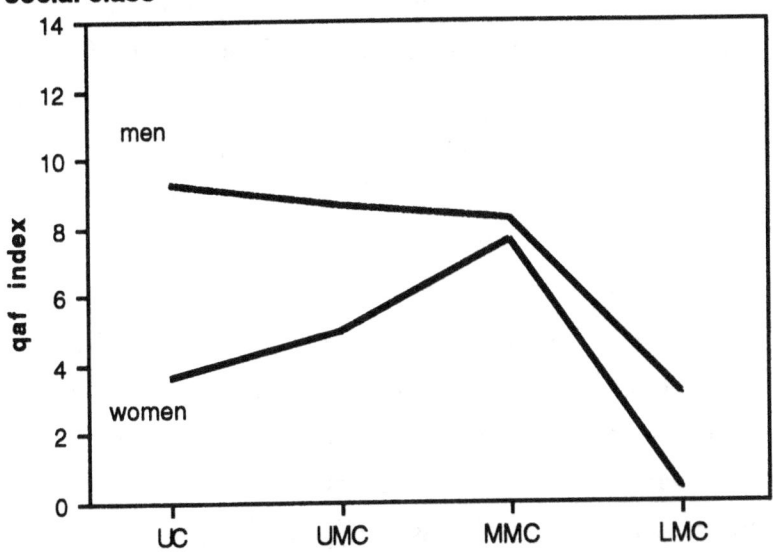

Social class plays an even more complex role for women. Middle Middle Class women have higher indices of qaf usage than women in the two higher social classes. Chi-square tests show a high level of significance for men in LMC and MMC; as well as between the MMC and the two upper class groups ($p < .001$). The same is true for women. However, there is no statistical significance for either men or women between the UMC and the UC, ($p < .10$).

Table 11:
Social Class

	Women	Men
Lower Middle Class	0.37	3.14
Middle Middle Class	7.60	8.20
Upper Middle Class	4.91	8.59
Upper Class[12]	3.57	9.76

The Re-appearance of a Classical Sound: The Qaf

Emerging Questions

A number of interesting questions are raised by the foregoing results. What kind of "standard" is Classical Arabic? Do lower frequencies of qaf usage, or lack of usage signify choosing a "non-standard" form as opposed to a "standard" form? Whose patterns are more "conservative"—women who use it less, or men who use it more? Why is it that neither women nor men in the highest educational level have the highest indices of qaf usage? What role is social class playing in affecting the use of the qaf—why do women in the highest social classes have lower indices? Can the gender differences be explained by such factors as differential access to education; the general "conservativeness" of women; and differences between the "public" and "private" domains? What factors are at work such that the relations between education, social class, and qaf usage seem to be different for those in the Middle Middle Class group, and those in the higher social classes?

These and similar questions will be addressed in the Chapter 5. To the empirical findings of this chapter we will add ethnographic observations to create a wider perspective of language use in Cairo. Before concluding this chapter, however, we will attempt a formulation of the particular kind of variation that the qaf represents.

The Re-appearance of a Sound and the Formation of a Sociolinguistic Variable: What Happens to Old Variables in a Diglossic Setting

Before the qaf merged completely with the glottal stop, there must have been a period during which it was a sociolinguistic variable—operating on extralinguistic dimensions such as bedouin/sedentary, rural/urban, and as some have said "native" vs. "non-native" speakers. Once the merger was complete, however, notwithstanding its continued use in the restricted domains that we enumerated earlier, the regular variability between it and the glottal stop (or any other reflex) also ceased. That is, between the merger and the emergence of mass education in the early decades of the 20th century, several centuries passed during which there was no regular variability. Up to this point, there is nothing unique about the sound change.

What makes the situation distinctive beyond this point is that the choice of Classical Arabic as the medium of secular mass education and of bureaucracy after its "stagnation" and "decline" between the 11th and the 18th centuries (Chejne 1969), brought this language into an increasing number of domains, and made it more accessible to the population at large. The choice of Classical Arabic as opposed to the national vernaculars, has had its own specific linguistic and sociolinguistic consequences.[13] The more active knowledge of Classical Arabic afforded by mass education brought forth the possibility of using lexical borrowings in non-formulaic, expanded contexts, and among an increasing group of speakers. The regularity of the use of qaf lexical items also outside of formulaic genres and outside of written language again made its use as well as its alternation with the glottal stop into stylistic devices. Hence, an old sociolinguistic variable becomes once more a stylistic variable, but this time the extralinguistic dimensions are far more complex and numerous. It is difficult to imagine such a process without the choice of Classical Arabic as the medium of (secular) mass education.

The use of qaf has social meanings, as has been shown by this and other studies. However, these social meaning are not solely based on the *alternation* between it and the glottal stop. The use of borrowed forms has social meaning by virtue of the fact that they belong to a language or a variety that is socially evaluated in the speech community. For example,

The Re-appearance of a Classical Sound: The Qaf

speakers use lexical items with a [q] that often lack dialectal equivalents. In this case, the forms are not alternating with dialectal forms, and yet the use of such forms is socially meaningful. Clearly, code-switches between the latter and non-classical Arabic has itself meaning, as when within a political speech, the speaker switches to one or the other variety.

The distinctive features of the qaf presented in this section make it necessary to find a more precise and descriptive term than the general one of a "sociolinguistic variable." This is in particular desirable since the latter term has been used for linguistic variations which are not quite similar to the case at hand. As such, I suggest that the term "diglossic variable" be used to denote linguistic phenomena which are the specific consequences of a diglossic setting. There is no reason to believe that the kinds of influence which Classical Arabic has exerted on the dialects will diminish. So it is preferable to have a term which captures the feature of processes that reflect this influence. In terms of language change, "diglossic variables" such as the qaf are changes from above the level of social awareness (Labov 1994). Not only are they initially introduced through conscious linguistic decisions, but their use continues to be commented on by members of the speech community. It is also important to distinguish between linguistic phenomena which are due to contact between Classical Arabic and the present-day national varieties, on the one hand; and phenomena which are due to other dynamics. In this way, we are better able to specify in which ways sociolinguistic processes operating in various speech communities may or may not be comparable. I believe that the term "diglossic variable" is descriptively more adequate and can be useful.

Chapter Four

1. How the social meanings of Classical Arabic and of any of its particular features have transformed through time and for different speakers, is a question of immense interest that has not been investigated.

2. Sallam gives the example of six words in which he says the occurrence of [q] and [g] are "impermissible." That is, the occurrence of the urban and rural reflexes. He then generalizes the syllable structure of such words and provides a rule consisting of six syllable types where only the [q] can occur. All six syllable structures contain a glottal stop followed by a high front vowel [i], with the exception of one where the glottal stop is word-final. However, such sequences are not part of the synchronic phonotactics of the modern dialects, since as was explained in the diachronic section above, the glottal stop changed into the semi-vowels [y] and [w] in prevocalic position. And word-finally, it completely disappeared. Thus when such sequences do occur, they occur as part of borrowed items. That the reflexes of /q/ do not co-occur with some other phoneme, some of whose allophones have disappeared in those positions should not be interpreted as "phonological constraints." In addition, Sallam's quantification of his data is problematic. Although he is interested in frequencies of occurrence and provides percentages of frequencies for various social categories, he uses the following criteria for counting the lexical items concerned: "If the same item occurred in the speech of one interlocutor more than twice, only the first three examples were considered" (Ibid: 90). This procedure then renders his data on frequency of each reflex, inaccurate. Since, as compared to the modern reflexes, the [q] is far less frequent, the percentages are then biased to provide a balance in frequency. Secondly, though he notes the existence of lexical items where no variation is possible, he does not exclude these items from his coding. It would seem that such words should be excluded from a measurement of *variation*.

3. The entire sura reads: "Qul huwwa allaahu aHad allaahu Samad lam yalid walam yuulad walam yakun lahuu kufuwan aHad."

4. It proves rather difficult at times to follow some of the discussion. If both [g] and [dz] are "colloquial" and the author does not measure their use vs. the [q], as it seems to be the case, then what is being "colloquialized"? The [dz] is used between 3%-9% vs. the [g] that is used between 91%-97% in three styles (Ibid: 134, Table 5.3b). There seems to be hardly any variability here. Secondly, between the [q] and the [ɣ], the latter is used between 4%-7% while the former is used between 93% to 96% in four styles (Ibid: 134). Again, if both are "standard" what is being "standardized"; and their respective percentages of use indicate little variation.

5. I would like to thank Charles Ferguson for this idea which came out of our discussions on this chapter.

The Re-appearance of a Classical Sound: The Qaf

6. Classical Arabic diphthongs were changed to long vowels, thus [æw] →[oo].

7. As was explained in Chapter 2, my assistant carried out this experiment in group sessions where he and the other children tried to help the interviewee choose the "right" word. But he also did this experiment with three children individually, and these are included here. Due to such problems, my original intention of comparing boys and girls; and asking the children to tell the story in fuSHa could not be fully realized. In the final sample of 8, there is only one girl.

8. Abu-Haidar (1989) which is a study of the Baghdadi dialect among fifty educated informants, found the opposite pattern. However, the methodology in this study is not comparable to the others cited above, since, among other reasons, the investigator had to prompt the speakers directly in order to obtain data on some of the variables. (cf. p. 477). Furthermore, the study does not provide the number of instances of any of the variables investigated; and with the exception of one variable, the differences between men and women are small with no statistical tests of significance. Finally, the author equates every form that is Classical as "prestigious," and every form that is not as "stigmatized." (cf. p. 477). This is a very simplistic model of variation in any speech community. Due to several serious methodological problems in this study, it will not be further investigated here. Clearly, it is possible that the gender pattern is different in Baghdad. However, an investigation that is methodologically rigorous is necessary.

9. This study was carried out in Buffalo, New York, among the Palestinian community.

10. Cited in Ibrahim (1986). This work was unavailable through interlibrary loan.

11. The number of tokens does not equal our total of 1168 in the section on linguistic analysis. The reason is that for that section, I included two speakers, who I interviewed due to their high use of Classical Arabic lexical items. They were both my friends and knew the purpose of the interview. However, they cannot be included in the social analysis since they were fully aware of my interest in their language, in particular in their use of Classical Arabic vocabulary, and therefore cannot be directly compared to the other speakers. I include them again in Chapter 5 where a comparison is made between private and public schools.

12. There is only one man in this category. See Chapter 2 for an explanation.

13. The "print elevation" of "humble vernaculars" in Europe that resulted in the replacement of Latin by national vernaculars which later became standardized (Anderson 1983:77), did not take place in the Arab world.

Chapter Five
Searching for Explanations: Gender, Class, and Education

The question that has been posed most frequently with regard to sociolinguistic studies of Arabic concerns the linguistic behavior of women and men. Since in other speech communities women have been found to employ forms belonging to the "standard" variety more than men in situations of stable variation, their linguistic behavior has been characterized as more "conservative." In Arabic speech communities the surprise finding has been that women use "standard" Arabic forms *less* than men, and hence their linguistic behavior is also *less* "conservative." This conclusion has then been followed by another question: How can women in Arab societies behave less conservatively than men given their subordinate social position? In answer, it has been argued that their less conservative behavior is only due to their lower access to education and other institutions where the "standard" language, that is, Classical Arabic would be learned. But the results presented in Chapters 3 and 4, together with the ethnographic data to be described below, make it clear that before any such questions and characterizations can be formulated, we need a deeper understanding of the dynamics of the sociolinguistic setting in Egypt. One crucial aspect that requires probing has to do with the role and place of Classical Arabic within the hierarchy of linguistic varieties in Egypt. Through an investigation of this question to which we turn first, and our general search for explanations of patterns found in previous chapters, we will also address others posed at the outset of this study. Such questions center on what kinds of standard varieties there may be in different speech communities; whether they can be assumed to be the same sociolinguistic entity everywhere; and whether in some settings there may be more than one kind of standard variety. Only after such questions are explored, are we in a position to characterize linguistic behavior more accurately; and perhaps attempt to explain it.

The Sociolinguistic Market of Cairo: "Standard" Arabic

I will use the concept of the "linguistic market" taken from theories of social reproduction developed in the field of sociology (Bourdieu 1977, 1982, 1991; Bourdieu and Passeron 1977; Sankoff and Laberge 1978) to address the question of "standard" varieties in Egypt. Empirical and theoretical studies of the relations between social class and use of the "standard" language have explicated a linear relation such that the official standard language is defined as belonging to or representing the speech of those in the highest social classes. Sociolinguists have repeatedly found empirical evidence of a direct link between the variety considered as the standard/official language, and the variety used most frequently by and associated with members of the upper classes. They speak of the official as the language of the corporate world and the one required for upward social mobility. Generally, macro-sociological indices have been used to determine the social class membership of the speakers. This approach to class has been criticized on various grounds by a number of authors working within and outside the field (Milroy 1987: 98); (Williams 1992: 82). Yet, no matter how social class has been constructed, few have cast a doubt on the equation of the official language with the language of the upper classes.

Thus, despite Bourdieu's more nuanced construction of social class, he also defines the "dominant" or official language as that of the "dominant group."

> We must pause for a moment to look at the relation to language which characterizes the members of the dominant class (or at least those of them who originate in this class). Having acquired the dominant usage by early familiarization, . . .they are able to produce, continuously and apparently without effort, the most correct language, not only as regards syntax but also pronunciation and diction, which provide the surest indices for social placing. *In short, the dominant usage is the usage of the dominant class* (Bourdieu 1977: 659, emphasis added).

Speakers that I interviewed ranged from those who had not had any schooling and were, for example, janitors and maids, to clerks and secretaries, to diplomats and physicians with advanced degrees. Depending on a number of factors, I classified the latter kinds of speakers as members of the "dominant" or upper classes (see Chapter 2). In all interviews, a major topic of discussion was the speakers' experiences at the specific schools they attended and their education more generally. As was already mentioned in previous chapters, with few exceptions, it turned out that these speakers had received all their education in a foreign language in Cairo, Alexandria and other cities and towns. The schools that they had attended were for the most part private Catholic missionary schools in which the main languages of instruction were (and continue to be) English, French, Italian and German.[1] Classical Arabic was taught as a subject a few hours a week. Not all private language schools (*madaaris il-*

luya) teach in a foreign language, but these are more limited in number. In any case, from elementary school onward, those attending private foreign language schools had been taught to read and write in a foreign language and not in the official language. They often commented on their limited knowledge of Classical Arabic, pointing out that the particular kind of education they had received had been in another language. In this regard, one could observe a degree of linguistic insecurity which is often said to be a feature of the lower middle classes (especially women) in studies of New York (Labov 1966, 1972), and Philadelphia (Labov 1990). I found more pronounced linguistic insecurity among men and women of the upper classes in Cairo. In addition, such speakers and the class or classes that they represent are regarded by others as unfamiliar with Classical Arabic. Among some, this is a stereotype. In two earlier studies of Cairo, as well as a study carried out in Irbid, Jordan a similar perception of the language abilities of the upper classes with regard to Classical Arabic was also noted (Schmidt 1986; Royal 1985; Sawaie 1987). Historians and linguists, among others, make repeated claims in the literature that Classical Arabic is used by the "elite." However, they are never explicit about who is included in this "elite," (besides writers and religious scholars); and to what social class or classes they belong. It is reasonable to assume that this elite includes the upper classes.

Based on the patterns of qaf usage that we found in Chapter 4; and the educational backgrounds of most upper class speakers, the direct link between the "dominant" language and the "dominant" group does not hold for Egypt. This is not to say that all members of the upper classes, or more generally the dominant classes, have the same relation to the official language. But it appears that by and large members of the upper classes in Egypt are not the ones who know the official language the best or use it the most. In fact, speaking with a number of Egyptian sociologists and anthropologists, I was told that I should use the criterion of foreign language school attendance as central to my classification of speakers.

Let us go back to Bourdieu's conception of the relation between the dominant usage and the linguistic market.

> Linguistic exchange—a relation of communication between a sender and a receiver, based on enciphering and deciphering, and therefore on the implementation of a code or a generative competence—is also an economic exchange which is established within a particular symbolic relation of power between producer, endowed with a certain symbolic capital, and a consumer (or a market), and which is capable of procuring a certain material and symbolic profit (Bourdieu 1991:66)

Thus in this theory, the forms chosen in linguistic exchanges are defined within the larger set of power relations that are reproduced through economic and symbolic exchanges. Bourdieu goes on to say that the "price" of linguistic varieties on the market is determined in relation to the "price" of the official variety. He emphasizes greatly the role of institutions such as the school and family in creating and perpetuating the value of the official variety on the market. However, he specifies that the educational system creates linguistic value only to the degree that it controls access to the labor market (Bourdieu 1982: 33).

To what degree does the educational system in Egypt control access to the labor market? What is the relation between these speakers' linguistic capital, and the labor market? Looking at the occupations that they hold, it becomes clear that it is their education and their bi- or multilingualism which are important and not their knowledge of the official language. I speak here of such occupations as the ownership of small and large businesses, (construction, boutique, pharmacy), medicine,

Searching for Explanations

television production, positions in international firms of banking as well as research, movie and stage acting. Even for such positions as diplomatic posts which are directly related to the state bureaucracy, requirements regarding the official state language seem to be flexible. A young diplomat told me that he had all along been educated in English. When I asked if he ever needed to compose letters in Classical Arabic, he replied: "Oh yes, but thank God for my secretary. I tell her what I want to say and she writes it for me." The situation is surely more complex with respect to other posts within the diplomatic corps. For instance, I interviewed another diplomat, a woman who had been educated in German and in fact addressed her daughter in German when she came in for some cookies. She explained to me that her application to the foreign ministry met all requirements except that she had to pass a written examination in Classical Arabic. She said that she therefore took intensive tutorials in Classical Arabic to pass the exam. It should be mentioned that although most members of the upper classes do not receive their education in the classical language, and although the stereotypical image of them is one of limited knowledge, they can and do use classical words and expressions in their speech depending on context. Speakers the world over use borrowed words from other languages or from learned varieties without knowing those languages. Thus lack of knowledge on the part of the upper classes does not mean that they never use learned borrowings at all, in particular if they have certain posts where some knowledge is expected of them. Still, a generalization can be made that not only some schooling, but the kind of schooling influence the frequency with which features of Classical Arabic are used. This can be seen in Graph 1 where both private and public school speakers have more frequent qaf usage than those with no schooling, but at the same time, those in private schools use fewer qafs than speakers who have attended public schools.

Chapter 5

Access to what kinds of labor markets then is controlled by the public educational system, which contributes to determining the linguistic value of the classical language? The largest employer of occupations requiring this knowledge is the state: its public schools, and its colossal bureaucracy. Those who teach and those whose jobs involve reading and writing government documents have to have some knowledge of the classical language. Yet it is clear that the degree of this knowledge required by the state varies according to status, role and occupation. In a

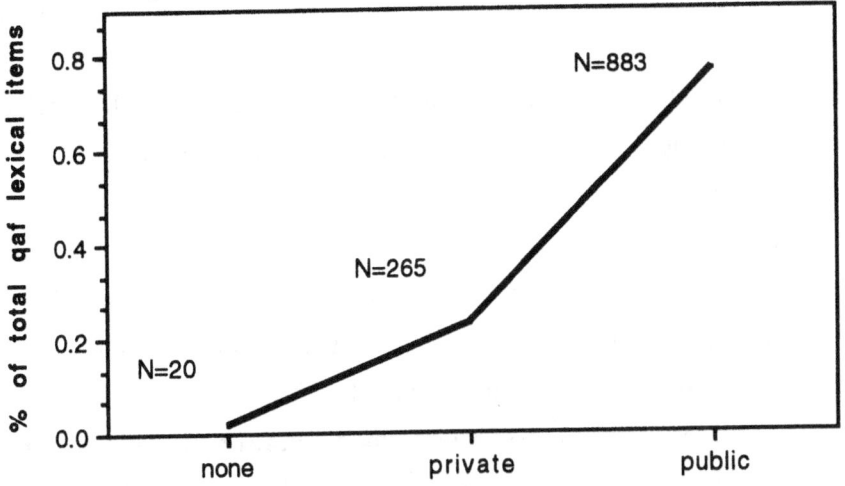

Graph 1: Proportion of qaf lexical items used according to schooling

state hospital, for example, physicians, nurses, directors, public relations agents, and secretaries would have different language skill requirements. Hence, for any kind of bureaucratic position, its relation to the degree of knowledge of the official language cannot be assumed to be linear, as the example of the diplomat and his secretary demonstrates.

There are thus two educational systems in Egypt, a public one supported by the state, and a private one, missionary and secular, in whose curricula the state has some say, but which remains largely independent.² In any case, Bourdieu's assertion that the labor market is the primary determinant of linguistic value seems to be *in part* borne out by this data, except that if one is a member of the dominant group, one does not have more of what others have less. One has an entirely different capital. Thus the relation between the educational system, the labor market and linguistic value is not the same for all classes. The public educational system does not control all access to the labor market and thus does not alone create linguistic value. Non-state private education does not always contribute to the creation of different linguistic values. In the United States, the public and private educational systems do provide their clients with access to somewhat different labor markets, but both reinforce one standard variety. In Egypt, the segmentation of the market has helped create multiple and at times contradictory linguistic values. Thus while the public school system produces and reproduces values for its medium which is Classical Arabic, the private schools create values for other languages. The foregoing are some of the consequences of the inclusion of Egypt in the capitalist world market. Among the languages of currency in this market, Classical Arabic is not included.

The Jordanian linguist Muhammad Ibrahim has articulated differences between standard English and Classical Arabic in this way:

> there is an important difference between standard Arabic (H[igh]) and standard English. It is possible for an individual to acquire standard English simply by belonging to a particular socioeconomic class [. . .] Social status and mobility in any Arab society, however, are insufficient for the acquisition of the H[igh] language [i.e. Classical Arabic] (1986: 119).

Chapter 5

If members of the upper classes in general do not know or use the official "dominant" language; if there is an educational establishment that reproduces values for other languages and helps place its clients in important occupations; and if the official language is not the native language of any of the "dominant" groups, then what is it that makes Classical Arabic a "standard" variety? Although a full treatment of this question would require nothing less than a social history of Arabic, a few brief remarks will be made here.

The status of Classical Arabic as the most "correct," powerful, expressive, authoritative, and *in these senses* "standard" or supra-standard norm is a result of its associations with the most significant texts of Islamic civilization, and of the institutional enforcement and reproduction of those values. No social group that is or has been dominant, has by extension given power to Classical Arabic *on the basis* of claiming that the latter represents its own speech habits. All standard varieties derive some authority from texts (religious and literary), and indeed the similarities between "standard English" and "standard Arabic" are in the realm of written language. But whereas in the case of some standards, there is a coincidence between the speech of powerful groups and institutional and literary norms (Leith 1987 [1983]), Classical Arabic derives its dominance first and foremost from texts that are fundamental to Islamic culture and civilization. The linguistic ideology embodied in such texts is further affirmed by the production of some of the earliest and most detailed grammatical studies ever (see Bohas, Ghillaume, and Kouloughli 1990) undertaken to pre-empt the changes that were foreseen as a result of conversions of millions of non-native speakers of Arabic to Islam.

In addition to mosques and their madrasas, the establishment of centers such as the Al-Azhar mosque-university in Cairo by the Fatimids in 972 has been of utmost importance (Berkey 1992, Hourani 1991b) in preserving and disseminating Classical Arabic as the main medium of all scholarly productions in the centuries to follow. Notwithstanding the imposition of English in diverse domains by British colonial rule for several decades, the end of the 19th century saw the great "revival movement" (*nahDa*[3]) which resulted in a surge of writings in Classical Arabic. It also furthered the gradual development of Classical Arabic into a medium of bureaucracy, *and* of secular public education (Baer 1969).

Returning at this point to a central question of this study posed in Chapter 1 as to whether the standard varieties of all speech communities can be assumed to represent the same sociolinguistic entity, we would have to respond in the negative. From this brief outline it is clear that "standard English" and "standard Arabic" have distinct social histories, and therefore represent different kinds of standard varieties. And some speech communities may simultaneously have more than one standard variety in their repertoire, as I will argue to be the case in Egypt. Having delineated the specific ways in which Classical Arabic may be called a "standard" variety, we are now in a better position to re-examine cross-linguistic comparisons.

Urban Cairene: A Non-classical "Standard"

The surprising reversal of gender patterns in non-Western speech communities was articulated in Labov (1982: 78):

> The general principle that emerged from studies in Europe, Canada, the United States, and Latin America is that women are more conservative in their reaction where stable and socially recognized variation is concerned. But this generalization has

been reversed for a number of societies in the Near East and South Asia.

Men in Arabic-speaking speech communities showed patterns of usage that went against expectations: their linguistic behavior turned out to be more "conservative" than women because men used features of Classical Arabic more frequently than women. The implications of these patterns created a long-lasting controversy in sociolinguistics. Given the general understanding of the social position of women in the Middle East as being less equal to that of men, and to that of women in Western speech communities, the expectation was that their linguistic behavior would reflect more "conservative" uses. Instead, even in studies carried out since 1982, the same findings were replicated. Women consistently turned out to be the speakers who use the urban, non-classical, and therefore less "conservative" variants more than men.

We will return to discussions of the term "conservative" later on, but for now we may note that what renders the comparison of results across speech communities possible is the assumption that "standard English" or "standard French" represent essentially the same entity as Classical Arabic. In the preceding section, however, we established that the two kinds of standards are not directly comparable to each other and hence the reversal of gender patterns must be re-examined. Focusing on Cairo, we may note that its dialect is a long-standing urban variety with national and regional prestige. This status is due to many factors including the historical role of Cairo as a major intellectual, cultural, and commercial center; its export of teachers, trained personnel, and movies and television series (the latter are almost always in Egyptian, not Classical Arabic). Cairene Arabic, as Schmidt (1974, 1986), Royal (1985) and the present study demonstrate reflects and reproduces the social structure. Thus it has its own hierarchy of varieties in which gender, social class, and education play crucial roles. Although Cairene Arabic is not an institutionally accepted medium of writing, the variety spoken by the educated classes is one that comes closest to what has come to be called "standard" in non-diglossic speech communities. Note that to consider a variety of Cairene Arabic as "standard" is not to argue for the existence of a separate and distinct language that distinguishes all educated speakers from others (see Chapter 1). We may thus reformulate a comparison of gender differences across diglossic and non-diglossic settings in the following manner.

Recalling that Labov's comparison was based on studies that investigated the use of Classical Arabic forms in contrast to those found in urban dialects, we may define the urban *dialectal* forms as the "standard" variants. This "standard" may be associated with the language of non-classical literature, even though *its* texts (written and/or oral) do not invoke the high claims of Classical Arabic to empire, Islam, pan-Arab nationalism, science, poetry, and grammatical studies.[4] Equally importantly, the non-classical standard derives status from the power and prestige of groups whose speech it represents. Writing on Classical Arabic and dialectal varieties of Arabic, Altoma (1969: 3) states: ". . .there is in each case a standard or semi-standard colloquial based on the dialect of the capital city." Ibrahim (1986) and Ferguson (1988) both comment on this kind of urban standard varieties. On the process of standardization as a type of language spread, which is in turn a form of convergence, Ferguson writes:

> In the Arab world a number of recent studies of such convergence agree in showing that the dominant lines of convergence are toward regional standard, namely, prestigious urban educated speech patterns of various communicative centers, rather than

toward a single unified prestige norm for the Arab world as a whole (Ibid: 126).

Schmidt (1986) speaks of a "norm" other than Classical Arabic: "both upper class men and upper class women seem to be responding to a prestige *norm* which distinguishes between classes but which is not in the direction of classical Arabic." Thus in Arabic speech communities, there are two kinds of standard varieties, one based on the classical language; and another based on the non-classical languages whose associations with the speech habits of prestigious and higher status social groups in the capital cities place them higher in the hierarchy than other social dialects in the city and outside. The presence of variables such as palatalization make it clear that a distinction must be made between "standard" Cairene and "non-standard Cairene." That is, palatalized dental stops are the non-standard variants of non-palatalized dental stops, which are the older and the standard variants. Those who use palatalized variants less, for example, are employing standard Cairene forms more.

Reviewing the results of previous studies, in Cairo, Schmidt (1974) found that women used the glottal stop as opposed to the qaf more than men; in Amman, Abdel-Jawad (1981) found the same result, and so did Shorrab (1981) among Palestinians living in New York. In Basra, Bakir (1986) found that women use the urban reflex [č] as opposed to the classical [k]; and described their behavior as emulating the socially prestigious Baghdadi dialect. Kojak (1983) who looked at the classical [θ] vs. [s, t] and [ð] vs. [z, d] found women to use the non-classical reflexes more frequently than men. And finally, Royal (1985) found that women had weaker pharyngealization than men, where strong pharyngealization is the proper norm for Classical Arabic. In the present study, our data point to the same direction of differences—women as a group use the glottal stop, that is, the urban Cairene form more than men. Hence, women employ the urban "standard" forms more. In this respect their linguistic behavior is similar to that of women in non-diglossic settings. There is no reversal of the patterns: in "Western" as in Arabic-speaking speech communities, women use "standard" forms more. However, the variants that men use more frequently such as the qaf are also some kind of "standard"—perhaps we should call these "supra-standard" or "official standard" forms. Whose behavior can then be evaluated as more or less "conservative"? I would argue that if the interpretation of the linguistic behavior of women in non-diglossic settings is that it is conservative (cf. Labov 1982, 1990), then the linguistic behavior of women in Cairo *with respect to* the use of Classical Arabic forms versus dialectal ones is different. It is standard but not conservative since the sociolinguistic paradigm in Cairo includes Classical Arabic—another co-existing standard variety.

If we separate the simultaneous senses of the term "conservative" in sociolinguistics, and consider only its reference to forms that are older, the view point of Arabic dialectologists must be discussed. In comparing older with younger *rural* speakers, Arabic dialectologists characterize the speech of the older, uneducated speakers as "non-standard" and "conservative" in the sense that their speech conserves "archaic" dialectal features. They contrast such speakers to younger, educated ones whose speech shows more borrowings both from urban varieties, and from Classical Arabic. Dialectologists characterize all such borrowings as "innovations" in the speech of younger speakers. Thus, for them, the speech of older rural speakers is more "conservative" partly because it does not show borrowings or "innovations" from urban non-classical varieties, and from Classical Arabic. This terminology is based both on the premise that Classical Arabic has not been in continuous use, and that urban dialects are later stages of rural ones. These are certainly warranted premises, and from the point of view of rural dialects, both urban and classical borrowings may indeed be "innovations." Moreover, if the main analytic concern is with the historical development of a dialect—when it loses or acquires different forms and features—and not simultaneously with social meanings and social evaluation, then the task is somewhat simpler. However, where we are concerned with distinctions that are at once social and linguistic within an urban variety; and with evaluations of those distinctions, the issues are more complex. This is not only because social meanings are more difficult to investigate, but also because such meanings and evaluations can affect the course of linguistic change.

A sociolinguistic variable such as palatalization is an *innovation* in the dialect of Cairo. There is more evidence to suggest that it was not a feature of Cairene phonology several generations ago. And while we may also analyze the "re-appearance" of a sound such as the qaf as an "innovation," it seems to me that the terminology would obscure rather than illuminate the specificities that were brought out in Chapter 4. Had it not been for the fact that Classical Arabic was deemed the appropriate medium for education, the qaf may not have reappeared. The "newness" of the qaf or any other classical feature is inescapably framed and affected by the fact that it belongs to and is recognized as belonging to the prescriptive variety, namely, Classical Arabic—an outcome that does not await innovations such as palatalization. Although in purely historical terms, a feature of Classical Arabic that has been borrowed may be "newer" than its urban dialectal reflex (if there is one) in the sense that the former may be a more recent event, it is simultaneously part of that variety that is the older, prescriptive norm. The speech of some speakers, such as the sheikhs of Al-Azhar shows more Classical Arabic borrowings than others, and some of these features may indeed be "new." Yet one could hardly characterize their linguistic behavior as "innovative" or outside of the standards of the prescriptive variety, even though dialectologists would perhaps be correct in that assessment in purely historical terms. As will be seen in the next chapter, evaluations of the speech of sheikhs and teachers of grammar as "backward" and "archaic" are offered repeatedly by some of the Egyptians that I interviewed. In fact, the use of the qaf is an example of a feature that speakers are highly aware of. Many, for example, evaluated their own speech as containing Classical Arabic elements. Asked why they thought so, they referred to their use of words such as /aȋtaqid/ 'I believe' even when in most cases they had used it only a few times. But what seemed to be crucial was the presence of the qaf. The point is that for the purposes of understanding the *socio*linguistic dynamics of urban varieties, and the causes of language change, the dialectological approach, as has been pointed out by others (Weinreich, Labov, and Herzog 1968; Chambers and Trudgill 1980), is limited since it does not concern itself directly with phenomena whose linguistic and socio-cultural aspects are inseparable from each other. For these and similar reasons, the sociolinguistic framework is better suited for the goals of this study, and therefore the terms that are employed are based on their usage in sociolinguistics.

So far in this chapter, our concern has been a relatively detailed exploration of sociolinguistic entities that come to be characterized as standard varieties. We turn next to potential explanations that would shed light on the causes of gender differences in the use of classical and non-classical forms.

Explaining Gender Differences: A Matter of Access?

Let us begin first with a word of caution. Empirically, our knowledge of the various aspects of the linguistic behavior of both genders in Arabic speech communities is quite limited. All studies, including the present one, have concentrated on the use of a few phonological variables. A fuller understanding of the linguistic behavior of individuals and groups would require far more than that: lexical, syntactic, and prosodic variation; as well as examinations of gender-differentiated genres of speaking. With the exception of palatalization and possibly degree of pharyngealization, the phonological variables themselves have all been of one type involving the alternation of classical and non-classical forms. Thus, available formulations of gender differences are generalizations based on limited kinds of data. With such reservations in mind, I will proceed to offer an analysis of my own data while making use of the results of previous studies. My main aim is to bring out a number of issues whose consideration is crucial to any eventual explanations of the linguistic behavior of the specific and varied groups of women and men that we study.

The central explanation put forward in accounting for the differential use of Classical Arabic features by women and men relies on the notion of "access." Using the constructs of "public" and "private" domains (Rosaldo and Lamphere 1974), it is argued that Classical Arabic is the language of the "public" domain. Because women in Arab countries have less access to this domain than men and, hence also, less access to education, they have fewer opportunities to acquire its norms. Therefore they use such features less than men (Abdel-Jawad 1981; Labov 1982). In a revisiting of the putative reversal of gender patterns in Arabic speech communities, Labov (1990: 213) notes the lack of parallel between "Western" norms and Classical Arabic and concludes that there may not be a reversal. But, he goes on to suggest that the principal that women use "standard" features more than men, must be qualified by the observation that for women to use standard norms that differ from everyday speech, they must have access to those norms.[. . .] It stands to reason that the conservative tendency of women applies only when the opportunity for it to apply is present.

This explanation may be critiqued on a number of grounds. To begin, Classical Arabic is the written medium of all officialdom and institutions. But even within institutions, employees speak to each other and to their clients in Egyptian Arabic. Outside of institutions, aside from political speeches, the nightly televised news program, and some debate oriented programs on radio and television, the variety used orally by the overwhelming majority of people in most "public" settings is not Classical Arabic. Men and women who might be very active in this domain, come across Egyptian Arabic far more frequently than Classical Arabic. Thus both Classical Arabic and Egyptian Arabic are languages of the "public" domain, and since people communicate to each other far more frequently through oral channels than written ones, it is Egyptian Arabic that dominates.

It is unclear why the "conservative tendency" of women is treated as a given in Labov's analysis, so that with access and opportunity, it "applies." The data presented in this study clearly demonstrate that women's linguistic behavior both with respect to palatalization and with respect to qaf usage can hardly be interpreted as "conservative." And they are based on the speech of a majority of women who are educated and are in various professions. These women can hardly be said to have lacked opportunities to realize their "conservative tendency." But more fundamentally, the question is whether linguistic behavior is so simply and directly a matter of "access"—without any mediating factors that govern all kinds of social practices (see below).

Chapter 5

The timeless claim that all Muslim Middle Eastern women are "sheltered," "secluded," and confined to the "private" domain, and the dichotomous conceptualization of domains have both been challenged successfully by a vast literature in several fields (Nelson 1974; Tucker 1985; Badran and Cooke 1990; Early 1992; Ahmed 1992, among others). In this section, rather than repeating the discussions of this literature, I will attempt to contribute to it by bringing a sociolinguistic perspective to the issues. In Chapter 4, we established that the differential use of the qaf could not be due to lower levels of education on the part of women since our comparisons were based on the speech of women and men who had had equal amounts of education. Although the concept of the "public" domain is not limited to work outside the home, holding a job and all that it entails are at the center of this construct. Thus we need to examine qaf usage also according to occupation.

Among the 50 women that I interviewed, only 14 did not work. Four were under 22 and had just finished high school or college. The other 10 were housewives some of whom had at times held various jobs. The rest had diverse occupations such as university teaching, accounting, public relations, acting, housekeeping, owning and operating small businesses, diplomatic positions and so on (see Appendix 1). Based on these data, and the census data provided in Chapter 2, the number of women who work is so large that one has to make a point of searching for women who do not. In lower income families, women cannot afford not to work. In higher income ones, they often become professionals and start work early on. Among the 16 women whose speech was analyzed for qaf usage, only 4 did not work at the moment of the interview. One was a retired diplomat, another a former airline employee who was temporarily out of work, the third was a college student, and the fourth had a Masters in architecture but had never worked. What accounts in part for differences that we found in

Chapter 4 is thus not a division between those who operate in the "public" domain and those who do not, but between different *kinds* of occupations. There are occupations that require to varying degrees knowledge of Classical Arabic, and those that have no such requirement.

Table 1: Comparison of qaf indices for women in different occupations

Requiring Classical Arabic	Not Requiring Classical Arabic
9.04	7.36
7.94	4.12
7.13	2.53
7.0	2.54
6.0	0.47
	0.27
37.11/5=7.42	17.29/6=2.88

Table 1 shows a comparison of the working women's qaf indices depending on whether their occupations require knowledge of Classical Arabic. The difference in frequency of qaf usage between women whose occupations require knowledge of Classical Arabic, and those that do not, is rather large. Occupations of those in the first column are: accountant and secretary in an Egyptian company, public relations agent in a state hospital, and two university professors of Classical Arabic. The occupations in the second category range from ownership of a pharmacy, secretaries in foreign firms, interior design, ownership of a small *makwagi* ('laundry/clothes ironing shop'), to domestic help. Thus occupation according to language requirement has some explanatory power in distinguishing both groups of women. And note that the women in the

Chapter 5

second column are also very active in the "public" domain, so in this respect the issue is not one of differential "access."

The woman who I will call Omm Ali has one of the two lowest indices (.047) in Table 1.[5] A brief discussion of her life history will illustrate the exigencies of the lives of a large number of Cairene women who cannot afford not to operate in the "public" domain. Omm Ali was 55 years old at the time of the interview and lived in a poor section of Cairo. She had 5 adult-age children and had never attended school. She had married at a young age, and during an emotional narrative explained that when she was around 25, her husband suddenly disappeared. She had little idea of where he was until a few years later when she heard that he had taken a second wife. Alone, Omm Ali worked hard as a maid and at various odd jobs and saved about 1000 Egyptian pounds (at the time the equivalent of about $400.00 U.S. dollars). A community supermarket was opening in her neighborhood and was asking for local investors. She invested her money there and began receiving monthly interest. She used part of this money and opened up a *makwagi* (laundry/clothes ironing shop). She said that she was finally living a relatively comfortable life, especially since all her children had finished high school and found decent jobs. Omm Ali has clearly not lived a sheltered life and constraints that lead her to participation in the "public" domain can be found in the lives of a very large sector of women (and men) in Cairo. The point is that even if we accept such a differentiation of domains, it applies differently to women and men of diverse social class backgrounds. There *are* probably some women who spend most of their lives in the "private" domain, but we cannot use their case to provide a *general* explanation for the linguistic behavior of all women in Arabic-speaking speech communities.

Table 2: Comparison of qaf indices for men in different occupations

Requiring Classical Arabic	Not Requiring Classical Arabic
13.84	11.96
13.15	11.09
10.5	9.7
10.0	4.24
8.03	1.81
7.62	1.22
6.65	0.96
5.9	
4.65	
80.34 / 9 = 8.92	40.98 / 7 = 5.85

In Table 2, the same comparison is carried out among men. As a group, men whose jobs require knowledge of Classical Arabic have a significantly higher index than men whose jobs lack that requirement. Hence also for men, this factor plays a role in explaining differential uses of the qaf. The former group hold jobs such as: acting (employee of Ministry of Culture), purchasing for a government office, clerk, high school teacher of Classical Arabic, engineer working for the state electric company, Egypt Air employee, policeman, professor of Classical Arabic, and high school teacher. In the second column, there is a physician, an engineer, a salesman, an independent actor (not an employee of the Ministry of Culture), a refurbisher, a house painter, and a hospital janitor. We find again that among women and men whose occupations do require knowledge of Classical Arabic, men have a higher group index (7.42 vs. 9.22); and among those whose occupations lack that requirement, men's index is higher than women's (2.88 vs. 5.95). What also stands out is that as a group, men whose occupations do not require knowledge of Classical Arabic, have a *lower* qaf index than women whose occupations do require it (7.42 vs. 5.95). This difference is significant not because it confirms a truism—that speakers' occupations are relevant to their linguistic behavior. But so far every other categorization we have examined has shown the opposite pattern. For the first time, we find a group of women who use a feature of Classical Arabic more than a group of men.

We should note a few shortcomings of this division of occupations. For example, while obtaining a particular occupation can require various degrees of knowledge of the official language, the occupation itself may not. One clear illustration of this is provided a policeman who was interviewed. He had to attend the Police Academy and take exams toqualify. But once he obtained his position, he did not have to use the classical language on a regular basis. Furthermore among occupations which do not require such knowledge, disparate individuals like a janitor and a physician end up in the same group—one who has barely had a few years of elementary school, and another who holds the highest degree in his field. I have chosen to divide speakers according to whether or not the acquisition of their jobs required knowledge of Classical Arabic.[6]

Thus although the divisions in Table 1 and 2 capture a significant difference between speakers, they are not without problems. Still, this kind of distinction between occupations shows us that the language requirement is important both in explaining the group differential among women; and among men. It also locates a group of women who use the qaf more than a group of men. However, we still have to explain the difference between men and women in both categories. That is, when comparing men and women in the first columns of Tables 1 and 2 (9.22 vs. 7.42); and those in the second columns (5.95 vs. 2.88), we find that men have higher indices in both groups.

It should be clear that to explain this repeated differential, we cannot invoke the factor of participation in public "domains" as defined by holding a job. These are all women and men who work, and at times hold similar jobs. However, a factor that has been overlooked is that both in the kinds of education that these speakers have received, and in the kinds of occupations they hold, Classical Arabic has had a primarily non-religious function. That is, we may separate the functions of Classical Arabic according to two very broad divisions—domains in which it has a primarily religious function, and those in which it has non-religious functions. Are there gender-based daily practices in which Classical Arabic functions exclusively as a religious language? All the data presented in this study, as in other sociolinguistic studies, are from the use of Classical Arabic and its features in domains where it does not function as a religious language. But even without data on the use of Classical Arabic for religious purposes, a number of potentially significant observations can to be made.

Differentials of "access" and practices seem far more pronounced where the classical language has religious functions. Most people whom I interviewed said that they performed the five daily prayers (which are in Classical Arabic). But whereas men recite these prayers *outloud*, women must whisper their recitations. Given that accurate realizations of the phonetic intricacies of the classical language has historically been highly valued, men both have occasion to and must conform more to correct pronunciation, especially since they can be heard. Whispering the prayers, on the other hand, provides neither an occasion nor a stage for strict conformations to the ways in which the prayers must be recited. This differential practice in a regular daily activity is highly significant. It also cuts across the social classes, and degrees of education.[7]

Women are not allowed to become reciters of the daily *azaan* emanating from loudspeakers in mosques and announcing the time for prayer. Although I do not have data on actual participation rates, there seemed to be many more young boys in Quranic recitation contests than girls. The same could be said about the performance of daily prayers and Quranic recitations in Iran. In any case, we might generalize that in spheres where the use of Classical Arabic is strictly connected to religion, diverse gender-based practices lead to differentials in linguistic behavior with regard to the use of features of Classical Arabic in other spheres as well. But where Classical Arabic does not have a primarily religious function, as is the case in public state schools and bureaucracies, there does not seem to be a significant difference in access for women and men. Hence I suggest that women's lower qaf indices in Tables 1 and 2, may be in part a result of the use of Classical Arabic in domains where its function is primarily that of a religious language.

Language Change, Linguistic Behavior, and Ideology

One important and difficult issue that remains to be explored involves the relation between linguistic behavior, ideology, and language change. Sociolinguistic theory makes a distinction between changes from above and below social awareness:

> 'Above' and 'below' refer here simultaneously to levels of social awareness and positions in the socioeconomic hierarchy. Changes from above are introduced by the dominant social class, often with full public awareness. Normally, they represent borrowings from other speech communities that have higher prestige in the view of the dominant class. Such borrowings [. . .] appear

primarily in careful speech, reflecting a superposed dialect learned after the vernacular is acquired (Labov 1994: 78).

Qaf borrowings represent a change from above the level of social awareness, and those who introduced this change may have been from the "dominant class." What is important for the purposes of our discussion is that borrowings from Classical Arabic constitute a historically conscious goal of educational institutions. At present, speakers frequently comment on the use of qaf lexical items. In contrast to changes from below, changes from above are subject to overt reactions and evaluations by speakers. In changes from above, there is therefore the possibility for speakers to convey their ideology and construct social identities both through the way they talk, *and* through metalinguistic comments on socially sensitive forms. Such comments include characterizations of their own ways of talking (self-reports), and general comments on the use of sociolinguistic varieties. So long as forms involved in changes from below have not become stigmatized or otherwise risen to the level of social awareness, that possibility does not exist for such changes. Speakers would only be "signalling" and identity through their rates of use of such forms.

At times the social meanings of the use of forms involved in changes from above, and of the source language, become parts of larger societal discourses. In Egypt, for example, the use of Classical Arabic and its features such as the qaf are implicated and embedded in very significant debates on "modernity," "tradition," "secularism," and Egyptian versus pan-Arab nationalism. For many people, one's position on such matters is an important and consequential part of one's social identity. And in the expression of such an identity, *both* linguistic behavior, and overt evaluations contribute. The social meanings and roles of Classical Arabic have been a site of ideological battles. The religious establishment has fought fiercely to maintain its monopoly on all aspects of the reproduction of Classical Arabic—from defining what is or is not Classical Arabic, to teaching and controlling its use for non-religious purposes (e.g. fiction writing), to its political significance. In addition to important figures, whole social movements such as the *nahDa* have attempted to wrest Classical Arabic from this monopoly by arguing that it is not just a religious language, but one fit for all secular and "modern" purposes (Reid 1990; Gershoni and Jankowski 1986; Hussein 1954). Hence, what Classical Arabic is and represents has been and continues to be a significant topic of debate. In my interviews, middle and upper middle-class men provided commentary on the cultural and political significance of Classical Arabic, and on the necessity to use the language, more than women from the same classes. Men expressed strong and positive evaluations of Classical Arabic, some stressing its significance for Muslims, others emphasizing more its role in keeping Arab nationalism alive. Such commentary seemed to contribute to projections of an identity that relied in part on having positive personal views and opinions of Classical Arabic.[8] In the kinds of identities projected by many women (as reflected in their language use, tastes in clothing, music, literature, and friends), Classical Arabic seemed to play a less important role. This can at least partly be explained by the fact that historically they have had less power to engage in the politics of the language situation.

If it is true that in the case of changes from above both actual usage and overt commentaries are used to construct social identity, there is also the possibility that speakers' linguistic behavior may not fully match either their position in the "social grid," or their commentaries and self-characterizations (Eckert and McConnell-Ginet 1992).[9] *In other words, speakers may articulate views that are not reflected in their actual rates*

Searching for Explanations

of usage. This is in fact what I found with many of the men that I interviewed.

Men in the upper classes in particular seemed to preach a linguistic ideology that they did not follow in practice. For example, a physician who had attended an English language private school, spoke of the importance of Classical Arabic in forging a pan-Arab identity, resisting colonial domination, bringing about political unity among all Arabs, and as a cultural and political weapon against the more recent forms of foreign domination. This speaker, however, has a total qaf index of 11.09—11 qaf lexical items in 45 minutes of speech—far lower than his views would lead us to expect.

The same speaker recalled that in high school, he and his classmates were forced to speak English outside of class during recess, and they had to pay a small fine if they were caught speaking Egyptian Arabic. It is reasonable to assume that they would not be speaking Classical Arabic in those circumstances in any case. He spoke of this experience with some measure of resentment and anger. I asked him why then was he sending his own children to the same schools, and why in general people who can afford it, make this decision. Referring to the English language, he replied: "I think because it is the language of the banks, this foreign language is the language of the banks. It is the language of travel. It is the language of all the beautiful things which they see. And they want their children to learn this language which may give them that level of life." What is evident is that, on the one had, his identity is tied to going to an English school and sending his own children there; and on the other, to his positive evaluations of the cultural and political significance of Classical Arabic for Egypt. Based on his views, his qaf index may be low. But considering that his entire education has been in English, perhaps his knowledge of Classical Arabic exceeds what would be expected from his educational background. Attempts to understand language change have to take into account the effects of competing social pressures.

We might draw a useful parallel to the case of (r) in New York City as another example of a change from above (Labov 1966). In that study, Labov gathered a rich body of data on linguistic behavior, subjective reactions to variables, self-evaluations, and overt commentaries on the New York dialect. In general, he did not find "accurate" and consistent correlations between self-evaluations, and speakers' linguistic behavior. The case of Mrs. Mollie S. is particularly instructive for our purposes. She was a 36-year-old lower middle-class housewife from a Jewish background. Together with her daughter, Mrs. Mollie S. "were greatly amused by the stigmatized forms of speech used by the speakers on the S[ubjective] R[eaction] test" and "ridiculed" such forms in the speech of others that they knew (Labov 1966: 470). In the case of (r), both "insisted that they always pronounced all of their r's as (r-1). They had ridiculed Speaker LMC for dropping a single (r-1), and they could not believe that they would make such a mistake themselves" (Ibid: 471). Mrs. S's (r) index in casual speech was (r)-00, and in careful speech (r)-23—that is, no postvocalic [r] at all in one style, and less than one third in a more formal style. So, there is a large difference between her metalinguistic comments and reactions and her actual linguistic behavior.

In discussing Mrs. Mollie S., Labov explains that New Yorkers "combine an extraordinarily keen perception of the speech of others with a completely unrealistic view of their own speech. The combination of outer perception with self-deception is fundamentally a product of the phonemic principle, as it applies to socially significant variation in language" (Ibid: 470). It is unclear whether the fact that linguistic behavior may be different from speakers' overt judgments and characterizations should best be described as "unrealistic" and "self-deception." This is a way of bracketing as irrelevant ideology writ large. But because ideology influences language change, we must pay more systematic attention to it. If differences between linguistic behavior and perception are due to the phonemic principle, then how can we explain listeners' "keen" perceptions of other speakers? Why does the phonemic principle fail to apply when listeners become speakers? A sociolinguistic variable such as the (r) that is also a change from above cannot be compared to a phoneme whose variants bear no social significance and remain largely below the level of awareness. The fact that Mrs. S. was "disheartened" when she listened to her own speech and conceded that she was an "r-less" speaker, may or may not have to do with "self-deception." The task of the sociolinguist is to explain how and why linguistic behavior and ideological positions in the form of overt commentaries on that behavior may not go hand in hand. It is the job of the sociolinguist to explain why speakers go about their lives without having to be consistent in these respects, and what is the effect of this "inconsistency" on language change.[10] The treatment that is being advocated here seems also to have been shared by Weinreich, Labov, and Herzog (1968). In discussing the "evaluation of linguistic variables," they state that:

> For some variables, the level of social awareness is so high that they are prominent topics in any discussion of speech. *These linguistic 'stereotypes' are not related to linguistic behavior in any one-to-one fashion.* [. . .] The study of overt statements about language yields many insights into the social factors which bear upon language change, and into the sources of irregularity which disturb the course of sound change; but to relate these data to the evolution of the basic vernacular is a matter which requires a

detailed knowledge of the speech community and considerable sociolinguistic sophistication (Ibid: 181-183, emphasis added).

The fact that behavior and ideology may not be in a one-to-one relation has been addressed by the concept of "covert prestige" (Labov 1966, 1972; Trudgill 1972).[11] Trudgill's comparison of men's and women's self-reports with their actual rates of usage brought out the covert prestige of working-class speech for men in higher social classes. But the issue has not received the systematic treatment it deserves. "Unconscious" evaluations such as those accessed through matched guise tests continue to be given more weight in so far as their status as "data" is concerned.[12]

If a distinction between changes from above and below in the sense that is being argued is tenable, then understanding why women use qaf lexical items consistently less than men becomes inseparable from understanding why men have lower indices than their ideologies would lead us to believe. I have tried to show that sociological categories and differentials of access are insufficient in explaining this gender-based linguistic differential. Behavior and ideology are not, and as far as the speakers are concerned, do not have to be "balanced" against each other. We may ask why there seems to be more of a "discrepancy" between men's ideological positions and their linguistic behavior than is the case with women. How is this related to power differentials in defining the meanings and roles of Classical Arabic? And similar to the questions Gal pursued in her analysis of bilingualism in Oberwart (Gal 1978, 1979), we may ask what is at stake for women and men in their use and evaluation of Classical Arabic features? Answering these and similar questions would constitute significant progress in understanding the reasons behind gender-based differences in Arabic-speaking speech communities' ideology.

Searching for Explanations

In this chapter, we set out to answer a number of questions that were raised in the course of previous chapters. A central aim was to show that in order to formulate questions and search for explanations of gender differences, we first need a better understanding of the hierarchization of linguistic varieties in Cairo. The social class differences that were found in the previous chapter are partly explained by the existence of private foreign language schools whose clients are from the upper classes. Once such specificities were brought out, it became clear that earlier comparisons of gender differences were based on the untenable assumption that the standard varieties of all speech communities may be directly equated to each other. Patterns of usage by different social classes, and the roles of the public and private educational systems indicated the multivalent and conflicting social evaluations of Classical Arabic. Our search for explanations lead to a consideration of the effect of occupations that require knowledge of the official language, and those that do not; and to a separation of the functions of Classical Arabic. We concluded that differential practices in domains where Classical Arabic functions as a religious language may explain in part the less frequent use of Classical Arabic features by women also in other domains. In addition, our discussion with regard to kinds of language change, points to the need for for a more complex theorization of the relations between behavior, ideology, and their mutual impact on the course of language change.

There is also a strong need in sociolinguistic studies for ethnographic approaches that do not take as *already known* the social meanings of Classical and non-classical Arabic varieties and their features. It may be recalled that when we used the concept of the linguistic market to analyze the sociolinguistic situation in Cairo, we concluded that Bourdieu's theory illuminates its dynamics only in part. The reason for this assessment may have become clear by now. For while educational establishments and the labor markets are crucial to the reproduction of linguistic values, they do not wholly determine the actual linguistic behavior of speakers. Criticizing Bourdieu's overemphasis of the role of formal institutions, Woolard (1985) argues that the "work of making meanings in social life, responds to far more than just the messages of the formal media and institutions of communication in society" (Ibid: 743). Thus while an analysis based on the construct and metaphors of the linguistic market (with certain modifications) sheds light on the situation in Egypt, it is not sufficient for an understanding of the actual linguistic practices of different speakers.

---

1. See Heyworth-Dunn (1968 [1939]) for data on the large number of such schools in Egypt since the mid 1800s (cf. pp. 406-424). See also Hourani 1991:302-3.

2. This is not just the case in Egypt, but in many post-colonial, "Third World" societies.

3. In English, the movement is variously referred to as the "Arab Revival" "Renaissance," or the "Arab Awakening."

4. The Egyptian playwright Mahmoud Taymour is quoted in Chejne 1969 as having written : "In our overt and covert awakening, we are endeavoring to perpetuate our imperial bond by means of the Arabic language as if we were revivifying with this bond our bygone empire. . .Thus our faith in the literary language is born out of our faith in that empire, which embodies our long-cherished glories" (Taymour 1956, in Chejne 1969: 165).

5. Omm Ali was interviewed by Mr. Yahya Abdel-Latif who was my assistant in Cairo.

6. In Amman, Abdel-Jawad (1981) found that both among men and women, those in the 'civil servant' category had high frequencies of qaf lexical items in their speech.

7. In the context of group prayers, for example, on Fridays in the mosques, except the Imam, most men do not pray outloud. But within the home, men can and do recite their prayers outloud. I have not seen any circumstances under which women can do the same. Almost all the speakers said that they usually pray at home.

8. As we will see in the next chapter, when asked whether they would prefer to speak Classical Arabic or Egyptian Arabic in daily life, both women and men say that they prefer to speak Egyptian Arabic.

9. In critiquing the exclusive reliance of sociolinguistics on demographic categories, Eckert and McConnell-Ginet write: "Sociolinguistic variables are seen first and foremost as passive 'markers' of the speaker's place in the social grid (particularly in the socioeconomic

hierarchy). Correlation of a linguistic variable (or a certain level of frequency of its use) with a demographic category gives a rudimentary social meaning to that variable within the community – what the variable 'means' is membership in the demographic group with which its use is correlated. Speakers are seen as making strategic use of sociolinguistic markers in order to affirm membership in their own social group, or to claim membership in other groups to which they aspire" (Eckert and McConnell-Ginet 1992: 9).

10. A serious methodological problem in this respect is that in most sociolinguistic studies, data are obtained solely from one context and that is the context of the interview. Speakers' reasons for their linguistic behavior are then inferred in other contexts as well, to explain for example, covert prestige factors such as group or local solidarity. Labov (1972:249) points out this problem in attempting to answer the question of why speakers do not speak in the way they believe they should: "Careful consideration of this difficult problem has led us to posit the existence of an opposing set of covert norms, which attribute positive values to the vernacular. In most formal situations in urban areas, such as an interview or a psycholinguistic test, these norms are extremely difficult to elicit. Middle-class values are so dominant in these contexts that most subjects cannot perceive any opposing values, no matter how strongly they may influence behavior in other situations."

11. Other constructs that have been employed for taking ideology into account are "local" and "national identity." But such constructs have not been developed satisfactorily.

12. For an insightful discussion of the ambivalence of anthropology on the status of "self-description" from local informants, see Keane 1995.

Chapter Six
Language Attitudes and Ideologies

> The colloquial is one of the diseases from which the people are suffering, and of which they are bound to rid themselves as they progress. I consider the colloquial one of the failings of our society, exactly like ignorance, poverty and disease.
>
> Naguib Mahfouz (in Cachia 1967: 20)[1]

An important part of the study of language in its social context is to investigate speakers' attitudes towards the varieties of speech available in the linguistic repertoire of their communities. The powerful disdain for "colloquial" Arabic in the quotation above is shared by a sizable number of famous public figures and by religious and secular institutions. In addition, scholars often project the same views onto the "masses": "Arabic has maintained a strong hold on the literati and the masses alike" (Chejne 1969: 5) where "Arabic" refers to Classical Arabic. In the sociolinguistic interviews that were carried out for this study, a number of questions were designed to address potentially covert attitudes with regard to Classical and Cairene Arabic. Given the prominence of negative public characterizations of non-Classical Arabic, examinations of speakers' articulations of their feelings and perceptions vis-à-vis both varieties is necessary for a fuller contextualization of their actual usage. As Woolard

(1985) has pointed out, to understand the dynamics of linguistic exchanges, behavior and attitudes have to be examined in relation to each other. In recent years, a growing body of literature on language attitudes in Arab countries has emerged. Most are article-length studies and use questionnaires. Although all provide valuable insights and data, the exclusive use of questionnaires is a methodological drawback for addressing the complexity of the issues involved. I will briefly review some of their findings before proceeding to my own data from Cairo.

Review of the Literature

El-Dash and Tucker (1975) and Herbolich (1979) are both investigations of language attitudes in Cairo. El-Dash and Tucker used the technique of matched guise tests in their study, and chose five varieties to be tested: "Classical Arabic (Modern Literary Arabic), Colloquial Arabic, American English, British English, and Egyptian English." They define "Egyptian English" as the "form of English spoken by well educated Egyptians."

One of the most important methodological problems the authors faced was the use of stimuli segments that are not artificially composed by researchers, but are "spontaneous." However, as the authors note "we had the most difficulty in obtaining acceptable sequences of 'spontaneous' Classical Arabic" (Ibid: 36). Although the authors state that they were finally able to obtain "acceptable" segments, they are not explicit about what rendered these "acceptable." In addition, for the "colloquial" passages, the authors found that "[the speakers recorded] seemed to 'elevate' slightly their style of colloquial speech for our recording." The problem is that what may seem "slightly elevated" from the point of view of the authors may be highly elevated from the point of view of others, or perhaps not elevated at all. The point is that it depends on who the listener is. This is a very difficult problem to overcome in matched guise experiments and cannot be overlooked.

Four groups of listeners in four educational levels served as judges: grade school children, high school students, national university students, and students of the American University in Cairo (AUC). The judges were to listen to the recordings and rate the speakers on four personality traits: intelligence, likeability, religiousness, and leadership. The speakers who read the passages in Classical Arabic were in general rated the highest on all four traits, i.e. "most intelligent," "most likeable" and so on (Ibid: 42). But when the judges were asked about which language would be more "suitable" for which contexts, different preferences emerged. For example, "Colloquial Arabic" was judged to be "more appropriate for use at home than any other language variety" and "Classical Arabic was deemed significantly *less* suitable than any other variety" (Ibid: 48).

The issue of the "likeability" of the Classical Arabic speakers brings out the inherent limitations of "tests" however well constructed they may be. For example, high school students in general found "Colloquial Arabic" to be more suitable for a larger number of contexts than other speakers. They also rated speakers of Classical Arabic as the most "likeable." Considering that for high school students the main context in which they regularly come in contact with those who use Classical Arabic is the school; and that for all other contexts except at school they found "Colloquial Arabic" to be appropriate, we would have to conclude that they find their teachers, especially teachers of Classical Arabic ,very "likeable" people.

It may indeed be the case that such teachers are particularly liked by their students. However, I found the contrary in my interviews. A question that I asked frequently was whether the speaker had had a teacher in high school who had treated him/her unfairly.[2] In answer to this question, more than half named their Classical Arabic teacher specifically as the one who committed injustice, *Zulm*, against them. Frequent descriptions of such teachers were that they were full of complexes, *ʕuʔda*; that they were obnoxious and irritating *ɣilis*; and that they did not know anything about the world except *kaana wa ixwaatu* (literally: 'to be and its sisters', an allusion to one of the famous grammatical topics in Classical Arabic). That is, they were seen as "backwards" and not with the times. In addition, the figure of the teacher of Classical Arabic turned out to be the butt of many jokes and humorous anecdotes—indeed some of the liveliest personal narratives related by speakers had to do with various practical jokes played on this teacher. I would thus conclude that the "likeability" of speakers of Classical Arabic for high school students remains an open question. Still, it should be mentioned that it is due to the authors' careful discussion of their problems and dilemmas that we can further our understanding of what would constitute a more successful set of subjective reaction tests. El-Dash and Tucker are aware of the points raised in this discussion and tell us that the "results *must* be interpreted cautiously."

Herbolich (1979) carried out a study in Cairo in which he investigated attitudes of Cairene speakers toward "Arabic vernaculars." Herbolich recorded native Egyptian speakers; and in addition made two recordings each of Syrians, Libyans and Saudi Arabians speaking once in their own dialects ("native guise") and once in Egyptian Arabic ("Egyptian guise"). The speakers were all university students in Cairo. Eighty Egyptians listened to these recordings and served as judges. They were "professionals," university students, and high school students. Herbolich found that in general "Egyptian subjects rate speakers of their own Cairene vernacular Arabic the most favorably" (Ibid:301) as "truthful," "intelligent," "faithful," "principled," "respectable," with "good reputation," and "cooperative" (Ibid: 309). As will be seen later on in this chapter, I also found similar positive attitudes towards Cairene Arabic among the speakers that I interviewed.

In Jordan, significant aspects of language attitudes have been investigated in a variety of ways (Za'rour and Nashif 1977; Zughoul and Taminian 1984; Sawaie 1987; and Hussein and El-Ali 1989). The first two are both concerned with the choice of language of instruction in the teaching of sciences: Classical Arabic versus English (the term "Arabic" is used in both studies). Zughoul and Taminian (1984) explain that while the official language of the university is Arabic, "it is the exception rather than the rule for instructors to use Arabic, especially in sciences and engineering" (Ibid: 157). Both studies use questionnaires administered to university students. They find that there is little disagreement over the capability of the Arabic language to handle the sciences. Women were found in general to be more favorable toward the use of English than men in both studies. But strong divisions emerge over the utility of Classical Arabic in finding better paying jobs or continuing on to higher education. Many state that they believe English is more useful in these respects. Even so, immediately after stating that the "average Arab university student" views English as more instrumental in finding a good job, Zughoul and Taminian conclude that "Arab students feel that there is *no justification* for prescribing English as a medium of instruction at the university level" (Ibid: 174, emphasis added). Furthermore, the authors characterize "nonconservationists"—those with "less adherence to the exclusive use of Arabic" as "looking at English out of the historical context" (Ibid: 175) because many disagreed that the use of English is a "remnant of colonialism" and a "marker of our cultural backwardness" (Ibid:167). But although it is the case that the use and spread of English in many parts of the world is directly related to colonialism, the authors seem not to consider the moment of their own research in the history of Jordan within its "historical context"—hence they as well seem to hold ahistorical and unchanging views of the roles of Arabic and English in the lives of their informants. This is a general problem in most studies of language attitudes in the Arab world. Rarely is ambivalence or better multivalence acknowledged and articulated, notwithstanding results that clearly point in that direction (but see Stevens 1983).

Finally, a few of the findings of Sawaie (1987) will be reviewed here. Sawaie carried out his research in Yarmouk University located in Irbid, Jordan. A male native speaker was recorded reading the same sentence in four different ways: once with the qaf, then with the glottal stop, then with [g] and [k]. The qaf belongs to Classical Arabic, the glottal stop is the urban variant and the last two Sawaie classifies as "country varieties." The sentence was:[3]

qaabala	Taariq	Sadiiqa	hu	Tawfiiq	qabla	lmuHaaDarah
met	Tareq	friend	his	Tawfiq	before	the lecture

'Tareq met his friend Tawfiq before the lecture.'

A questionnaire was given to 223 university students, 115 males, and 108 females. For the sake of brevity, only two of the results will be discussed here. One is the listeners' assignment of likely professions to each of the "speakers." The profession most often assigned to the "qaf speaker" was a university professor or school teacher. Professionals in other categories who also have a high level of education such as physicians, lawyers, and judges were not considered as qaf users. While Sawaie concludes that this is due to a perception of the use of the "standard" by the "educated sector of society," it is clear that lawyers and judges are also part of this sector, and yet the qaf speaker is not assigned to such professions but only to those that involve teaching. The other finding of interest has to do with assignments of social class. Judges were asked which of the four "speakers" "belongs to a high social class" (Ibid: 9). The speaker with the glottal stop (and not the qaf) was assigned by a majority to belong to a "high social class." Although the speech communities of Cairo and Irbid are different in a number of ways, this result is in agreement with my findings on the use of the qaf and the glottal stop (see Chapter 4). Here, Sawaie has found that speakers do not associate its use with those in a high social class. Sawaie further explains this result as follows:

> It is the belief of this author that city speakers who generally tend to be [ʔ] speakers in the Jordan-Palestine regions are traditionally viewed culturally superior to country, town or village residents. Since [ʔ] is associated with urban centers, and since urban centers are viewed to be culturally superior, this may explain why [ʔ], in this case, receives the highest ratings as a marker of high social class (Ibid: 10).

The association of the glottal stop with urban centers has been documented both in diachronic and synchronic studies of Arabic speech communities. In addition, implicit in Sawaie's explanation is the association of "cultural superiority" with those in the upper social classes, since the former attribute was invoked to explain speakers' beliefs regarding the use of the glottal stop by speakers in a high social class. The presence of multiple and conflicting values with regard to features of Classical and non-classical Arabic is clear in such results. Both the qaf and the glottal stop are viewed ambivalently. The glottal stop is at once urban, cosmopolitan, and associated with those who are "culturally superior" but also it is "less correct" than the qaf.[4]

Language Attitudes and Ideologies

Signs of Ambivalence: Fear, Habit, and Identity

In the remainder of this chapter, my central goal is a description of language attitudes among the Cairenes that I interviewed. The number of speakers reported on varies from 31 to 73 depending on the question. Since the discussion of such attitudes was always left to the end of the interview, the time constraints of the interviewee sometimes made it necessary to cut short the number of the questions.[5] Although the issue of terms was discussed in Chapter 1, a brief note will again be made here. The two most frequently used terms were *ʕammiyya*, and *fuSHa* (respectively, Cairene or Egyptian Arabic, and Classical Arabic). The term *maSri* 'Cairene' came up in a number of contexts, as will be seen. Depending on the educational background of the speaker, and his or her own usage, other terms such as *il luɣa il ʕarabiyya*, 'the Arabic language', or *(il)naHawi*[6] were also used for Classical Arabic. *naHawi* was employed more often by less educated speakers who also opposed it to the term *baladi* 'local, Egyptian' instead of, or in addition to *ʕammiyya*. I was told by my college educated Egyptian friends that *baladi* and *naHawi* are more appropriate to use with speakers who are not highly educated. As it turned out, they were right.

A wide array of social and historical factors contribute to ambivalent feelings expressed by Egyptians toward both Classical Arabic and Egyptian Arabic, some of which have already been discussed in previous chapters. Egyptian Arabic is their mother tongue, the variety over which they have control, the one they use to convey humor, seriousness, intimacy, distance; what they can mold lexically, phonologically, and syntactically to convey myriad meanings without fear of strong prescriptive norms; and what distinguishes them from other Arabs. Writing in Egyptian Arabic remains largely institutionally unsanctioned. Simultaneously, it is the variety that educational establishments as well as many famous literary, religious, and political figures denigrate and stigmatize. In his "The Future of Culture in Egypt," Taha Hussein, one of the most famous intellectual and literary figures of Egypt who also became the minister of education in 1950, wrote:

> I am, and shall remain, unalterably opposed to those who regard the colloquial as a suitable instrument for mutual understanding and a method for realizing the various goals of our intellectual life because I simply cannot tolerate any squandering of the heritage, however slight, that classical Arabic has preserved for us. The colloquial lacks the qualities to make it worthy of the name of a language. I look upon it as a dialect that has become corrupted in many respects (Hussein 1954: 86 [1944]).

Classical Arabic has historically been exalted by religious and secular public figures as the "true" language of the "Arabs." While Classical Arabic is uniquely associated with the most important cultural achievements of the "Arabs," and viewed as the embodiment of Islamic civilization, Egyptian Arabic has no such historical and cultural claims. Such exaltations of Classical Arabic have created a strong emphasis on its purity, and its use without changes or mistakes. But this emphasis is precisely what prevents the contradictory but simultaneous goal of expanding its usage among the population. The contradiction between the requirement of purity on the one hand, and propagation of use on the other, is a problem that was faced by all defenders of classical languages such as Tamil, Greek, and Latin (Kahane 1986). This problem is best illustrated by the fact that "fear" is cited by many speakers, including those with graduate degrees, as a prime reason for why they do not use Classical Arabic. Egyptian Arabic, and indeed all non-classical varieties of Arabic remain largely uncodified through institutional means and are not taught. That they are often viewed by a majority as lacking "grammar," and being less "correct" than Classical Arabic contributes to their use—there is no fear of vulgarizing them or making mistakes in their grammar. At the same time, for Cairene speakers specifically, their dialect is not just another lowly non-classical variety. There is a hierarchy among rural and urban varieties, and urban varieties of different capitals within the Arab world, as was discussed in Chapters 4 and 5. Cairene speakers view their dialect to be in general superior to all other non-classical varieties (see below). Given such factors, dichotomous and black and white views of Classical Arabic as simply "prestigious" and Egyptian or any other non-classical variety as "stigmatized" would be surprising and are indeed quite rare. The foregoing is intended as a brief background to the speakers' own articulation of their language attitudes that is to follow.

My questions about language attitudes began first with queries about other dialects in Egypt.[7] I asked speakers about their travels within Egypt (*il muhaafiZaat*) and whether people in other parts immediately notice the speakers are from Cairo.[8]

lamma	tiruuH	muHaafiZa	taniya	humma
when	(you) go	province	other	they

yilaaHiZuu	ʃalaa Tuul	inta	min	maSr?[9]
notice	right away	you	from	Cairo

'When you go to another province, do they notice right away that you are from Cairo?'

Chapter Six

The answer which was always in the affirmative, was followed by:

min een   min libsak   min Tarii'it   kalaamak
from where   from clothes-your   from manner of   speech-your

'aw nuT'ak
or   pronunciation-your

'From what? Your clothes? Your manner of talking or your pronunciation?'

Speakers often responded that it had to do with their accent or dialect *laHga*. They were then asked to give examples of the features they were referring to. Most often, speakers cited differences in vocabulary items. The exception to this was the citing of the Upper Egyptian, *Saʕiidi*, /g/ instead of the Cairene /'/. As usually happens with those who live in the capital, speakers were better able to give examples of the specificities of *other* dialects rather than of their own. These questions were then followed by others focusing more directly on the speakers' feelings towards his/her own dialect. For example, they were asked:

law   'ult li-Hadd   inn   huwwa min maSr ʕašaan
if (you) told to someone that   he   from Cairo because

Tarii'it   kalaamuu   tu'Sud da   ka mugaamila
manner of   speech-his   mean   that as compliment

'If you told someone that he is from Cairo on the basis of his speech, do you mean that as a compliment?'

Speakers answered this question in the affirmative and generally went on to praise *maSri*, or Cairene, by stating that it is *n'ii'a*, 'soft', *aHlaa*, 'more beautiful' than all the other dialects in Egypt. A few speakers also thought I was opposing the Egyptian dialect to other national varieties such as Syrian, Lebanese, etc. and used the same adjectives to characterize *maSri*. For example, a woman in her 50s who was a designer said that even though Jordanians and *ilʕarab* 'people from the Gulf countries' speak *fuSHa*, Egyptians and the way they speak are rated highly because:

iHna binuʕtabar zayy il hulivood bitʃhum
we   count/considered like their Hollywood

'we are considered to be like their Hollywood'

They were then asked, not whether they like *maSri*, which they had already answered, but whether they like *ʕammiyya*. In this way, the contrast from their dialect versus other dialects was implicitly switched to a contrast between *ʕammiyya* and *fuSHa*, although the latter variety was not mentioned in the question. Tabulations of responses to this question are provided in Table 1. As we can see 47 out of 50 respondents said they like *ʕammiyya*. Again these responses were followed by more praise to justify the response. That Cairene speakers might have positive attitudes towards their own language may not come as a surprise to some. But it should be mentioned that strong claims to the contrary regarding how "Arabs" view "colloquial Arabic," abound in the literature.

Table 1:
Do you like *ʕammiyya*? (n=50)

	Women	Men	All speakers
Yes	24	23	47
	92%	96%	94%
No	2	1	3
	8%	4%	6%

Chapter Six

After some discussion of these and similar questions, speakers were asked whether they prefer ʕammiyya, fuSHa, or there is no preference for them:

bitfaDDal   il-ʕammiyya 'aw il-fuSHa   'aw litneen zayy baʕD
(you) prefer the ʕammiyya or the fuSHa   or   the two like each other

'Do you prefer ʕammiyya, fuSHa, or the two are alike (for you)'?

This question was left intentionally vague. Modifications such as: 'Do you prefer one or the other in speaking, writing, at home, etc.?' were more likely to bias the responses. Secondly, the vagueness of the question was

Table 2:
Do you prefer ʕammiyya or fuSHa, or both? (N= 50)

	Women	Men	All speakers
ʕammiyya	18 72%	16 64%	34 68%
fuSHa	5 20%	6 24%	11 22%
both	2 8%	3 12%	5 10%

meant to allow us to find out whether this is an issue from the point of view of the speakers, in which case they would not find it vague. On the other hand, if it does not represent a relevant issue, they would ask for clarification, and this in itself would be valuable information. As it turned out, a few of the highly educated speakers asked for clarification: they asked in what domain—for speaking, for everyday life, etc. However, most people responded without asking for clarification. Table 2 provides tabulated responses to this question. Sixty-eight percent of the speakers said that they preferred ſammiyya to fuSHa, 11% said they preferred fuSHa, and 10% said they liked both. Clearly, these Cairenes do not have negative opinions towards their own language. Doubtless many of the speakers who said they prefer ſammiyya, also believe that fuSHa is "beautiful," "powerful," "correct," and so on. Such simultaneous views cannot be considered as simply contradictory—to believe that a language is "beautiful" does not automatically serve as a motivating factor to actually use it. As will be made clear from speakers' responses, the question was interpreted to mean whether they preferred one or the other *in terms of their own daily language use*. This was indeed my intention, as I was not asking at this point for general commentary on their historical or cultural values. This may explain why the differences in language attitudes between men and women are quite small in Tables 1 and 2. For although men in general have more positive evaluations of Classical Arabic and although they use its features more than women, they did not claim that they switch to fuSHa completely in the course of their daily interactions.

We will now review some comments made by individual speakers in explaining their choices. I have attempted to pick comments for each category above which were articulated repeatedly by different speakers. Of those who said they preferred fuSHa, a 30-year-old school teacher who was highly religious (he quoted the Quran throughout his interview), said:

luɣa   il qur'aan   hiyya il luɣa   il ſarabiyya   il 'aSiila
language of the Quran it   the language   the Arabia of   original

'The language of the Quran is the original/pure Arabic language'

His wife had a similar opinion:

Chapter Six

huwwa il mafruuD fiʕlan in iHna niHaafiZ yaʕni ʕalaa qadr il imkaan
it the assumption really that we protect meaning to degree possible

bi il luɣa il qur'aan
to the language of the Quran

'It is proper and right (one should) that we preserve the language of the Quran to the degree possible.'

A female professor of Classical Arabic said:

il fuSHa mumtiʕa wa gamiila
the *fuSHa* enjoyable and beautiful

'*fuSHa* is enjoyable/pleasurable and beautiful.'

This speaker spoke for a while on how much she likes Classical Arabic, that she teaches it, lives it, and so on. But suddenly the tempo of her speech increased and as if she was delivering a punch line after a long story, said:

laakin il fuSHa miš malyaana Hayaa zayy il ʕammiyya
but the *fuSHa* not full of life like the *ʕammiyya*

'But *fuSHa* is not full of life like *ʕammiyya*.'

A man in his early 30s who was studying medicine said that he preferred *fuSHa*, but he added:

il ʕammiyya hiyya di il Ha'ii'a law 'ult ana ʕaayiz nixalli naas
the *ʕammiyya* she this (is) the reality if (I) said I want leave people

bititkallim maʕa baʕD bi il fuSHa yib'a ana basafsaT

Language Attitudes and Ideologies

speak   with each other in the *fuSHa* would be I (say) nonsense

'the *ʕammiyya* it is the reality. If I said that I want people to speak to each other in *fuSHa*, then I would be speaking nonsense.'

Of the speakers who said they like to use both varieties, a 67-year-old woman who holds a Ph.D. and was one of the first Egyptian women to work at the United Nations, said:

di   liiha wa't wa   il tanya liiha wa't   Hasab   bititkallimi miin
this to it time and the other to it time   depends (you) speak who

wa   fi 'ayy   Zarf
and in what   circumstance

'This one has a time and the other has a time. It depends on who you are talking to and under what circumstances.'

This opinion was echoed by others who said they like to use both varieties.

The speakers who said their preferred *ʕammiyya* gave many reasons. Frequently used adjectives for *fuSHa* were: 'heavy', *tiʔiila*; 'lacks humor' *mafihaaʃ xiffit Damm*; and there is 'pretense and affectedness' *takalluf* in it. A middle aged woman who owns a small business, for example, said:

fa   il luɣa il ʕarabiyya hiyya miʃ luɣa   ka luɣa   bass
and the language of Arabic she not language as language only

kalaam laazim il fatHa wa Damma wa taʃkiil
speech necessary the (vowel signs)

'and the Arabic language is not just language as language, but speech that needs the vowel signs for [a] and [u] etc.'

Here reference is being made to the dreaded case endings of Classical Arabic which are not present in Egyptian Arabic or any other non-classical variety. Another woman who was in college said:

il luɣa il ʕarabiyya il fuSHa miš ayyi Hadd yitkallimha
the language of Arabic of *fuSHa* not any person speaks it

fiih naas muʕayyana
there are people specific

wa dool aɣlabhum bituuʕ il diin wa il azhar innama
and those most of them belong to religion and the Azhar but

ba'iit il naas bititkallim bi il ʕammiyya
rest of people speak in the *ʕammiyya*

'The Arabic language of *fuSHa* is not a language that just anybody speaks. There are specific people most of whom belong to (have something to do with) religion and with al-Azhar, but the rest of the people speak in *ʕammiyya*.'

Several speakers used the notion of *taʕawwuD* 'habit, being used to' to explain their preference for *ʕammiyya*. The following comment was made by a 20-year-old woman in college:

xalaaS baladna xadit kida xadit ʕalaa ʕammiyya
finished country-our got used to got used to *ʕammiyya*

'It is over, our country has taken to/is accustomed to *ʕammiyya*'

Language Attitudes and Ideologies

Another speaker, a forty-year-old man said:

il fuSHa   il waaHid   matʕawwidš ʕaleyh
the *fuSHa* the one   not used   to it

'The *fuSHa*, one is not used to it.'

And finally, another female professor of Classical Arabic said:

miš Hikaayit tafDiil Hikaayit taʕawwud
not story   of preference story of habit

'It is not a question of preference but one of habit.'

A number of comments articulated the difficulties and tensions in actually speaking *fuSHa* in face to face interactions. A man in his 40s who was in sales said:

miš maʕʔuul   ana aaʕid maʕaaki   wa aʔuul
not normal/reasonable I (am) sitting with-you and say

"ana sa-   ataHaddaθ   ila kaza"
"I will (CA fut. tns. marker) discuss (Classical word) about such and such"

masalan   Hanuʕud niDHak.
for example (we) will sit   laugh.

'It is not reasonable (does not make sense) that I am sitting with you and say "I will expatiate on such and such" for example. We'd start laughing.'[10]

Such remarks were in accord with my own observations that the constraints of face to face interaction override factors such as formality of topic and level of education cited in the literature to play important roles in the oral use of Classical Arabic. Herbolich (1979: 302) quotes Mitchell as characterizing the oral use of "Modern Standard Arabic" in this way: "the man who wants to talk at all times like a book or a newspaper is a decided oddity." Knowledge and use of Classical Arabic bestows authority and power to the individual. But since Classical Arabic is not commonly employed as a medium of everyday communication, it simultaneously makes the use of that power treacherous. Thus, one has to take care not to appear "pompous" or "ridiculous" (Shouby 1951) in one's use of the classical language. Among friends, expressions from Classical Arabic are often used for humorous purposes.

The most frequent reason cited by speakers for their preference for ʕammiyya, however, had to do with speakers' *fears* of making mistakes in Classical Arabic. Out of 34 speakers who said they preferred ʕammiyya, nineteen said it is because ʕammiyya is *ashal* 'easier' (ten women and nine men) and that they would be afraid of making mistakes in *fuSHa* because it is difficult. A man of 45 who was a school teacher said:

Il luɣa   il ʕammiyya   ashal wa   asraʕ wa   bitooSal li il ʔalb
the language of the ʕammiyya   easier and faster and reaches to the heart

wa li il wugdaan   asraʕ min   il luɣa   il ʕarabiyya
and to the conscience   faster than the language of the Arabic

'The language of ʕammiyya is easier and faster and reaches the heart and the conscience faster than the Arabic language (*fuSHa*).'

Over and over different speakers mentioned the difficulty of Classical Arabic, and hence their fear of making mistakes. Another man in his early 30s who was an engineer said that when he speaks or writes *fuSHa*:

bab'a   xaayif aylaT fi   il Sarf   'aw 'a'uul kilma   miš fi
(I) would be afraid err   in the conjugation or   say   a word not in

maSdarha   'aw fi maɛnaahaa.
(source) place-its   or in meaning-its

'I would be afraid to make a mistake in the conjugation or say a word that is not in its (right) place or in its meaning.'

Speakers' notion of Classical Arabic as a difficult language and their fear of making mistakes came up as well in answers to the following question: 'In your opinion, should we write in *ɛammiyya* like we do in *fuSHa*?'

Table 3:
Should we write in *ɛammiyya*, like we write in *fuSHa*? (N= 35)

	Women	Men	All speakers
Yes	8	6	14
	42%	38%	40%
No	9	5	14
	47%	31%	40%
Both	2	5	7
	11%	31%	20%

'fi ra'yak mumkin niktib bi il ʃammiyya (*baladi*) zayma biniktib bi il *fuSHa* (*naHawi*)?'

Table 3 provides the tabulated results to this question with opinions divided equally. Many of the speakers who answered 'no' explained their answer by saying that they are used to writing in *fuSHa* and they would not know how to write in *ʃammiyya*. Those who said they would rather write in *ʃammiyya* generally continued by saying that they already do and that writing in *fuSHa* is hard for them. One woman and one man told me:

maʃarafʃ   aktib bi il naHawi
(I) not know write in the *naHawi*

'I do not know how to write in *naHawi*'

axaaf kitiir lamma aktib bi il naHawi
afraid a lot when   write in the *naHawi*

'I fear a lot when I write in *naHawi*'

Another man who was an engineer in his early 30s said:

lamma   aktib   il gawaab bi il luɣa   il baladi
when   (I) write   the letter in the language of the baladi

yaʃni baHiss inn   baTallaʃ kull   illi ʃandi   wa baHiss in
(I) feel   that (I) take out everything that in me and (I) feel that

ana kamaan ka'innik inti ʔuddaami   wa   binitkallim maʃa baʃDiina.
I   also   as if   you front of me and (we) speak   with each other

'When I write a letter in the language of *baladi*, you know, I feel that I take out everything that is inside me and I feel as if you are in front of me and we are speaking to each other.'

Parkinson (1991: 40) also found that some Egyptians "even express resentment toward the form [fuSHa] for its difficulty and the effect of the results of their Arabic school tests on their future career choices." Making mistakes in public seems to have embarrassing consequences experienced by many. Two brief examples from my own field observations will illustrate better the reasons for this fear.

I often attended the lecture series at the Dutch Cultural Center during my stay in Cairo. On one of these occasions, a presenter asked that her paper be simultaneously translated into "Arabic." A man from the audience volunteered and proceeded to translate into *Classical* Arabic. But several members of the audience, in particular an older man, almost immediately began to shout corrections to the translator's supposed grammatical mistakes, showing impatience and disappointment. At times the translator had to take long pauses to be able to proceed again, and he became clearly distraught. On another occasion, I watched a program on television that had several panelists discussing aspects of Islam. There was a studio audience who could ask questions and a young woman got up from her seat and addressed the panelists. She attempted to use Classical Arabic while speaking but she was corrected by the (male) panel members continuously and rather mercilessly. The woman was clearly distressed and embarrassed. Such public corrections are not rare and demonstrate why speakers would be afraid and hence would avoid using Classical Arabic. Stevens (1983) in his study of language attitudes in Tunisia calls Tunisian Arabic "the real prestige language." He also cites fear among reasons given by various speakers for why they do not use the classical

Chapter Six

language. He reports that a "Tunisian business executive explained to me [that] Tunisians, when they use Classical Arabic, insist on pure Arabic. But the insistence on purity leads to fear of using the language improperly. Hence, it is not used at all" (Ibid: 107).

Finally speakers were asked if they know anybody personally who speaks *fuSHa*, or are there people who they believe speak it. In Table 4, we see that 27 out of 31 respondents said 'no' to this question.

Table 4:
Do you know people– Are there people who speak *fuSHa*? (n=31)

	Women	Men	All speakers
Yes	2	2	4
	12%	14%	13%
No	15	12	27
	88%	86%	87%

As with all other questions, speakers were asked to elaborate on their answers. When a woman in college said that she did not know anybody like that, I insisted:

Interviewer:
yaʕni mafiiš Hadd   fi Hayaatik abadan biyitkallim fuSHa?
mean no there is nobody   in life-your at all   speak   *fuSHa*

Speaker:
la abadan
no at all

Language Attitudes and Ideologies

Interviewer:

wala   mudarris   il luɣa il ʕarabiyya?
not even teacher of the language of Arabic

Speaker:

mudarris il luɣa il ʕarabiyya biyitkallim il luɣa il fuSHa   'aw'aat
teacher of language of Arabic speaks   the language of *fuSHa* at times

il dars bass   'innama baʕd kida biyib'a   ʕaadi   xaaliS
of study only   but   after that would be normal completely

zayyina bi il ZabT
like us exactly

Interviewer:

you mean there is nobody in your life at all who speaks *fuSHa*?

Speaker:

no, nobody at all.

Interviewer:

not even the teacher of the Arabic language?

Speaker:

the teacher of the Arabic language speaks *fuSHa* at times of study (in class) only. But after that he would be normal, exactly like us.

Another speaker, a twenty year old woman in college said:

bi il nisba li maSr miš mooguud   wa law mooguud fa
with respect to Egypt not available and if available and

il naas biyaʕmiluuh ka'innu miš maSri

Chapter Six

the people treat him like   not Egyptian

ka'innu min   doola   ſarabiyya il muhim huwwa miš maSri
like he   from   country Arabic   the important   he   not Egyptian

'With respect to Egypt, there is no one and when there is people treat him like he is not Egyptian, like he is from (one of the) Arabic (Gulf) countries. The important thing is (in any case) he is not Egyptian.'

This comment is interesting when we relate it to the comment above: 'our country, *baladna*, is now accustomed/has adopted *ſammiyya*'. In her book on Egyptian identity, El-Messiri (1978) explores the topic with respect to the concept of "ibn/bint al-balad" (son or daughter of the country)[11] used to characterize those who are the "real" and "authentic" Egyptians. El-Messiri notes that "An obvious and typical characteristic of the 'real' Egyptian is his use of his mother tongue.[12] She goes on to say that:

> the 'real' Egyptian must be loyal to his country, love it and remain attached to it. The *ibn al-balad* also sees himself as being direct and simple in speech, not sophisticated. It is often said in conversation, when someone starts to philosophize and use classical Arabic words, 'Make your point in *baladi*' (Ibid: 3).

There are very few studies of the relations between local nationalist feelings in the Arab world and the national language. The overwhelming majority of studies in various fields ranging from linguistics, to history, to political science and others, mention the relations between "Arab nationalism" and "Arabic," meaning Classical Arabic (Khalidi et.al 1991; al-Duri 1982; al-Husri 1982; Chejne 1969). But surprisingly few scholars have problematized the tensions between pan-Arab nationalism, and local nationalisms with regard to language issues (but see Gershoni and

Jankowski 1986). The two are not necessarily mutually exclusive, but there are inevitable tensions that are rarely investigated and articulated. In the case of Egypt, preferences for ʃammiyya are often articulated in terms of "baladna" (our country) and its own language. One speaker, a 33-year-old man whose initial response was typical of others, said: 'Of course I like my language, it is my language and my country, and my people' *Tabʃan, di luɣati wa baladi wa ahli*. When he was pressed further to articulate the reasons behind his preference he responded quite eloquently in this way:

li'an   di luɣati   'aw il laHga bitaʃti
because this language-mine or the dialect mine

wa il laHga   illi Hawalaya
and the dialect that around me

wana Tiliʃt la'eet hiyya di il ʃammiyya hiyya illi sayyida   fi il beet
and I grew up found this the *ʃammiyya* this that prevalent in the house

wa fi ilʃaariʃ wa fi   il Hitta   wa fi il šuɣl   wa fi maSr kullaha.
in the street and in the neighborhood and in the job and in Egypt all of it

'Because this (*ʃammiyya*) is my language or my dialect and the dialect that is around me and I grew up (appeared, showed up) and found it is *ʃammiyya* that is prevalent in the house, in the street, in the neighborhood, at work, and in all of Egypt.'

One can hardly add to this comment. It may be that Egyptians are unique in the Arab world in being proud of their mother tongue. Royal (1985) who also studied Cairo found that the speakers in her sample have "positive evaluations" of their own speech. But also in Bahrain, Holes (1987) found that speakers of the prestigious Sunni dialect in do not "correct" towards Classical Arabic regardless of context or interlocutor. In discussing "Myths about Arabic" Ferguson states: "he [Arabic speaker] regards his own dialect as the nearest to classical, the easiest to learn, and the most widely understood" (Ferguson 1959c: 379). While Egyptians generally seemed to believe that their language is the most widely understood, they did not state that their own dialect is the closest to Classical Arabic. In fact, they often cited, for example Jordanians, or *il-ʕarab* (natives of the Gulf countries), as the ones whose dialects are closer to Classical Arabic.

It should be mentioned that the speakers who said they preferred *ʕammiyya* to *fuSHa* did not qualify their statement by enumerating contexts in which this preference would be reversed. Based on these data, it seems that linguists have generally tended to see the absolute prestige of Classical Arabic and its total lack for non-classical varieties of Arabic in highly dichotomous and one-dimensional ways. Writing about Iraq, Altoma (1969) notes:

> In spite of its use as the dominant medium of the spoken word in conversation, and in various cultural or artistic contexts such as songs, stage, and movies, the colloquial lacks the prestige enjoyed by the Classical and is looked upon, often with a considerable degree of contempt, as a stigma of illiteracy and ignorance (Ibid: 3).

Altoma's description may well be true about Iraq, or at least the Iraq of three decades ago. In any case, while comments to this effect are quite common in the literature, scholars are rarely explicit about *whose* views are being represented—exactly who has "contempt" for the "colloquial"? Surely some do, but empirical research is necessary to answer that question. Quite often such assertions tend to project the ideology of some highly literate elites onto all "Arabs" without any further qualifications.

Language Attitudes and Ideologies

To access speakers' language attitudes is a difficult task in any speech community. Investigations of such attitudes within the Arab world have to be particularly sensitive to the immense institutional and ideological support that Classical Arabic enjoys, in order to access speakers' views towards a language which is their mother tongue, but which has far less official sanction.

Perceptions of Differences in the Speech of Men and Women

For attitudes towards men's and women's speech, speakers were first asked whether they thought there are any differences at all in the way men and women speak (pronunciation, manner of speaking, choice of words). Many responded in the affirmative to this question: 49.3%, 22 women and 14 men. They cited expressions that men never use such as *yaxti* (< *ya uxti*) (lit. 'my sister' said in times of surprise, or sudden fright); voice quality; presence of 'authority' in men's language, but not in women's; and the fact that women speak 'softer, more delicate', *ri?ii?*, and men speak 'rough', *xišin*. Three men said they think men speak 'better', *aHsan*; and four women said that women speak 'better.'

A number of speakers commented that men use *fuSHa* more than women. One woman said that "men's speech tends more towards Classical Arabic": *kalaam il raagil amyal ila il luɣa il farabiyya aktar*. Another speaker who was a skilled refurbisher (*ostorgi*) commented that "women maybe speak in *baladi* a bit more than men": *il sitt yimkin bititkallim bi baladi šuwayya fan il raagil*. The speaker who was referred to earlier as "highly religious," made the following comment (Classical Arabic words are put in bold face):

haaza al qur'aan **la yiqraa'uu**   illa   il raagil Tabfan
This the Quran not   read   except the man of course

il sittaat mayiʃrafuuš yi'ruu il qur'aan yiʃrafuu yi'ruu
the women not know-not read the Quran (they) know (how to) read

innama il qur'aan   tiHiss kida Haaga kabiira
but   the Quran (you) feel like something big

Haaga Daxma giddan waaxad baalak inta ʃaayiz eeh
something heavy very understand you want what

il   maxaarig
the point of articulation

maZbuuTa il Huruuf maZbuuTa fa ana fi TaSSawuri   illi **yintaq**
exact the letters   exact   and I in opinion-mine who pronounces

il luɣa   il fuSHa fiʃlan maZbuuT giddan
the language of *fuSHa* really exact very

il raagil aktar min il sitt   yaʕni
the man more than the woman, that is.

'This Quran is not read except by men. Of course women do not know how to read the Quran. They know how to read but the Quran you feel like it is something big, something really heavy, you understand? It requires what? Good and exact articulation. And in my opinion, he who pronounces the language of *fuSHa* really well is the man more than the woman.' [13]

Such perceptions in terms of the more frequent use of Classical Arabic and its features by men have been found in other studies (Royal 1985) and as we saw in Chapter 4 are corroborated by data on actual use. Notwithstanding a general perception that there are many linguistic differences in the way men and women talk, with regard to pronunciation specifically, speakers had difficulty citing examples, and most said that they do not believe there are such differences. Table 5 shows tabulated responses to whether speakers believe there to be pronunciation differences

Table 5:
Are there differences in pronunciation in the speech of men and women? (n=73)

	Women	Men	All speakers
Yes	1	5	6
	2%	15%	8.2%
No	39	28	67
	98%	85%	91.8%

between women and men. Speakers who said there are pronunciation differences mostly referred to pharyngealization as a difference, saying that women pronounce their [T] or their [S] as [t] and [s], without pharyngealization. Royal reported this as a frequent comment made by Cairene speakers. Otherwise, most speakers did not believe there to be pronunciation differences.

We began this chapter with an emphasis on illustrating ambivalent language attitudes. To this end, we provided some of the socio-historical and ideological reasons for why dichotomous characterizations are unrealistic and empirically unfounded. On the basis of speakers' own characterizations, it is clear that on the one hand they concur with official views that *il luɣa il ʕarabiyya* represents the highest linguistic norms of the society, while *ʕammiyya* cannot match it in its "beauty,"

Chapter Six

"power," and "correctness." On the other hand, Classical Arabic lacks "humor," is "heavy" and full of *takallof*, and its use is mostly attributed to religious men and those who are from other Arab countries. In addition, the overwhelming prescriptive norms of Classical Arabic make speakers fearful of making mistakes, and therefore discourage them from using it.

But the characterizations that are provided here are still limited since speakers' feelings towards the use of Classical Arabic in different contexts and different genres are not explored. For example, it is quite likely that "fear" does not play a role when speakers hear recitations in Classical Arabic in a mosque—where they do not have to actively use this variety. Moreover, recitations of various kinds—at weddings, funerals, calls to prayer, and so on often have moving and nostalgic associations for many people. Nader (1962) did a brief study of language attitudes in Lebanon. She recorded a variety of ceremonial recitations (apparently in some version of Classical Arabic) performed by rural speakers and played these to groups of urban speakers to elicit their reactions. She found that most reacted very positively to these recitations. Nader rightly implies that aesthetic judgments with regard to the beauty or purity of speech genres cannot be simply reduced to whether or not those utilizing such genres enjoy social "prestige" through affluence. In fact, this point is similar to our own discussions in Chapters 1 and 5 with regard to Classical Arabic: that it represents the highest linguistic norms does not have to do with the fact that these norms are found in the speech of "affluent" speakers. Thus a more complete exploration of language attitudes will have to include views of and reactions to a variety of genres.

---

1. Originally appeared in Fu'ad Duwwarah (1965: 286). I thank Roger Allen for providing me with this citation.

2. Questions taken from the Language Modules of the Project on Change and Variation in Philadelphia, Labov, 1981.

3. This sentence is said by Sawaie to have been "chosen as a natural utterance, which avoids artificiality of the test sentence." Since the setting is a university, the content is clearly natural, and the form may also be natural in Irbid. However, in spontaneous speech, the presence of five qafs in one sentence has to be shown to be natural and not assumed. In the more than 130 hours of interviews that I recorded in Cairo, for example, never did a sentence with so many qaf's occur even in the speech of highly educated speakers.

4. In Badawi and Hinds (1986: 682) the expression "bi-yitakallim bil-qaaf" is cited and is said to mean "he speaks in a pompous way." Intrigued by the meaning, I asked a number of informants at the beginning of my fieldwork about it, and what they thought it meant. Most said that they had not heard it, but a few older speakers (those in their 50's and 60's) said that though they were not sure, they thought it meant "huwwa Hanbali" meaning that "he is rigid and puritanical" (Ibid: 228).

5. This seems to be a general problem with long interviews where language attitude questions are left to the end of the interview. Labov (1966) describes a very similar problem with his investigation of language attitude questions: "In many cases, the interview had already lasted an hour or more before this section was reached [...] The linguistic attitudes section was therefore administered as if it were not part of the formal interview, and the completion rate for various questions was somewhat irregular. If the informant had only a limited amount of time, other sections of the interview were given priority." (p. 483).

6. This term comes from the root n–H–w, meaning 'grammar' or 'syntax' of Arabic. (Badawi and Hinds, 1986: 852). Badawi's dictionary translates /naHawi/ only as an adjective meaning 'pompous, posh' said of speech. But it is also used as a noun to refer to language in particular in contrast to /baladi/ 'Egyptian language'; or 'very colloquial Egyptian'.

7. A note about the interviewers' language should be mentioned here. I had a number of Classical Arabic lexical items in my speech such as /aʕtaqid/, 'I believe'; /qarrart/, 'I decided', among others. Moreover, my original training in Classical Arabic revealed itself, for example, in my pronunciation of the emphatics which were more heavily pharyngealized than is the norm in ʕammiyya. In a conversation in ʕammiyya with a university professor, I said: "ana Taaliba fi gamʕat binsilvanya", 'I am a student at the University of Pennsylvania', with heavy pharyngealization of the [T] of Taaliba. The professor chuckled and said "iHna mabinʔulʃ 'T' kida, binʔuul 't' ʕaadi", 'We don't say 'T' like that, we just say 't', normal'. But this, as I found, was a hard habit to break. The male interviewer also had a number of Classical Arabic lexical items in his speech during the interviews. Moreover, as he generally interviewed the people in his own neighborhood, speakers were aware of his high educational background which was a Masters in electrical engineering.

8. See footnote 2.

9. The transcriptions of responses is an attempt in phonemic representation. Lexical items such as /muhaafiZaat/ 'provinces'; /Zarf/ 'circumstance'; /laHaZa/ 'to notice'; and /maZbuuT/ 'exact' were often pronounced with little or no pharyngealization of the /Z/ as [z]. In Badawi and Hinds dictionary, derivations of Z-b-T are cited both with [Z] and [z] (see pp. 555-6; 214; and 782).

10. Parkinson (1991: 40) relates an interesting anecdote from his fieldwork with regard to the constraints of the oral use of Classical Arabic. It concerns a "passionate supporter of *fuSHa*" who had vowed to use it at all times while speaking to his children. But, as a friend of his tells the story, one day the man gets separated from his three-year-old daughter while getting on the bus. To locate his daughter, he yells for her using fuSHa. As a result "the entire bus started laughing outloud. It was rude, but they couldn't help themselves."

11. "Balad" depending on context can mean Egypt, or another locality such as a village (see El-Messiri, p. 1).

12. The rest of that paragraph reads: "The *ibn al-balad* speaks Arabic in the local Egyptian dialect and not 'broken Arabic.' If an Egyptian does not master his mother tongue, which has happened often enough as a result of westernization, foreign occupation and the emphasis on foreign education, he may be referred to sarcastically as a *khawaaga*" (El-Messiri 1978: 2). *Khawaaga* can be briefly translated into "foreigner."

13. In Badawi and Hinds' Dictionary of Egyptian Arabic, /taSSawor/ is translated as 'fantasy'. In this context, I believe it may more appropriately be translated as 'imagination' or 'opinion'.

Chapter Seven
Conclusion

One of the central theoretical issues with which we began in Chapter 1 was how sociolinguistic variation in Arabic-speaking speech communities has been conceptualized. In examining this conceptualization, the term "colloquial Arabic," its underlying assumptions and its implications were critiqued. The arguments need not be repeated here, except to emphasize that since Egyptians can and do use Egyptian Arabic to discuss philosophy, literature, politics, as well as the more mundane matters of daily life, what they speak cannot be viewed as a "colloquial" language. That all sorts of Classical Arabic elements *may* be employed in their conversations, (some of which may not be classical from their point of view) does not cause a metamorphosis of Egyptian Arabic into another entity, but *serves to widen its scope of variability*. The nature of this variability cannot be fully captured by approaches that focus exclusively on the contributions of the classical language. Stylistic variation is a product of the simultaneous resources of the varieties in contact (see also Heath 1989). Much has been written on the criteria for determining whether the use of words (expressions, or phrases) belonging to one language while speaking another is to be considered "code-switching," or "borrowing," (Myers-Scotton 1993, Poplack, Sankoff, and Miller 1988, among others). In my data, for those speakers who used the resources of Classical Arabic, the great majority employed only its lexical resources. This kind of variation is part of the many ways in which Egyptian Arabic speakers use to style shift in Egyptian Arabic. English, for example, has many borrowings from Latin, some that are well-integrated, and some that are not. It may be argued that such borrowings are rarely used in "colloquial English." But even if we grant that to be the case, no one has argued that as a result of such borrowings, a new "third English" has emerged. That borrowing is still part of "English"—or more precisely a style of English. Similarly, Egyptian Arabic has integrated and unintegrated borrowings from Classical Arabic. The use of these, along with the use of other linguistic resources together define variation in Egyptian Arabic. Thus there is no separate entity called "Educated Spoken Arabic" as distinct from a style that educated speakers of *Egyptian Arabic* sometimes employ.

The two kinds of sociolinguistic variables that were analyzed in detail in Chapters 3 and 4 shed light on the nature of stylistic variation in Cairo. The contrast in their histories, social meanings, linguistic and extra-linguistic constraints brings us closer to an understanding of variability that may also be generalizable to other Arabic-speaking speech communities. The phonological variable of palatalization represents one of the many stylistic resources of Cairene Arabic that exhibits social differentiation. It is a variable whose emergence does not involve Classical Arabic and one which is quite similar to other phonological variables investigated in numerous other speech communities. Palatalization is to my knowledge the first report of a sound change in progress in an Arab-speaking speech community. Moreover, it seems to be one of the few documented cases of an innovation originating among the upper classes,

Conclusion

since "no cases have been reported in which the highest status social group acts as the innovating group" (Labov 1994: 78). However, a review of sociolinguistic literature shows that the speech of the upper classes has not been investigated—their speech habits seem to be often inferred (but see Kroch 1978). Thus, the fact that upper class innovations have not been documented may be simply due to the fact that they have not been studied.

Palatalization, strength of pharyngealization (Royal 1985), and other similar variables (see below) comprise one specific kind of variation. There is also the kind of variation that is created as a result of the use of Classical Arabic features and lexicon. In the case of the qaf, for example, the use of lexical borrowings containing this sound has created a kind of variation that has brought back an older sound with them. In so far as the reasons behind the "re-appearance" of the qaf are concerned, this sociolinguistic phenomenon may be unique to those diglossic settings where the classical language serves as a medium of mass education. However, as far as the ways in which the use of the qaf is mitigated by social and ideological factors, it is similar to other sociolinguistic variables. In other words, the social embedding of this variable is not radically different from variables in other settings. In Chapter 4, we suggested the term "diglossic variable" to refer to the reappearance of features of Classical Arabic. The contrasts between the variables that we have analyzed representing two kinds of linguistic changes, is summarized in Figure 1. The conceptualization of Figure 1 is inspired by Guy (1990).

Figure 1:

Contrasts in Types of Linguistic Change in Cairo

	Qaf	Palatalization
Result of Contact with Classical Arabic	Yes	No
Agents of Change	Men	Women
Class Origin	Varied*	Upper
Social motivation	Extra-national identity?	National identity?
Institutional norm	Yes	No
Change from above	Yes	No
Linguistic motivation	Lexical gaps?	Phonetic

* Qaf belongs to the speech of no particular social class. It has never been identified as such. "Varied" means that those who acted as agents of re-introducing it were probably not from one social class.

Conclusion

Through a focus on gender differences, a number of significant empirical and theoretical problems were addressed. Having established one kind of variability in Cairene Arabic that does not involve the resources of Classical Arabic, we examined the simultaneous questions of whether the standard variety in all speech communities represent the same sociolinguistic entity; and whether there may be more than one kind of standard in Egypt. In this discussion, the concept of the linguistic market proved useful in differentiating the roles of two educational systems in Egypt which serve clients from distinct class backgrounds; and values for the official language are reproduced mostly by the public educational system. We concluded that Egypt has one standard variety as represented by the urban dialect of Cairo; and a supra-standard variety that is also the official language of the country.

In Chapter 3, an attempt was made to reconcile the "paradoxical" nature of the linguistic behavior of women. It was argued that this behavior has been seen as "paradoxical" because it has been assumed that the social meanings of stable and changing variables can be evaluated in the same manner. That is, the question has been asked why women use the "non-standard" variants of stable variables less than men; but the "non-standard" variants of changing variables more than men. We argued that these two kinds of "non-standard" forms have to be *shown* to be evaluated equivalently by speakers, and not assumed. In the case of stable variables, all variants have long acquired stable social meanings and associations; and the non-standard variants often bear negative evaluations that speakers are socialized into through diverse means. However, in the case of changes in progress, depending on the stage of their development, the social meanings of non-standard variants go through a period of negotiation and are in flux. Hence the two kinds of forms are not necessarily evaluated as simply "non-standard." And if that is the case,

Chapter Seven

then in this sense there seems to be no "paradox" in the linguistic behavior of women. This particular formulation of the problem of social meanings and evaluations still needs further specification, but the general point is that unless theoretically and methodologically we are able to improve upon our understanding of the social meanings of linguistic forms, characterizations such as "paradoxical" presume empirical bases that are in fact lacking.

In Chapter 4, we compared women and men with the same educational backgrounds and found, just as other studies had, that women have lower frequencies of qaf usage. In attempting to explain this repeated finding in Chapter 5, the explanation based on differential "access" was rejected. Instead, a division between occupations that require knowledge of Classical Arabic versus those that do not; and the differential in daily practices where Classical Arabic has an exclusively religious function were suggested. In addition, sociolinguistic theory's treatment of the relations between linguistic behavior, ideology, and language change was critiqued. We argued that in the case of changes from above, both linguistic behavior and metalinguistic commentaries including self-characterizations contribute to constructions of social identities. As such, the role of ideology in language change needs a more systematic treatment than it has been so far accorded. Sociolinguistic theory does not seem to recognize commentaries as data, although the disappearance of certain innovations are attributed to strong stigmatization so that it has long acknowledged the role of evaluation in affecting the course of linguistic change.

Without repeating our findings with regard to the use of palatalization and the qaf by women and men, we may summarize the dynamics of the role of gender in the sociolinguistic setting of Cairo in Graphs 1 and 2. These graphs confirm the findings of many studies in showing that men are more often the propagators of the reappearing forms of Classical Arabic; while women propagate a kind of variability that involves more often the resources of Cairene Arabic, and those offered by the contact of the latter with languages other than Classical Arabic.

Graph 1: Use of a non-classical stylistic resource (=Graph 1, Ch. 3)

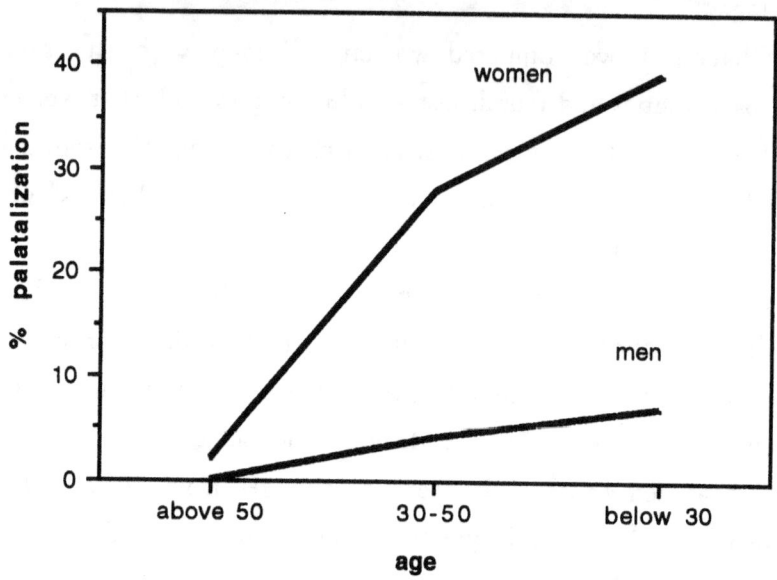

In Chapters 3, 4, and 5, gender, social class, age, level and type of education, and kinds of occupation, were all shown to play crucial roles in the degree to which palatalization and the qaf are used by different social groups. More than three decades of research within the variationist paradigm in many speech communities around the globe has found these and similar factors to correlate with stylistic variation and partly explain causes of linguistic variation and change. Yet, for Arabic, the situation is claimed to be somehow radically different. Writing on "Dimensions of style in a grammar of educated spoken Arabic" Mitchell (1986) states:

Chapter Seven

No attempt will or need be made here to characterize variation in form or structure in terms of regional dialect, generation, religion, education, sex, and similar variables, much less those of a socio-economically determined class structure—ESA [Educated Spoken Arabic] is better defined ostensively by reference to *the practice of the overwhelming majority of the professional classes* whose representatives have provided the extensive corpus of data on which the Leeds project is based (Ibid: 90, emphasis added).

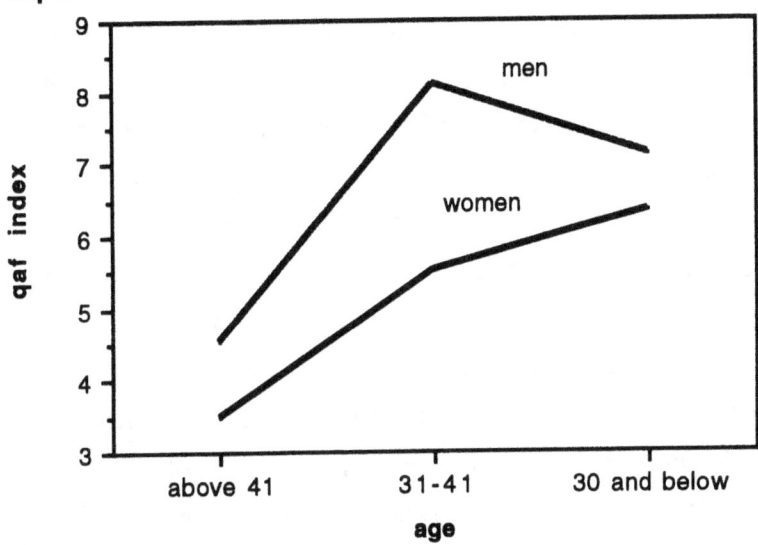

Graph 2: Use of a classical stylistic resource

The question is how can "practice" emerge in a seeming social vacuum where all the myriad factors that influence and shape all aspects of the social behavior of people are rendered as irrelevant to their linguistic behavior? Further, the extremeness of the claim is not helped by the circularity of the argument: "ESA" is defined as the "practice" of the "professional classes," and who they are has nothing to do with their social class, education, gender and so on—they need not be *defined* since if they

Conclusion

speak ESA then they are the professional classes. The data provided in Chapter 5 show that speakers who could be members of what is called the "professional classes" have heterogeneous backgrounds in type of education, ideology, social class, and other social factors. Those who have attended private language schools, and later received their graduate degrees in specializations in which a foreign language served as the medium; and those who went to public schools and acquired higher degrees in areas where Classical Arabic served as the medium, are both "educated." And both become members of the professional classes. Were we to construct a category such as the "speech of the professional classes," we would have to include not only Egyptian Arabic and Classical Arabic (and all their varieties), but also English, French, Italian, German, and still other languages. There is no doubt that educated speakers exhibit certain linguistic habits and practices that are different from those who are not educated. But due to factors just mentioned (and others) their habits do not form one clear-cut, distinct, and stable linguistic variety. It may be that for Mitchell those in the "professional classes" only include speakers who have attended public schools, and have been otherwise educated to be literate in Classical Arabic. But this would not only be inaccurate and ahistorical, it would also lead to neglecting the kinds of social dynamics that have a direct bearing on the sociolinguistic practices of the diverse members of the "professional classes." Indeed it would be hard to explain how any variability of interest to sociolinguists could exist in this variety since all social factors that have been identified as underlying sociolinguistic variation (with the exception of one kind of education) have been rendered as irrelevant.

Chapter Seven

Evaluations and Categorizations of Linguistic Varieties

In Chapter 6, we reported on a variety of linguistic attitudes among Egyptians. A majority of speakers articulated positive feelings towards ʕammiyya. It was praised for being "easy," "soft," "Egyptian," "full of life," "full of humor" and so on. With regard to using it as a medium of writing, speakers showed more ambivalence. While *fuSHa* was praised as the language that is more "correct," "powerful" and "beautiful," it was also characterized as one that speakers "feared"; as "pretentious," "lacking humor," "heavy," and one that cannot really be used in face to face conversations. Thus, we did not find dichotomized, black and white views that attributed absolute prestige to Classical Arabic, or an absolute stigmatization of Egyptian Arabic.

Research on language ideology is greatly advanced by explorations of speakers' own potential categorizations of linguistic varieties. Parkinson (1991) attempts to examine how Egyptians "conceive of and talk about" varieties such as Modern Standard Arabic (or "modern *fuSHa*"). Parkinson explains that:

> Naming and carefully defining distinct intermediate styles (such as Oral Literary Arabic, Educated Spoken Arabic, etc.), while it focuses our efforts and helps look for consistencies we might otherwise miss, also has a tendency to reify that style and give it an independent existence which it may not have for native speakers who apparently have no category for thinking or talking about it, and whose behavior simply may not be so consistent as to warrant a named style (Ibid: 37).

He thus carries out three experiments to elicit speakers' reactions to "mixed texts, to written texts of various levels of formality, and to a variety of oral performances of *fuSHa* texts." In these experiments, speakers were given sets of written texts taken from newspapers, and listened to passages where combinations of case endings, phonological and morphological features were altered to find out what they consider to be *fuSHa* on a scale from 1 to 7. Briefly, Parkinson found great diversity in which texts were considered *fuSHa* and how they were ranked vis-à-vis others: "Every text was rated both 1 and 7 by at least one subject." Some speakers' judgments seemed to be influenced by topic (religion, sports, etc.), others by comprehensibility; presence of "archaic Arabic style"; and still others by the presence of even a "little colloquial" in an otherwise *fuSHa* text. Parkinson summarizes his results by dividing the speakers into three broad categories: the "expanded-fuSHa" group for whom modern written Arabic is also *fuSHa*, and who seem to prefer the latter to more rigid classical norms; the "pro-narrow-fuSHa" group whose idea of it is not only "grammatical Arabic" but also "archaic Arabic style"; and finally the "anti-narrow-fuSHa" group who "see fuSHa as limited to classical Arabic but do not think it should be the standard for modern writing" (Ibid: 53). The speakers' judgments in the listening experiment were equally revealing. It was found that a text with all the correct case endings of *fuSHa*, correct pausal forms, and correct pronunciation except for interdentals which were pronounced according to Egyptian rather than Classical Arabic phonology, was judged as *lower* on the *fuSHa* scale than one that only had partial case endings, incorrect pausal forms, but which had the Classical Arabic interdentals: "the rankings [of] the phonological variable far outweighs the other variables" (Ibid: 57). Such results argue against the practices and claims of linguists who on formal or purely theoretical grounds divide up the Arabic stylistic continuum. It is not that forms do not matter, but that differences or similarities between them have to be demonstrated to coincide (or not) with the judgment of different speakers. In this regard, it should be mentioned that while Parkinson provides brief backgrounds on his informants, it would have been more illuminating if their judgments were given alongside more detailed biographies. Two of the main conclusions Parkinson draws are that "Egyptian native speakers of Arabic are not of one mind when it comes to their formal language"; and that "they disagree about what to call the form" (Ibid: 60). The first is amply supported by the data Parkinson presents, whereas for the second conclusion no data is provided. So far as can be determined from this study, speakers did not report that they had difficulty in naming the varieties that they were presented with, although one may well have expected the articulation of such a problem. In any case, this study addresses one of the most complex and most interesting problems in the sociolinguistic setting of Cairo, with potentially generalizable methods and concerns for other Arabic-speaking speech communities.

Diglossia Without Contact?

The issue of how different speakers perceive and characterize the linguistic varieties that they may be exposed to brings us to yet another crucial question in the study of Arabic. The problem which was already alluded to at the beginning of Chapter 4 has to do with an understanding of the nature and frequency of contact of different speakers with Classical Arabic (and all its versions). First the nature of this contact is of fundamental importance. Apart from contact in educational settings, some speakers may be exposed to Classical Arabic through personal relations with friends who use it from time to time, others may be exposed to it through largely impersonal means such as what they hear on radio and television, utility bills and notices from state companies, and letters from various bureaucracies. Some may mostly come in contact with it

Conclusion

when they attend mosques, read or hear the Quran, and pray. These are only examples of the many ways different speakers may be exposed to Classical Arabic. The kinds of contact speakers have and their frequency can greatly affect what they do or do not perceive as "*fuSHa*" and what aspects of it they master enough to use actively in the right contexts (lexical items, negation system, proverbs, the demonstratives, and so on). A systematic understanding of the nature and frequency of contact with Classical Arabic not only will shed light on the diversity of perceptions that Parkinson found, but significantly on the diversity of production as well. The ever present idea of the "continuum" that locates Classical Arabic on one end and "colloquial" Arabic on the other might in this way be substantiated, rejected, or its discontinuities better understood. Though the literature on "diglossia" is vast, as can be gleaned from the two most recent bibliographies (Hudson 1992; Fernández 1993), rarely can one find a study that has examined such questions.

The general practice of reducing diglossia to "functional differentiation of language use" has tended to overshadow many other aspects of diglossic settings. Whether our interest lies in understanding the causes of the particular formal properties of utterances, or in a characterization of the stylistic continuum, or the social and ideological facts of language use, we need to examine the nature and frequency of contact. Attention should be re-focused on processes of childhood socialization and acquisition, and adult contact. While functional differentiation of language use has served to shed light on aspects of sociolinguistic settings in a wide variety of speech communities, the concept itself tends to discourage historical and dynamic outlooks. Which language or variety is used in which domain(s) is often described in a rather timeless framework so that neither the emergence of new domains, nor an expansion in the use of a formerly restricted variety, nor the blurred boundaries of some "formal" and "informal" domains are considered. In the case of Arabic, for example, according to received wisdom Classical Arabic is used in "formal" domains while "colloquial" Arabic in "informal" ones. On the one hand, such a view, perhaps encouraged by the charts Ferguson (1959) provided in his diglossia article, is simplistic. For example, what constitutes the formality of instructions of use on commercial products such as nose sprays or insect repellents that are written in some version of Classical Arabic? And how "informal" are plays and poems written in Egyptian Arabic? (see also El-Hassan 1977: 113). On the other hand, functional differentiation in Arabic diglossic settings has been claimed by some and interpreted by others (Bynon 1977; Fasold 1987 [1984]; Lehiste 1988) to mean that speakers go back and forth and codeswitch routinely in the course of their daily lives depending on their interlocutor or topic of conversation. And failure to switch to the appropriate code would expose the speaker to ridicule. But these claims have not been empirically supported either by previous research, or by the present one.

Sociolinguistic Variables for Future Research

Beside the rather frequent use of qaf lexical items, no other Classical Arabic phoneme was used in my interviews with even a low degree of frequency to warrant further examination. The classical voiced affricate /ǯ/ and the interdental fricatives were used once or twice by a few speakers in the course of more than hour-long interviews. This of course does not mean that no one uses them, nor that they will not in time emerge with as much frequency as the qaf.

In so far as other sociolinguistic variables in Cairene Arabic are concerned, there are a few that merit variationist treatments. Among them, we can mention the following:

Conclusion

1. Gemination of final dental stops, as in:

    /bint/ → [bɪtt]   'girl'

    /kunt/ → [kott]   '(I) was'

2. Flapping of intervocalic [d] in particular in the speech of lower-class young men; as in:

    /kida/ → [kiɾa]   'like that'

3. Voice assimilation of stops and fricatives to the following consonant. This seems to be a stable sociolinguistic variable, commented on in the dialectological literature (e.g. Garbell 1958):

    /akbar/ → [agbær]   'bigger'

    /usbuuʃ/ → [ozbuuʃ]   'week'

4. Variation in the deictic/definite system. There are at least three systems which are used in my interviews:

Masculine Singular	**Feminine Singular**	**Plural**
da 'this, that'	di 'this, that'	dool 'these, those'
dawwat 'this, that'	diyyat 'this, that'	doolat 'these, those'
dawwan 'this, that'	diyyan 'this, that'	doolan 'these, those'

Still other systems are mentioned in Badawi and Hinds (1986).

Variation in Arabic-speaking speech communities involves stylistic resources that originate from within the non-classical languages, from Classical Arabic, and from foreign languages. It is the reliance of different social groups on one or all such stylistic resources that provides for the dynamics of the sociolinguistic setting in Egypt. Cairene Arabic,

Chapter Seven

far from a monolithic "colloquial" language reflects and reproduces the heterogeneity of its speakers. The complex role of gender in these dynamics seems to be a rather consistent differential in the degree to which women and men make use of the resources of Classical and non-classical Arabic.

Appendix 1

Brief descriptions of Speakers including age; occupation; education; and neighborhood.

Women

Pseudonym	Age	Occupation	Education	Neighborhood
1. Nawal	20	maid	two years elementary school	Bulaq
2. Omm Hossein	45	maid	no schooling	Massaka
3. Su'ad	36	maid	no schooling	Maadi
4. Sabah	19	clerk	high school diploma	Imbaba
5. Bahiiga	19		college student	Shubra
6. Aida	19	does not work	high school diploma	Imbaba
7. Fatheya	18	does not work	high school diploma	Imbaba
8. Hanaa	19	does not work	some high school	Ard il Gamaliya
9. Omm Ali	55	self-employed	no schooling	Imbaba
10. Samira	25	does not work	high school diploma	Imbaba
11. Hosna	18	does not work	high school diploma	Imbaba
12. Mervett	15		high school	Imbaba
13. Rawya	17		high school	Imbaba
14. Farida	23	housewife	B.A.–Advertising	Imbaba
15. Manal	30	housewife	high school diploma	Zawya il Hamra
16. Ibtesam	25	housewife	B.A.–Business	Imbaba
17. Houayda	19		2nd year college Philosophy	Dokki

Appendix 1

Pseudonym	Age	Occupation	Education	Neighborhood
18. Nahid	25	accountant	high school diploma	Old Cairo (Masr il 'adima)
19. Madiha	31	public relations mgr.	B.A.	Heliopolis
20. Samiha	22	does not work	high school diploma	Imbaba
21. Ferial	22	secretary	B.A.–English	il Hussein
22. Amal	28	actress	B.A.–Literature	Abdin
23. Sausan	24	secretary	B.A.–Library Science	Imbaba
24. Sobheya	32	actress	B.A.–Literature	Masr il 'adima
25. Nour	55	housewife	B.A.–English	Maadi
26. Hend	24		student–Anthropology	Zamalik
27. Amina	31	prof. Classical Arabic	M.A.–Arabic Linguistics	Agouza
28. Zekiya.	58	housewife	high school diploma	Agouza
29. Moshira	13		high school student	Giza
30. Malek	41	housewife	M.A.–Architecture	Giza
31. Hekmat	13		high school student	Giza
32. Lamis	17		high school student	Giza
33. Lubna	16		high school student	Giza
34. Ghada	48	housewife	high school diploma	Heliopolis
35. Saneya	31	owns business	M.D.–Pharmaceuticals	Heliopolis
36. Mohga	32	writer and researcher	M.A.–Sociology	

Appendix 1

Pseudonym	Age	Occupation	Education	Neighborhood
37. Mounira	34	prof. Classical Arabic	M.A.– Political Science	Ramsis
38. Samya	40	housewife	high school diploma	Dokki
39. Fatma	50	self-employed	high school diploma	Muhandesin
40. Nadya	27	admin. secr't	B.A.–Economics	Giza
41. Nermine	23		2nd year business school	Dokki
42. Nadine	26	secretary	B.A.– Communication	Central Cairo (Wost il Balad)
43. Faiza	42	T.V. producer	M.A.–English	Zamalik
44. Randa	30	housewife	B.A.–English	Maadi
45. Reema	48	diplomat	M.A.– Political Science	Giza
46. Nabila	68	university professor	M.A.–English	Zamalik
47. Yasmine	53	self-employed	high school diploma	Zamalik
48. Sherine	48	prof. Classical Arabic	M.A.–Languages	Zamalik
49. Hala	15		high school student	Zamalik
50. Nessrine	15		high school student	Zamalik

Men

Pseudonym	Age	Occupation	Education	Neighborhood
51. Hani	38	skilled laborer	self-educated	Bulaq
52. Hassan	17		high school student	Dokki
53. Hosni	40	theatre help	some high school	Bulaq
54. Raouf	17		high school student	Imbaba

Appendix 1

Pseudonym	Age	Occupation	Education	Neighborhood
55. Mansour		house painter	none	Imbaba
56. Bahgat	79	custodian (farrash)	none	Imbaba
57. Shauki	20		2nd year Agricultural college	Shubra
58. Fathi	39	electrician	junior college	Zawya il Hamra
59. Shakir	34	house decorator	B.A.–Agricultural Engineer	Imbaba
60. Fathi	68	policeman	Police Academy diploma	Imbaba
61. Hatem	30		B.A.–Arabic	Imbaba
62. Younis	33	electrical engineer	M.A.–Engineering	Imbaba
63. Taher	31	architect	M.A.–Architecture	Muhandesin
64. Farouk	33	high school teacher	high school diploma	Imbaba
65. Hamdi	29	refurbisher (ostorgi)	high school diploma	il Goriya
66. Amin	41	salesperson	high school diploma	Imbaba
67. Fadel	25	graphic design	M.A.–Fine Arts	Heliopolis
68. Sherif	28	auditor	B.A.–Accounting	Heliopolis
69. Sabri	40	sales rep.	B.A.–Business	Heliopolis
70. Aziz	31	mechanical engineer	B.A.–Engineering	Heliopolis
71. Metwali	68	ret. gov't clerk	high school diploma	Shubra
72. Farag	33	actor	B.A.–History	Abdine

Appendix 1

Pseudonym	Age	Occupation	Education	Neighborhood
73. Slah	50	oil company employee	B.A.–Economics	Roda
74. Adli	29	bank accountant	B.A.–Business	Heliopolis
75. Mohsen	58	retired	B.A.–English	Maadi
76. Ayman	31	self-employed	M.A.–Engineering	Muhandesin
77. Nabil	30	airline steward	B.A.–Business	Heliopolis
78. Yasin	31	self-employed	M.A.–Engineering	Muhandesin
79. Farid	27	actor	M.D.–Dentistry	Daher
80. Muhammad	17		high school student	Giza
81. Kamal	58	prof. Classical Arabic	M.A.–Linguistics	Garden City
82. Roushdy	30	researcher	M.A.–Architecture	Dokki
83. Hasan	30	actor	B.A.–Acting	Agouza
84. Yousef	31	self-employed	M.A.–Engineering	Muhandesin
85. Sadik	41	medical doctor		Maadi
86. Galal	24	does not work	B.A.–Political Science	Muhandesin
87. Magdi	27	movie director	M.A.–Business	Daher

Appendix 2

Example of Goldvarb run

Women speakers only; strong palatalization as application.

CELL CREATION • 4/16/91 • 5:18 PM

Name of token file: allpal
Name of condition file: lingsoc.cnd
Number of cells: 341
Application value: 2

Style Factor-group

Factor	Style		Application	Non-Application	Total	%
3 (6)						
c	(Response)	N	235	519	754	20
		%	31	69		
b	(Non-narrative)	N	562	1135	1697	44
		%	33	67		
a	(narrative)	N	448	798	1246	33
		%	36	64		
w	(Word List)	N	70	60	130	3
		%	54	46		
Total		N	1315	2512	3827	
		%	34	66		

Appendix 2

Age Factor-Group

Factor	Age		Application	Non-Application	Total	%
4(9) f	(below 30)	N %	849 42	1150 58	1999	52
k	(30-50)	N %	458 31	1030 69	1488	39
x	(above 50)	N %	8 2	332 98	340	9
Total		N %	1315 34	2512 66	3827	

Education Factor-Group

Factor	Education		Application	Non-Application	Total	%
5(11) 6	(high school)	N %	811 42	1116 58	1927	50
0	(no education)	N %	229 32	483 68	712	19
8	(college)	N %	177 31	401 69	578	15
9	(beyond)	N %	98 16	512 84	610	16
Total		N %	1315 34	2512 66	3827	

Appendix 2

Social class Factor-Group

Factor 6(12)	Social Class		Application	Non-Application	Total	%
1	(LMC)	N %	697 44	877 56	1574	41
a	(MMC)	N %	322 40	478 60	800	21
b	(UMC)	N %	266 28	688 72	954	25
c	(UC)	N %	30 6	469 94	499	13
Total		N %	1315 34	2512 66	3827	

Sex of interviewer Factor-Group

Factor 7(13)	Sex interviewer		Application	Non-Application	Total	%
m	(male)	N %	767 51	741 49	1508	39
f	(female)	N %	548 24	1771 76	2319	61
Total		N %	1315 34	2512 66	3827	

Appendix 2

TOTALS

	Application	Non-Application	Total
N	1315	2512	3827
%	34	66	

Group	Factor	Weight	App/Total	Input & Weight
3:	c	0.419	0.31	0.19
	b	0.484	0.33	0.23
	a	0.549	0.36	0.28
	w	0.696	0.54	0.42
4:	f	0.381	0.42	0.16
	k	0.805	0.31	0.57
	x	0.034	0.02	0.01
5:	6	0.589	0.42	0.31
	0	0.403	0.32	0.18
	8	0.531	0.31	0.27
	9	0.310	0.16	0.13
6:	l	0.683	0.44	0.41
	a	0.469	0.40	0.22
	b	0.440	0.28	0.20
	c	0.147	0.06	0.05
7:	m	0.780	0.51	0.53
	f	0.305	0.24	0.12

Total Chi-square = 1009.9139

Chi-square/cell = 2.0611

Log likelihood = -1853.362

Execution time: 9 min, 16.2 sec

Bibliography

Abdel-Jawad, Hassan. 1987. Cross-dialectal variation in Arabic: competing prestigious forms. *Language in Society*, 16: 359-368.

———1981. *Lexical and Phonological Variation in Spoken Arabic in Amman*. Ph.D. dissertation, University of Pennsylvania.

Abu-Haidar, Farida. 1989. Are Iraqi women more prestige conscious than men? Sex differences in Baghdadi Arabic. *Language in Society* 18: 471-481.

Abu-Lughod, Janet. 1971. *Cairo: 1001 Years of the City Victorious*. Princeton, NJ: Princeton University Press.

Abu-Lughod, Lila. 1988. *Veiled Sentiments: Honor and Poetry in a Bedouin Society*. Berkeley: University of California Press.

Ahmed, Leila. 1992. *Women and Gender in Islam: Historical Roots of the Modern Debate*. New Haven: Yale University Press.

Al-Ani, Salman (ed.). 1978. *Readings in Arabic Linguistics*. Indiana University Linguistics Club. Bloomington, Indiana.

———1976. The development and distribution of the Arabic sound 'qaf' in Iraq. In Al-Ani 1978.

Altoma, Salih. 1969. *The Problem of Diglossia in Arabic*. Harvard Middle Eastern Monograph Series, 21. Cambridge MA: Harvard University Press.

Anderson, Benedict. 1991. *Imagined Communities: Reflections on the Origin and Spread of Nationalism* London: Verso. [1983].

Aroian, Lois. 1983. *The Nationalization of Arabic and Islamic Education in Egypt: Dar Al-Alum and Al-Azhar*. Cairo Papers in Social Science, Vol. 6, Monograph 4. Cairo: The American University in Cairo Press.

Badawi, El-Said and M. Hinds. 1986. *Dictionary of Egyptian Arabic*. Beirut: Librairie du Liban.

Bibliography

Badawi, El-Said. 1973. *Mustawayaat al-arabiyya al-mu'aasira fi misr*. Cairo: Dar al-Ma'arif.

Badran, Margot and M. Cooke (eds.). 1990. *Opening the Gates : A Century of Arab Feminist Writing*. Bloomington: Indiana University Press.

Baer, Gabriel. 1969. *Studies in the Social History of Modern Egypt*. Chicago and London: University of Chicago Press.

Bakalla, M.H. 1983. *Arabic Linguistics: An Introduction and Bibliography*. London: Mansell.

Bakir, Muhammad. 1986. Sex differences in the approximation to standard Arabic: A case study. *Anthropological Linguistics* 28, 1: 3-10.

Barbot, Michel. 1981. *Evolution de l'arabe contemporain*.Vol 1. Bibliographie d'arabe moderne et du Levant - Introduction au parler de Damas; Vol. 2. *Les sons du parler de Damas*. Publications de la Sorbonne, Recherches 47. Paris: Maisonneuve.

——1961. Emprunts et phonologie dans les dialectes citadins Syro-libanais. *Arabica* 8: 175-188.

Beeston, Alfred. 1970. *The Arabic Language Today*. London: Hutchinson University Library.

Bell, Alan. 1984. Language style as audience design. *Language in Society* 13, 2:145-204.

Berkey, Jonathan. 1992. *The Transmission of Knowledge in Medieval Cairo: A Social History of Islamic Education*. Princeton, New Jersey: Princeton University Press.

Bhat, D.N.S. 1978. A general study of palatalization. In J. Greenberg, C. Ferguson, and E. Moravcsik (eds.), *Universals of Human Language*. Vol. 2, Phonology. Stanford: Stanford University Press.

Birkeland, Harris. 1952. *Growth and Structure of the Egyptian Arabic Dialect*. Oslo: Dybwad.

Blanc, Haim. 1974. The *nekteb-nektebu* imperfect in a variety of Cairene Arabic. *Israel Oriental Studies* 4: 206-226.

Bibliography

———1964. *Communal Dialects in Baghdad*. Cambridge: Harvard University Press.

———1960. Stylistic variation in spoken Arabic: a sample of interdialectal educated conversation. In C. Ferguson (ed.) *Contributions to Arabic Linguistics*. Harvard Middle Eastern Monograph 3. Cambridge: Harvard University Press. 78-161.

Bohas, Georges, J.P. Guillaume and D.E. Kouloughli. 1990. *The Arabic Linguistic Tradition*. New York: Routledge.

Booth, Marylin. 1992. Colloquial Arabic poetry, politics, and the press in modern Egypt. *International Journal of Middle East Studies*, 24: 419-440.

Bourdieu, Pierre. 1991. *Language and Symbolic Power*. Cambridge MA: Harvard University Press.

———1982. *Ce que parler veut dire*. Paris: Fayard.

———1977. The economics of linguistic exchanges. *Social Science Information* 16, 6: 645-668.

Bourdieu, Pierre and J.C. Passeron. 1977. *Reproduction in Education, Society and Culture*. London: Sage.

Bourdieu, Pierre and L. Boltanski. 1975. Le fetichisme de la langue. *Actes de la recherche en sciences sociales* 4: 2-32.

Broselow, Ellen. 1976. *The Phonology of Egyptian Arabic*. Ph.D. dissertation, University of Massachusetts, Amherst.

Bynon, Theodora. 1977. *Historical Linguistics*. Cambridge: Cambridge University Press.

Cachia, Pierre. 1967. The use of the colloquial in modern Arabic literature. *Journal of the American Oriental Society* 87, 1 [Reprinted in Pierre Cachia, *An overview of Modern Arabic Literature*, Islamic Surveys 17. Edinburgh, 1990].

Cantineau, Jean. 1960. Études de linguistique arabe. Mémorial Jean Cantineau: Études Arabes et Islamique, Études et documents II. Paris: Librairie C. Klincksieck.

Bibliography

———1950. Communications (A propos des sons G, K, Q dans les langues sémitique). *Bulletin Societé de Linguistique de Paris*, 46, no. 132: xxv-xxviii.

———1946. Esquisse d'une phonologie de l'arabe classique. *Bulletin Societé de Linguistique de Paris* 43, 1: 93-140.

———1939. Remarques sur les parlers des sedentaire syro-libano-palestiniens. *Bulletin Societé de Linguistique de Paris* XL, 1: 80-88.

Catford, John. 1988. *A Practical Introduction to Phonetics*. Oxford: Clarendon Press.

Caton, Steven. 1991. Diglossia in North Yemen: A case of competing linguistic communities. In A. Hudson (ed.) *Southwest Journal of Linguistics* 10, 1: 143-159.

Cedergren, Henrietta. 1973. *The Interplay of Social and Linguistic Factors in Panama*. Ph.D. dissertation, Cornell University.

Central Agency for Public Mobilization and Statistics (CAPMAS) 1978. [Cairo census of 1976] Cairo governorate, Vol. 1.

Chambers, Jack and P. Trudgill. 1980. *Dialectology*. Cambridge: Cambridge University Press.

Chejne, Anwar. 1969. *The Arabic Language: Its Role in History*. Minneapolis: University of Minnesota Press.

Coates, Jennifer and D. Cameron (eds.). 1989. *Women in Their Speech Communities*. London: Longman.

Cowan, William. 1960. *A Reconstruction of Proto-colloquial Arabic*. Ph.D. dissertation, Cornell University.

El-Dash, Linda and G. Tucker. 1975. Subjective reactions to various speech styles in Egypt. *International Journal of the Sociology of Language* 6: 33-54.

Douglas, Allen and F. Malti-Douglas. 1994. *Arab Comic Strips: Politics of an Emerging Mass Culture*. Bloomington: Indiana University Press.

Bibliography

Al-Duri, 1982. The historical roots of Arab nationalism. In K. Karpat (ed.) *Political and Social Thought in the Contemporary Middle East*. New York: Praeger. 21-27.

Early, Evelyn. 1993. *Baladi Women of Cairo. Playing with an Egg and a Stone*. Boulder: Lynne Reinner Publishers.

Eckert, Penelope and S. McConnell-Ginet. 1992. Think practically and look locally: Language and gender as community-based practice. *Annual Review of Anthropology* 21: 461-490.

Eckert, Penelope. 1989a. *Jocks and Burnouts: social categories and identity in the High School*. New York: Teachers College Press.

———1989b. The whole woman: sex and gender differences in variation. *Language Variation and Change* 1: 245-267.

Fasold, Ralph. 1987. *The Sociolinguistics of Society: Introduction to Sociolinguistics*, Volume 1. Oxford, New York: Basil Blackwell. [1984]

———1986. Linguistic analyses of three kinds. In D. Sankoff (ed.) *Diversity and Diachrony*. Current Issues in Linguistic Theory, 53. Philadelphia: John Benjamin Publishing Company. 361-366.

Ferguson, Charles. 1991. Diglossia revisited. In A. Hudson (ed.), *Southwest Journal of Linguistics* 10,1: 214-234.

———1988. Standardization as a form of language spread. In Peter H. Jowenberg (ed.) *Language Spread and Language Policy: Issues, Implications, and Case Studies*. Georgetown University Roundtable on Language and Linguistics 1987. Washington DC: Georgetown University Press. 119-132.

———1960. (ed.) *Contributions to Arabic Linguistics*. Harvard Middle Eastern Monograph 3. Cambridge: Harvard University Press.

———1959a. The Arabic Koiné, *Language* 35: 616-630.

———1959b. Diglossia. *Word* 15: 325-40.

Bibliography

———1959c. Myths about Arabic. Reprinted in J. A. Fishman (ed.) *Readings in the Sociology of Language*. 1968. The Hague: Mouton de Gruyter. 375-381.

———1957. Two problems in Arabic phonology. *Word* 13: 460-78.

Fischer, John. 1958. Social influences on the choice of a linguistic variant. *Word* 14: 47-56.

Fleisch, Henry. 1974. *Études d'arabe dialectal*. Recherches publiées sous la direction de l'Institut de Lettres Orientales de Beyrouth, Nouvelle Sèrie: A. Langue arabe et pensé Islamique 4. Beirut: Dar El-Mashreq Editeurs.

———1968. *L'Arabe Classique: Esquisse d'une structure linguistique*. New Edition. Recherches publiées sous la direction de l'Institut de Lettres Orientales de Beyrouth, Sèrie 2, Langue et Litterature Arabe, Tome V. Beirut: Dar El-Mashreq.

———1964. Arabe classique et arabe dialectal. In *Travaux et Jours* 12, 23-62.

Gal, Susan. 1979. *Language Shift: Social Determinants of Language Change in Bilingual Austria*. Academic Press, New York.

———1978. Peasant men can't get wives: Language change and sex roles in a bilingual community. *Language in Society* 7: 1-17.

Garbell, Irene. 1978. Remarks on the historical phonology of an East Mediterranean Arabic dialect. Reprinted in Al-Ani (ed.) *Readings in Arabic Linguistics*. Indiana University Linguistics Club. Bloomington, Indiana. 203-241. [1958]

Gershoni, Israel and J. Jankowski. 1986. *Egypt, Islam, and the Arabs: The Search for Egyptian Nationhood, 1900-1930*. New York: Oxford University Press.

Guy, Gregory. 1988. Language and social class. In F.J. Newmeyer (ed.) *Language: The Socio-Cultural Context*. Linguistics: The Cambridge Survey IV. Cambridge: Cambridge University Press.

———1990. The sociolinguistic types of language change. *Diachronica* VII, 1: 47-67.

Bibliography

Haeri, Niloofar. 1994. A linguistic innovation of women in Cairo. *Language Variation and Change* 6: 87-112.

———1992. Synchronic Variation in Cairene Arabic: The case of palatalization. In E. Broselow, M. Eid, and J. McCarthy (eds.), *Perspectives in Arabic Linguistics IV*. Philadelphia: John Benjamin Publishers. 169-180.

———1992. Beyond conservation and innovation: gender and negotiations of social meaning. Paper presented at NWAV-XXI, University of Michigan. Ann Arbor, Michigan.

———1991. *Sociolinguistic Variation in Cairene Arabic: Palatalization and the Qaf in the Speech of Men and Women*. Ph.D. dissertation, University of Pennsylvania.

———1989. Diglossia and the sociolinguistic variable. Paper presented at NWAV-XVII, Duke University. Durham, North Carolina.

———1987. Male/female differences in speech: an alternative interpretation. In K.M. Dennig, S. Inkelas, F.C. McNair-Knox, and J.R. Rickford (eds.), *Variation in language: NWAV-XV*. Stanford: Stanford University, Department of Linguistics. 173-182.

El-Hassan, Shahir A. 1977. Educated Spoken Arabic in Egypt and the Levant: A critical review of diglossia and related concepts, *Archivum Linguisticum* 8: 112-132.

Haugen, Einar. 1950. The analysis of linguistic borrowing. *Language* 26: 210-231.

Herbolich, James B. 1979. Attitudes of Egyptians toward various Arabic vernaculars. *Lingua* 47: 301-321.

Heyworth-Dunn, James. 1968. *An Introduction to the History of Education in Modern Egypt*. London: Frank Case and Co. [1939].

Hoenigswald, Henry. 1960. *Language Change and Linguistic Reconstruction*. Chicago: University of Chicago Press.

Bibliography

Holes, Clive. 1987. *Language Variation and Change in a Modernising Arab State: The Case of Bahrain*. London, New York: Kegan Paul International.

———1983. Patterns of communal language variation in Bahrain. *Language in Society* 12: 433-457.

Holmes, Janet. 1992. *An Introduction to Sociolinguistics*. London: Longman.

Hourani, Albert. 1991. *A History of the Arab Peoples*. Cambridge: The Belknap Press of Harvard University Press.

Hussein, Taha. 1954. *The Future of Culture in Egypt*. Washington, DC: American Council of Learned Societies. [1944]

Hussein, Riyad F. and Nasser El-Ali. 1989. Subjective reactions of rural university students towards different varieties of Arabic. *Al-Arabiyya* 22: 37-54.

Ibrahim, Muhammad. 1989. Communicating in Arabic: Problems and prospects. In F. Coulmas (ed.) *Language Adaptation*. Cambridge: Cambridge University Press.

———1986. Standard and prestige language: A problem in Arabic sociolinguistics. *Anthropological Linguistics* 28: 115-126.

———1983. Linguistic distance and literacy in Arabic. *Journal of Pragmatics* 7: 507-515.

Al-Jehani, Nasir Muhammad. 1985. *Sociostylistic Stratification of Arabic in Makkah*. Ph.D. dissertation, University of Michigan.

Kahane, Henry. 1986. A typology of the prestige language. *Language* 62: 495-508.

Kahn, Margaret. 1975. Arabic emphatics: the evidence for cultural determinants of phonetic sex-typing. *Phonetica* 31: 38-50.

Karmiloff-Smith, Annette. 1981. The Grammatical marking of thematic structure in the development of language production. In W. Deutsch (ed.), *The Child's Construction of Language*. London: Academic Press. 121-147.

Bibliography

Kay, Allen. 1972. Remarks on diglossia in Arabic: well-defined vs. ill-defined, *Linguistics* 81: 32-48.

Keane, Webb. 1995. The spoken house: Text, act, and object in eastern Indonesia. *American Ethnologist* 22, 1: 102-124.

Keating, Patricia. 1988a. Palatals as complex segments: X-ray evidence. *UCLA Working Papers in Phonetics*, Vol. 69.

Keating, Patricia. 1988b. A survey of phonological features. Distributed by the Indiana University Linguistics Club.

Khalidi, Rashid, L. Anderson, M. Muslih, and R. Simon. 1991. (eds.), *The Origins of Arab Nationalism*. New York: Columbia University Press.

Kojak, W. 1983. Language and Sex: A Case Study of a Group of Educated Syrian Speakers of Arabic. M.A. thesis, University of Lancaster.

Kroch, Anthony. 1978. Toward a theory of social dialect variation. *Language in Society* 7: 17-36.

Labov, William. 1994. *Principles of Linguistic Change: Internal Factors*. Oxford UK & Cambridge USA: Blackwell.

———1990. The intersection of sex and social class in the course of linguistic change. *Language Variation and Change* 2, 2: 205-254.

———1984. Field methods of the project on linguistic change and variation. In J. Baugh, and J. Sherzer (eds.), *Language in Use*. Englewood Cliffs: Prentice Hall. 28-53.

———1982. Building on empirical foundations. In W. Lehmann, and Y. Malkiel (eds.), *Perspectives on Historical Linguistics, Current Issues in Linguistic Theory*, Vol. 24. Amsterdam, Philadelphia: John Benjamin Publishers. 17-92.

———1981. Field methods used by the project on linguistic change and variation. *Sociolinguistic Working Paper 81*. Austen, Texas: South Western Educational Development Laboratory.

———1980. The social origins of sound change. In W. Labov (ed.) *Locating Language in Time and Space*. New York: Academic Press. 251-266.

———1972. *Sociolinguistic Patterns*. Philadelphia: University of Pennsylvania Press.

———1971. Some principles of linguistic methodology. *Language in Society* 1: 97-120.

———1966. *The social stratification of English in New York City*. Washington, DC: Center for Applied Linguistics.

Ladefoged, Peter. 1975. *A Course in Phonetics*. New York: Harcourt Brace Jovanovich.

Lambert, Wallace, R. Hodgson, R. Gardner, and S. Fillenbaum. 1960. Evaluational reactions to spoken language. *Journal of Abnormal Psychology* 60 (1): 44-51.

Lehiste, Ilse. 1988. *Lectures on Languages in Contact*. Cambridge MA: MIT Press.

Leith, Dick. 1987. *A Social History of English*. London and New York: Routledge and Kegan Paul. [1983]

Mahmoud, Youssef. 1986. Arabic after diglossia. In J. Fishman, A. Tabouret-Keller, M. Clyne, B. Krishnamurti, and M. Abdulaziz (eds.), *The Fergusonian Impact: In Honor of Charles A. Ferguson*, Vol. 1. Berlin, New York, Amsterdam: Mouton de Gruyter. 239-251.

Malkiel, Yakov. 1984. A linguist's view of the standardization of a dialect. In Aldo Scaglione (ed.), *National Languages*. Ravenna: Longo Editore.

Marçais, William. 1930. La diglossie Arab. *L'enseignement Public* 97: 401-409.

Matthews, Roderic and Matta Akrawi. 1949. *Education in Arab countries of the Near East*. Washington, DC: American council on Education.

Meiseles, Gustav. 1980. Educated spoken Arabic and the Arabic language continuum. *Archivum Linguisticum* 11: 118-143.

El-Messiri, Sawsan. 1978. *Ibn al-Balad: The Concept of Egyptian Identity*. Leiden: E.J. Brill.

Bibliography

Meyers-Scotton, Carol. 1993. *Social Motivations for Codeswitching: Evidence from Africa.* Oxford: Clarendon Press.

Milroy, Lesley and James Milroy. 1992. Social network and social class: Toward an integrated sociolinguistic model. *Language in Society* 21: 1-26.

Milroy, Lesley. 1987. *Observing and Analyzing Natural Language.* Oxford: Basil Blackwell.

———1980. *Language and Social Networks.* Oxford: Basil Blackwell.

Mitchell, Terence F. 1990. *Pronouncing Arabic I.* Oxford: Clarendon Press.

———1986. What is educated spoken Arabic? In B.H. Jernudd & M.H. Ibrahim (eds.), Issues in Arabic sociolinguistics. *International Journal of the Sociology of Language* 61: 7-32.

———1982. More than a matter of 'writing with the learned, pronouncing with the vulgar': some preliminary observations on the Arabic koiné. In W. Haas (ed.), *Standard Languages Spoken and Written.* Manchester: Manchester University Press. 123-155.

———1980. Dimension of style in a grammar of educated spoken Arabic. *Archivum Linguisticum* 11: 89-106.

———1956. *An Introduction to Egyptian Colloquial Arabic.* London: Oxford University Press.

Al- Muhannadi, Munira. 1991. *A Sociolinguistic Study of Women's Speech in Qatar.* Ph.D dissertation, University of Essex.

Nader, Laura. 1962. A note on attitudes and the use of language. *Anthropological Linguistics* IV: 24-29.

Nelson, Cynthia. 1974. Public and private politics: Women in the Middle Eastern world. *American Ethnologist* 1, 3: 551-563.

Nichols, Patricia. 1983. Linguistic options and choices for black women in the rural South. In B. Thorne, C. Kramarae, and N. Henley (eds.), *Language, Gender, and Society.* Rowly MA: Newbury House. 54-68.

Nyrop, R.F. 1982. *Egypt: A Country Study*. Washington, DC: U.S. Government Printing Office.

Ohala, John. 1981. Listener as a source of sound change. In C. S. Masek, R. A. Hendrick and M.F. Miller (eds.), *Papers from the Parasession on Language and Behavior*. Chicago Linguistic Society. 178-203.

Owens, Jonathan. and R. Bani-Yasin. 1987. The lexical basis of variation in Jordanian Arabic. *Linguistics* 25, 4: 705-738.

Owens, Jonathan. 1990. *Early Arabic Grammatical Theory: Heterogeneity and Standardization*. Studies in the History of the Language Sciences, 53. Philadelphia: John Benjamin Publishing Company.

Parkinson, Dilworth. 1991. Searching for modern fusha: Real life formal Arabic. *Al-Arabiyya* 24: 31-64.

Poplack, Shana, D. Sankoff and C. Miller. 1988. Borrowing: The social correlates and linguistic processes of lexical borrowing and assimilation. *Linguistics* 26: 47-104.

Rand, David and D. Sankoff. 1990. GoldVarb Version 2: A Variable Rule Application for the Macintosh. Distributed by Centre de recherche mathématiques, Université de Montréal.

Reid, Donald M. 1990. *Cairo University and the Making of Modern Egypt*. Cambridge: Cambridge University Press.

Rosaldo, Michelle and L. Lamphere (eds.), 1974. *Woman, culture and society*. Stanford: Stanford University Press.

Royal, Ann-Marie. 1985. *Male/Female Pharyngealization Patterns in Cairo Arabic: A Sociolinguistic Study of Two Neighborhoods*. Texas Linguistics Forum 27. Austin: University of Texas.

Sallam, A. M. 1980. Phonological variation in Educated Spoken Arabic: A study of the uvular and related plosive types. *Bulletin of the School of Oriental and African Studies*. 43, 1.

Sankoff, Gillian. 1980. *The Social Life of Language*. Philadelphia: University of Pennsylvania Press.

Bibliography

Sankoff, David and S. Laberge. 1978. The linguistic market and the statistical explanation of variability. In D. Sankoff (ed.), *Linguistic Variation: Models and Methods*. New York: Academic Press.

Sawaie, Muhammad. 1987. Speakers' attitudes toward linguistic variation: A case study of some Arabic dialects. *Linguistische Berichte* 107, Westdeutscher Verlag. 3-22.

Schmidt, Richard. 1986. Applied sociolinguistics: The case of Arabic as a second language. B. Jernudd and M. Ibrahim (eds.), *Anthropological Linguistics* 28: 55-72.

——1974. *Sociolinguistic Variation in Spoken Arabic in Egypt: A Reexamination of the Concept of Diglossia*. Ph.D. dissertation, Brown University.

Schultz, Eugene. 1981. *Diglossia and Variation in Formal Spoken Arabic in Egypt*. Ph.D. dissertation, University of Wisconsin-Madison.

Seckinger, Beverly. 1988. Implementing Morocco's Arabization policy: Two problems of classification. In F. Coulmas (ed.), *With Forked Tongues: What Are National Languages Good for?* Ann Arbor: Karoma.

Shaklee, M. 1980. The rise of Standard English. In T. Shopen and J. Williams (eds.), *Standards and dialects in English*. Cambridge MA: Winthrop Publishers.

Shorrab, Ghazi. 1981. *Models of Socially Significant Linguistic Variation: The Case of Palestinian Arabic*. Ph.D dissertation, State University of New York at Buffalo.

Shouby, E. 1951. The influence of the Arabic language on the psychology of the Arabs. *The Middle East Journal* 5: 284-302.

Stevens, Paul. 1983. Ambivalence, modernization and language attitudes: French and Arabic in Tunisia. *Journal of Multilingual and Multicultural Development*. 4: 101-114.

Tignor, Robert. 1982. Equity in Egypt's recent past: 1945-1952. In G. Abdel Khalek and R. Tignor (eds.), *The Political Economy of Income distribution in Egypt*. New York : Holmes & Meier.

Bibliography

El-Tonsi, Abbas and Kristen Brustad. 1981. *An Advanced Reader in Egyptian Colloquial Arabic*. Part one. Cairo: American University Center for Arabic Studies.

Trubetzkoy, Nikolai. 1969. *Principles of Phonology*. Berkeley: University of California Press. [1939]

Trudgill, Peter. 1986. *Dialects in Contact*. Oxford: Blackwell.

———1983. *On Dialect: Social and Geographical Perspectives*. New York: New York University Press.

———1974. *The Social Differentiation of English in Norwich*. Cambridge: Cambridge University Press.

———1972. Sex, covert prestige and linguistic change. *Language in Society* 1: 79-95.

Tucker, Judith. 1985. *Women in Nineteenth Century Egypt*. Cambridge: Cambridge University Press.

Vatikiotis, Panayiotis. 1991. *The History of Modern Egypt from Muhammad Ali to Mubarak*. Baltimore: Johns Hopkins University Press. 4th edition.

Versteegh, Kees. 1984. *Pidginization and Creolization: The Case of Arabic*. Current Issues in Linguistic Theory, Vol. 33. Philadelphia: John Benjamin.

Wahba, Kassem. 1991. An acoustic study of vowel variation in colloquial Egyptian Arabic. Paper presented at the Fifth Annual Symposium of Arabic Linguistics. Ann Arbor, Michigan.

Walters, Keith. 1989. *Social Change and Linguistic Variation in Korba, a Small Tunisian Town*. Ph. D. dissertation, University of Texas, Austin.

Weinreich, Uriel. 1974. *Languages in Contact*. The Hague: Mouton Publishers. [1954].

Weinreich, Uriel, W. Labov and M. Herzog. 1968. Empirical foundations for a theory of language change. In W. Lehmann and J. Malkiel (eds.), *Directions for Historical Linguistics*. Austin: University of Texas Press.

Williams, Glyn. 1992. *Sociolinguistics. A Sociological Critique*. New York: Routledge.

Woolard, Katherine. 1989. *Double Talk: Bilingualism and the Politics of Ethnicity in Catalonia*. Stanford: Stanford University Press.

———1985. Language variation and cultural hegemony: Toward an integration of sociolinguistic and social theory. *American Ethnologist* 12, 4: 734-748.

Za'rour, George I. and Rwadah Z. Nasif. 1977. Attitudes towards the language of science teaching at the secondary level in Jordan. *Linguistics* 198: 109-118.

Zughoul, Muhammad Raji and L. Taminian. 1984. The linguistic attitudes of Arab students: factoral structure and intervening variables. *International Journal of the Sociology of Language* 50: 155-179.

Index

Abdel-Jawad 1, 13, 121, 122, 147, 171, 175
Abu-Lughod, J. 20, 21
Abu-Lughod, L. 24
Al-Ani 115, 116
Al-Azhar 7, 167
Al-Muhannadi 125
Altoma 1, 170, 219
Arabic dialectologists 172-174
Aramaic 113
Aroian 133
Badawi 136
Badawi and Hinds 56, 135, 240
Baer 168
Bakir 146, 171
Barbot 109, 111, 112, 113
Bhat 45-47, 61, 63
Birkeland 108, 112
Blanc 60, 71, 114, 116
Borrowings,
    and kind of education 165
    as change from above 184
    compared to French 130
    integration of 16
Bourdieu 6, 160-161, 163
Broselow 60, 62
Cachia 193
Cairene phonology,
    and qaf 138
    syllable stress 60
    vowel height 58-60
    word boundary 61
Cairo,
    safety of 22
Cantineau 108, 109, 110, 111, 113
Caton 5
Cedergren 82
Chambers and Trudgill 94, 174
change in progress,
    and style patterns 73, 85
    and variation in meaning 94
Chejne 8, 155, 193
child language,
    elicitation of qaf 140
childhood games 29
Classical Arabic,
    ambivalent feelings towards 200
    and reading-writing elites 7
    as lingua franca 7
    as "standard" variety 167
    compared to English 167, 168
    contact with 7
    domains 8-9
    in mass education 105
    language of the public domain 175
    "likeability" of its speakers 196
    public corrections of 214

Index

    prestige of 115
    religious functions 182
    teachers of 196
    textual authority 3, 167
coinages 127
Cowan 107
diglossia,
    and actual language use 5
    and contact between varieties 104, 238
    and functional differentiation 5
diglossic variables 156
dissimilation 53, 62
domains of language use,
    and class 180
    and men's occupations 181
    and women's occupations 177
    public and private 175
doublets 127
Eckert 2, 68
Eckert and McConnell-Ginet 92, 93
Educated Spoken Arabic,
    and social context 232
    and variability 234
education,
    and knowledge of Classical Arabic 165
    and labor markets 165
    and production of linguistic values 166
    private schools 83, 162, 163
    public schools 83
    two systems of 165
Egyptian Arabic,
    ambivalent feelings towards 200
    dialect of Cairo 169
    domains 8-9
    language of public domain 176
    maSri 200
    movies 9, 20
    positive views on 203
    scope of variability 226
    "standard" Cairene 170, 171
    television 9
    Upper Egyptian 203
El-Dash and Tucker 194, 196
El-Hassan 14, 75, 239
El-Messiri 217
Fasold 239
Ferguson 15, 108, 112, 127, 170, 219, 239
Fernández 238
Fleisch 113, 114
French 64
Gal 189
Garbell 105, 106, 109, 113
Gershoni and Jankowski 8, 185
Guy 95, 228

Index

Haugen 14, 129, 132
Heath 226
Herbolich 194, 196, 211
Heyworth-Dunn 8, 133
Holes 115, 118, 124, 137, 218
Hourani 8
Hudson 238
Hussein 185, 201
Hussein and El-Ali 197
Ibrahim 115, 166, 170
ideology,
    (r) in New York 187
    and gender differences 189
    and linguistic behavior 184, 186
    and self-reports 184
    and use of questionnaires 194
    men on Classical Arabic 185-187
interviews,
    use of assistants 26
Jordan,
    teaching of science 197
Kahn 56
Keating 45-47, 55
Kroch 95, 228
Labov 168, 175, 184, 68, 92, 95, 228
language change,
    and Arabic dialectologists
        172-174
    and ideology 189
    morpho-semantic congruity 121
    summary of features 229
Leith 167
linguistic market,
    and global economy 6
    and the labor market 163
    and the official variety 163
    defined 6
Mahfouz 193
Meiseles 15
men's linguistic behavior,
    and palatalization 97
    and religious practices 182-183
    individuals 96
    working class men 95
Milroy and Milroy 2, 95
Milroy, L. 2, 95, 160
Mitchell 13, 59, 211, 232
Modern Standard Arabic 18, 115
morpho-semantic congruity 124
Nader 223
Ohala 62
Owens and Bani-Yasin 123
Parkinson 214, 236--237
pharyngealization 55, 57, 222
Poplack, Sankoff and Miller 130
qaf,
    and phonological variation 106
    as change from above 184

Index

hypercorrection of 122
in Amman 121, 133, 147, 148
in Baghdad 116
in Bahrain 124
in Basra 116
in daily prayers 103
in Doha city 125
in names 133
in Palestinian Arabic 120
in sedentary dialects 108, 110
Irbid 198-199
"Q-Colloquialization" 118, 120, 125
"Q-Standardization" 121, 125
reversal of merger 122
social evaluations of 114
Rosaldo and Lamphere 175
Royal 55, 162, 171, 218, 221, 222
Sallam 120
Sawaie 162, 197, 198, 199
Schmidt 1, 118, 119, 120, 162, 171
Schultz 120
Shorrab 120, 171
social class,
    and Classical Arabic 164
    and Egyptian Arabic 170
    and knowledge of foreign
        languages 161
    and occupation 163
    and "standard" variants 152
    linguistic innovations of 227
    linguistic insecurity of 162
    relation to the "standard" 160, 162
social meaning,
    and individual behavior 95-100
    and social awareness 80
    and sociolinguistic theory 4, 5, 91-100
    of "non-standard" forms 93, 97
    of changes in progress 79, 93
    of qaf 155
    of stable variables 93
sociolinguistic theory,
    and change in progress 11
    and conservative behavior 10
    and stable variation 10
    and "standard" variety 10
    and the evaluation problem 92
    and the transition problem 92
    and variation in meaning 94
Stevens 198
style,
    coding of 69
stylistic variation,
    and women 75
    "Educated Spoken Arabic" 13-14
    "Levels" of Arabic 16-17

conceptualization of 12-17
 style patterns 86
subjective reaction test 32-33
Trubetzkoy 103
Trudgill 94
Vatikiotis 8
vernacular, the 3, 106
Versteegh 112
Wahba 61
Weinreich 129
Weinreich, Labov, and Herzog 92, 174, 188
Williams 160
women's linguistic behavior,
 and religious practices 181-183
 "conservative tendency" of 176
 as controversy in sociolinguistics 169
 "paradox" in 4
 reformulation of 170
 reversal of the patterns 147, 172
Woolard 193
Word List 28, 31, 76
Za'rour and Nashif 197
Zughoul and Taminian 197

Glossary of Technical Terms

affrication	الانفجار الاحتكاكي
backing	التخليف
continuum	سلسلة متصلة
diachronic	تاريخي
dialect	لهجة
dialectal	لهجي
diglossic variable	المتغير المتعلق بالازدواجية
feature	ملمح (لغوي)
frication	احتكاك
fricative	صوت احتكاكي
fronting	التقديم (تحرك الصوائت من موقع خلفي الى موقع امامي)
high vowel	حركة مرتفعة
innovation	التجديد
interdental consonant	صامت ينطق بين الاسنان
merger	الاندماج
morphosemantic congruity	درجة التوافق الشكلي والمعنوي بين كلمة في اللغة الدارجة ونظائرها بالفصحى
palatalization	التّحنيك
pharyngealization	اطباق (الحروف)

phoneme	الفونيم/الوحدة الصوتية الوضيفة
phonetic	فوناتيكي
phonology	الفونولوجيا
social meaning	المعنى الاجتماعي
sociolinguistics	علم اللغة الاجتماعية
standard language/variety	اللغة القياسي
stigmatized	موصوم
stop consonant	انفجاري
stylistic variation	التغيُّر الاسلوبي
synchronic	وصفي
uvular	لهوي
variant	شكل لغوي يختلف عن شكل ثاني يشابهه اللغوي و الاجتماعي في المعنى او الوضيفة
variable	المتغيُّر
vowel height	ارتفاع الحركات

تطبيق نظريات ومناهج طورت لمجموعات المتخاطبين في مدينة كنيويورك مثلاً على مجموعات المتخاطبين في مدينة القاهرة. وبوسعنا أن نتساءل ما اذا كانت التشكيلات القياسيّة لمختلف مجموعات التخاطب يمكن مقارنتها ببعضها البعض بصورة مباشرة كوحدات تاريخيّة اجتماعيّة. والجواب الموجز هو انه يجب ان لا نفترض قابليّة المقارنة هذه، بل يجب بحثها ودرسها بالنسبة الى خاصيّات كل مجموعة من مجموعات التخاطب.

في الفصل الأول بحثت عدداً من القضايا المنهجيّة والنظريّة التي تتناولها هذه الدراسة. وفي الفصل الثاني قدّمت وصفا للنهج العلمي الذي استخدمته، وقسمت الفصل الثالث الى قسمين قدّمت في الأوّل منهما تحليلاً لغويا مفصّلاً لموضوع النطق حنكيّاً، وفي الثاني قمت بتحليل تأثير العوامل الاجتماعيّة في موضوع النطق حنكيّاً، وذلك عن طريق بيانات مقداريّة. أمّا الفصل الرابع فقد كرّسته لاستعمال "القاف" التي تُستعمل في اللغة العربيّة الفصحى، وأجريتُ فيه تحليلاً تاريخيا أتبعتُه بتحليل لغوي تزامني، ثم قمتُ بدراسة لاستعمال "القاف" من قبل المجموعات الاجتماعيّة المختلفة، وذلك في النصف الاخير من الفصل الرابع نفسه. وفي هذا الفصل أيضا قدّمتُ عرضا لتجربة تتعلّق بوجود "القاف" في لغة الاطفال. وأمّا الفصل الخامس فقد وقفتُ على البحث عن تفسيرات و إيضاحات الأنماط المقدّمة في الفصول السابقة، وفي قلب هذا البحث تحليل لدور مدارس اللغات الخاصة وللفروق بين طلاب هذه المدارس والطلاب الذين يتلقون تعليمهم في المدارس الحكوميّة، يشتمل الفصل السادس على دراسة لآراء المتخاطبين القاهريين ومواقفهم في ما يتعلّق بالعربيّة الفصحى والعربية المصريّة. أمّا الفصل الأخير فهو عبارة عن ملخّص لسُبُل البحث في المستقبل وتأملات في هذه السُبُل.

قُبيل انتهاء عملي الدراسي كطالبة للدراسات العليا في قسم علم اللغة في جامعة بنسيلڤانيا قرّرتُ ان أتناول في رسالة الدكتوراه موضوعا يتصّل باللغة العربيّة وليس باللغة الفارسيّة التي هي لغتي الأم. وكان لهذا القرار أسباب كثيرة منها اهتمامي الشديد بالتعرف على أجزاء أخرى من الشرق الأوسط وفهمها. ولقد أثبتت تجاربي في ايران و مصر الحاجة الى مثل هذا الاهتمام، ذلك انه يبدو ان المصريين والايرانيين يعرفون عن اوروبا والولايات المتحدة اكثر بكثير مما يعرفون عن بعضهم البعض، غير ان هناك قوة ثقافيّة يمكن تحقيقها عن طريق تعميق الوعي والاهتمام المتبادَلين. و هذه الدراسة، وهي ليست سوى صورة معدّلة لرسالتي للدكتوراه، إنما قصدتُ بها ان تكون إسهاما متواضعا في سبيل تحقيق هذا الهدف.

نيلوفر حائري

جامعة جونز هوبكينز

التغيّر في لهجة القاهرة المعاصرة: دراسة في اللسانيات العربية

اذا قمت بجولة في مدينة القاهرة، عبر الأسواق والمقاهي والمكاتب والجامعات والمساجد، طرقت أسماعك لغات ولهجات متعددة، وأتاح لك أذان المؤذن، ذو الوقع المؤثر باللغة العربية الفصحى، فترة قصيرة تُريحك من الجلبة واللّغط اللذين تشتهر بهما مدينة القاهرة، وأمكنك سماع اللهجات المحلية لمصر العليا التي يتخاطب بها البوّابون وهم يحتسون الشاي ويتحدثون امام العمارات التي يحرسونها. واللغة العربية القاهرية، محصوبة أو غير محصوبة برنين اللغة الفصحى، مع اللغة اليونانية أو الفرنسية أو الانكليزية، هي، من بين لغات أخرى لا تُحصى، وسيلة التخاطب والتعامل اليوميين لسكان مدينة القاهرة، ومن هنا فان الدراسة اللغوية الاجتماعية لهذه المدينة توفر لطلاب اللغة تحديات رائعة.

يهدف البحث الحاليّ الى الربط بين عدد من الدراسات التي أجريت في ميداني علم اللغة الاجتماعي (لابوف ١٩٦٦، ١٩٧٢)، وعلم اجتماع اللغة (بورديو ١٩٧٧، ١٩٩١)، ودراسات ميدان علم اللغة الاجتماعي في اللغة العربية (الطعمة ١٩٦٩، بَدوي ١٩٧٢، شمدت ١٩٧٤، عبدالجواد ١٩٨١، هولز ١٩٨٧)، تتضمن ايضا موضوع الازدواجية اللغوية وذلك في محاولة لمواجهة بعض من هذه التحديات. ولذلك شرعتُ في رسم صورة دقيقة لنواحي الوضع اللغوي الاجتماعي المعقد في القاهرة، ذلك الوضع الذي يطرح أسئلة تتعلق بالشكل الأسلوبي، من مثل الموارد الأسلوبية التي يستخدمها القاهريون في كلامهم، وهل هناك موارد مستعمَدَّة من العربية القاهرية، ومن اللغة العربية الفصحى في الوقت نفسه، وما هي العوامل الاجتماعية التي تؤثر في الاختيار من بين هذه الأشكال وفي تكرار استعمالها. وللاجابة عن هذه الأسئلة أجريت تحليلاً للمفردات التي تشتمل على صوت "القاف"، وكذلك للنطق الحنكي الذي هو المصدر الأسلوبي للّغة العربية القاهرية التي تظهر بصورة أوضح في كلام النساء.

وقد بدأتُ العمل الميداني لهذه الدراسة باستكشاف دور الجنس (من حيث الذكورة والانوثة) في استعمال اللغة العربية الفصحى وغير الفصحى في مدينة القاهرة. وفي تقديري ان هذه الخطوة كانت مثمرة لعدد من الأسباب، ذلك أن نظرة الى دور الجنس في الاطار المتغيّر تجربنا بالضرورة على استخدام فكرة التشكيلات اللغوية الاجتماعية "القياسية" و "المحافظة"، وذلك لتصوير أو وصف كلام مجموعات المخاطبين إزاء بعضهم بعضا. وهذه الفكرة تؤدّي الى بعض التحليل الطبقي الاجتماعي، كما أنّ مسألة الطبقية تعرض، بدورها، ومن بين قضايا أخرى كثيرة، قضية الحركية الاجتماعية التي تطرح التعليم كعامل تركّز عليه الأضواء الكشّافة. وهكذا فإن بحثا قوامه الدور الذي يقوم به الجنس، والطبقة الاجتماعية، والتربية، في الوضع الاجتماعي اللغوي في مدينة القاهرة، يشكّل الهدف الرئيسي لهذه الدراسة. غير ان هناك صعوبات يواجهها الباحث في

تقديم

لقد قطعت اللسانيات العربية الاجتماعية (Arabic Sociolinguistics) شوطاً كبيراً منذ أوائل الثمانينات، عندما ظهرت لأول مرة دراسات تعالج مسألة ارتباط التطور الاجتماعي والتغير اللغوي في العالم العربي. فقبل تلك الفترة كانت دراسة ما يُسمى بـ «اللغة العربية غير القياسية» (non-Standard Arabic) تقتصر على أبحاث في اللهجات الدارجة الاقليمية. وكان غرض معظم هذه الدراسات إما تاريخياً (لتمحيص العلاقة بين اللهجات المعاصرة والفصحى القديمة مثلاً) أو ثقافياً (لتسليط الضوء على أصول الشعر النبطي على سبيل المثال، أو على الآداب الشعبية بصورة عامة). ولكن مع ظهور حركة تطوير منهج علمي جديد، وهي الحركة التي قادها اللغوي الأمريكي المشهور «وليام لابوف»، بدأ اللغويون المختصون باللغة العربية الحديثة يوجهون نظرهم إلى أهمية عامل التراوح الاسلوبي والطبقي (Stylistic and Social Variation) في المجتمعات العربية المعاصرة. والجدير بالذكر في هذا الصدد أن زملاءهم المختصين باللغات الغربية كانوا قد سبقوهم في ذلك بما يقارب عشرين عاماً. ولا يخفى على القارئ أن التراوح اللغوي عامل اجتماعي كان موجوداً في كل مكان وزمان عبر التاريخ البشري، إلا أنه لم يكن يحوز انتباه المختصين باللغة العربية حتى الآونة الأخيرة. ففضل هؤلاء تركيز انتباههم إلى «الناطقين باللهجة الصرفة» ("pure dialect speakers") على حد قولهم - أي الكبار في السن بشكل عام، وغير المثقفين منهم بشكل خاص - ولكن خلال السنوات الخمس والعشرين الماضية، تمّ تنفيذ الكثير من الأبحاث الميدانية حول التراوح اللغوي في العالم العربي المعاصر، ولا حاجة للقول إن معظم هذه الدراسات تمت في المراكز السكانية الرئيسية في المشرق العربي. ومع أن البحث الذي تقدمه الدكتورة نيلوفر حائري هنا يتبع المنهج الذي ابتكره وليام لابوف، إلا أنه بعيد كل البعد عن تطبيق غير حسّاس لنظرياته. فالدكتورة نيلوفر تأخذ بعين الاعتبار الخلفية الاجتماعية المحلية وتأثيراتها على موضوع بحثها، كما تعالج السياق اللغوي العام الذي تندرج فيه القاهرة معالجة كاملة ودقيقة.

والبحث الذي بين يدي القارئ يمثل مساهمة قيّمة في ميدان الدراسات العربية الخاصة بالتراوح اللغوي الحديث، وهي دراسات تزداد أهميتها يوماً بعد يوم، كما يشكل مساهمة مهمة في دراسة العلاقة بين اللغة والجنس.

الدكتور كلايف هولز

الكتاب الثالث عشر

التغير في لهجة القاهرة المعاصرة:
دراسة في اللسانيات العربية

تأليف
الدكتورة نيلوفر حائري

مؤسسة كيغان بول العالمية
لندن ـ نيويورك
1418 هـ/ 1996 م

مكتبة اللسانيات العربية

هيئة التحرير
محمد حسن باكلاً
جامعة الملك سعود، الرياض، المملكة العربية السعودية
بروس أنغام
مركز الدراسات الشرقية والافريقية، جامعة لندن
كلايف هولز
كلية مودلن، جامعة اكسفورد

هيئة التحرير الاستشارية
بيتر فؤاد عبود، جامعة تكساس في هيوستن، الولايات المتحدة الأمريكية؛ محمد حسن عبدالعزيز، جامعة نيروبي؛ يوسف الخليفة أبو بكر، جامعة الخرطوم؛ صالح جواد الطعمة، جامعة انديانا؛ ارنه امبروس، جامعة فيينا؛ السعيد محمد بدوي، الجامعة الأمريكية في القاهرة؛ مايكل جي. كارتر، جامعة نيويورك؛ أحمد الضبيب، جامعة الملك سعود (جامعة الرياض سابقاً)؛ مارتن فورستنر، جامعة أوتبرغ في مينز؛ اوتو ياسترو، جامعة هيدلبرغ؛ رجا توفيق نصر، الكلية الجامعية في بيروت؛ سي. إتش. إم. فيرستيغ، الجامعة الكاثوليكية في نيميخن؛ بوغوسلاف آر. زغوريسكي، جامعة وارسو.

مكتبة اللسانيات العربية
دراسات في لهجات شمال شرقي الجزيرة العربية: بروس انغام
دراسة التعدية والسببية والبناء للمجهول: جورج نعمة سعد
اللغة والاصول اللغوية في البحرين دراسة في لهجة البحارنة العربية: مهدي عبدالله التاجر
دراسة لغوية عن تطور المصطلحات العلمية في اللغة العربية: عبدالصاحب مهدي علي
التغير اللغوي في دولة عربية متطورة: كلايف هولز
لهجات المملكة العربية السعودية: ثيودور بروخاسكا الابن
الاختلاط اللغوي في اللهجة العربية المغربية: جيفري هيث
سيبويه عالم الأصوات: ايه. ايه. الناصر
تطور نظام الأفعال في اللغة العربية الدارجة: تي. إف. ميشال وشاهر الحسان
اللغة العربية في صقلية: ديونيسيوس أجيوس

التغير في لهجة القاهرة المعاصرة:
دراسة في اللسانيات العربية

مكتبة اللسانيات العربية

الحمد لله وحده . والصلاة والسلام على من لا نبي بعده . أما بعد : فإن هنالك أسباباً عدة دعت إلى إنشاء هذه السلسلة من الكتب في حقل اللسانيات والصوتيات العربية.

أولاً : إن هذا الحقل يمر بتطور سريع في إطار الدراسات اللغوية المعاصرة. كما أن كثيراً من الجامعات العربية والغربية قد بدأت تدخل علم اللسانيات وعلم الصوتيات وبعض العلوم اللغوية الحديثة ضمن مواد التدريس بها. بالإضافة إلى الإهتمام المتزايد في الدوائر اللغوية العالمية بهذا الميدان.

ثانياً : ومع ازدياد الاهتمام بالدراسات اللسانية والصوتية العربية بدأت تصل هذه الدراسات إلى مرحلة مظلمة في النضوج ليست مستفيدة من معطيات علم اللسانيات العام والعلوم الأخرى النسبة فحسب. بل وأيضاً من معطيات الدراسات اللغوية العربية القديمة.

ثالثاً : بدأت تظهر في حقل اللسانيات العربية فروع ونظريات مختلفة تشمل الصوتيات والفونولوجيا والنحو والدلالة ، وعلم اللغة النفسي، وعلم اللغة الاجتماعي، وعلم اللهجات العربية، وصناعة المعاجم، ودراسة المفردات. وتدريس العربية أو تعلمها كلغة أولى أو ثانية أو أجنبية. وعلم الاتصال. وعلم الإشارات اللغوي. ودراسة المصطلحات. والترجمة. والترجمة الآلية ، وعلم اللغة الإحصائي. وعلم اللغة الرياضي. وتاريخ العلوم العربية العربية. وما إلى ذلك.

بإضافة إلى هذا كله أن الإقبال على اللغة العربية دراسة وتدريساً وبحثاً يزداد يوماً بعد يوم على الصعيدين المحلي والدولي. ولما لم يكن هنالك منبر يرتفع من نداء لغة الضاد وتعلو من أصوات الباحثين والمتخصصين فيها لنا وجدت ` مكتبة ` اللسانيات العربية`، لتسد هذا الفراغ الكبير والفجوة العميقة وتتلح بالبحث اللغوي العربي قدماً إلى الأمام خدمة للغة القرآن الكريم والتراث العربي الأصيل ، وسيراً بالبحث اللساني العربي للحاق بركب اللسانيات العامة المتقدم. وإثراءً للدراسات اللغوية واللسانية العربية.

وتحرص هذه السلسلة العلمية على تقديم الجديد من البحث اللغوي وإعطاء الفرصة للباحثين من العرب وغيرهم للمشاركة في بناء صرح اللسانيات العربية حتى تسعد الدراسات اللغوية بمجدها الماضي العريق.

ولأن هذه السلسلة تعد الأولى من نوعها في الدراسات اللسانية العربية المتخصصة. فإننا نهيب بكل باحث متخصص في مجال اللسانيات العربية بمختلف فروعها النظرية منها والتطبيقية أن يشارك بجهوده وأفكاره وأبحاثه وألا ينجل بتقديم أجود ما لديه من عطاء في سبيل دعم أهداف هذه السلسلة وتطوير مجالاتها الواسعة. والباب مفتوح أمام جميع الأقلام العربية والشرقية والغربية التي تخدم هذه الأهداف المثمرة.

ونسأل الله العلي القدير أن يحقق لهذه السلسلة ما تصبو إليه من نجاح وتقدم. قال سبحانه وتعالى :

«وقل اعملوا فسيرى الله عملكم»، صدق الله العظيم. والله الموفق لما فيه الخير والصواب لصالح أمتنا العربية الإسلامية المجيدة ولغتها العريقة الأصيلة. إنه سميع مجيب.

For Product Safety Concerns and Information please contact our EU representative GPSR@taylorandfrancis.com
Taylor & Francis Verlag GmbH, Kaufingerstraße 24, 80331 München, Germany

www.ingramcontent.com/pod-product-compliance
Lightning Source LLC
Chambersburg PA
CBHW052153300426
44115CB00011B/1655